Martin Newell was born father's career – he was a Medical Corps – Martin Hampshire, London, Cyprus, Dundee, Chester, Singapore, Malaya and Essex. As a teenager he learned to play guitar, keyboards, bass and mandolin. In 1973 Martin joined the Colchester glam-rock band, Plod. Subsequent bands were Gypp, The Stray Trolleys and Cleaners From Venus. In-between jobs included stints as a sawmill worker, window cleaner, kitchen porter, postman and gardener. He joined Captain Sensible as a lyricist and collaborated with XTC's Andy Partridge on the album *The Greatest Living Englishman*. Martin's latest album is *The Spirit Cage* (Cherry Red records).

In 1990 Martin began working as a performance poet and took up a poet's residency in Middlesborough. He has had seven books published: five collections of verse and two long poems, *Black Shuck* and *Wildman of Wivenhoe*. Martin is resident pop poet for *The Independent*, and as a result he is the most regularly published poet in the UK. He lives in north-east Essex.

this little ziggy

martin newell

HOUSE OF
STRATUS

This edition published in 2001 by House of Stratus, an imprint of
Stratus Holdings plc, 24c Old Burlington Street, London, W1X 1RL, UK.

www.houseofstratus.com

Typeset, printed and bound by House of Stratus.

A catalogue record for this book is available from the British Library.

ISBN 0-7551-0267-3

*This book is dedicated to Hank Marvin and The Shadows
– the first and the best*

ACKNOWLEDGEMENTS

This book could not and would not have appeared without the following people: Jane Lindsey, Emma Drew, Stix, Jack, Bachelor Johnny, Captain Terence Newell BEM, Mrs Beryl Violet Newell, Paul Wilkinson, Sarah Fergusson, Justine Bell, Sarah Byrne and the good folk at House of Stratus. Jane O, H E Wright, E Wright, Aero, wherever he is, the British army, the constabularies of Essex and Hertfordshire, the Metropolitan Police, Don Smith – who was right, Big Nik – who was always right, the Horkesley Savage, rock bands too numerous to mention – with The Pink Fairies and Stray right up there at the top. Bistro Nine, Colchester, *Melody Maker*, R J Okell, Hedley Pierre, Charlie Watkins, Smith, Kline & French, Ford Transit vans, Moulton bicycles and the spirit of The Mighty Plod. If there's anyone I've left out, I'm bloody sorry, right?

Martin Newell

INTRODUCTION

We have no extradition treaties with the past. That is, we can't bring our younger selves back into the present to account for our doings there. At best, all we may have are a few scribbled notes on faded paper and perhaps a handful of faded Polaroids to tell us that events ever really happened at all. These recollections begin in the late summer of 1964 and end in the early spring of 1975. They are not, therefore, an autobiography as such.

What began for me as a clutch of humorous stories about a provincial rock band, to be written down in idle moments for publication I knew not when, has turned into something rather different. The most recent of these stories took place over a quarter of a century ago. Most of the people mentioned herein are now living completely different lives. I have lost touch with some of them. A handful of them are dead.

Am I telling the truth? In so far as I can remember and to the best of my ability, yes. But it's only my version of the truth. Time has smeared its Vaseline on the camera lens and, at best, things are in soft focus, if not actually blurred to distortion. I have changed a few names and locations to protect people who may not wish to find themselves mentioned. I think very highly of the people I mention most. There are no villains as such, but there are one or two heroes.

The greatest of all of these are, of course, my parents, who although I didn't realise it, bore with me to the best of their ability, even though they appeared at the time not to understand the tumult I was going through. In retrospect, perhaps they understood me rather better than I thought. The other heroes are the young men I knew as Bachelor Johnny, Stix, Jack and Big Nik.

I don't think that the things that I recount are unique, at least not in isolation. Many of the events detailed here will be familiar to anyone who grew up in England in the same era. I was a boy who grew up in the sixties and came of age (sort of) in the seventies. Taken as a whole, however, my youth was not exactly typical.

I am the same age as our current Prime Minister, Mr Blair. Both of us must have gone to an infants' school with its smells of stale milk in the classroom and Izal in the outside lavatories. Both of us must have learned to read with *Janet and John* books. Both of us must have pored over comic books on wet Saturdays, known the smell of coal fires in the rain and the jangle of The Shadows from kitchen radios. Both of us must have awoken to the songs of The Beatles and dreamed of playing guitars.

Later, though, much later, when adolescence came, coinciding as it did with a period of social and cultural change at least as potent as the hormones coursing through us, only one of us hurled himself saucer-eyed into the maelstrom with no thought of where or when he might emerge. I'm rather glad it was me. I wouldn't fancy being Prime Minister. And I'd hate to think that Mr Blair might have conducted the kind of experiments on his health and sanity that I once did. You wouldn't want a bloke like me running the country. On the other hand, I don't think Mr Blair could have fronted a glam-rock band from Colchester in quite my haphazard style. That must remain his loss.

In the end I wanted to write these stories down. Many of them are funny and are intended for entertainment rather than as any kind of confessional. Comedy, like tragedy, is nearly always born of dashed expectation. And oh, I have had my turn at the wheel of that wonky ship, the *Dashed Expectation*. God bless her and all who sail in her. These chapters are some of the entries from her logbook.

Martin Newell, Essex, spring 2001

One

Coal and Kindling
Chester, England, July-August 1964

Mrs Lightfoot has seen something at the back of the classroom. It must be roughly parallel with the top of my head. I am sitting in the back row of the class, where they put the kids who are good at English. And English is the only thing I'm good at. In fact there's only a little Welsh girl called Enid with higher marks than me, so I get to sit right in the back row. I am eleven years old. Mr Jones, our usual form teacher, is away today, so Mrs Lightfoot is taking us for English. She's middle-aged, wears a black cardigan, a tweedy skirt and spectacles. We've heard that she's nice. That's all I know of her.

What can I say? It's a summer day, the holidays are approaching and I'm looking forward to the lesson. In the faint smell of stale milk, parquet floors and polish, I sit dreaming as the sun streams in through the high windows, lighting up the tiny specks of chalk dust like little stars. Mrs Lightfoot is walking more quickly now. She speeds up through the aisle between the desks, intent on remedying whatever it is she's seen at the back of the classroom. Perhaps one of the paintings behind me is hanging crooked. She's moving faster, getting closer. She'd better slow down soon, or she'll hit the wall. She stops just in front of my little desk. She draws back her hand. And she slaps me full force on my left cheek.

The result is dramatic. My face is burning with embarrassment, there's a high-pitched whine in my left ear, a tear is pushing its way out of my eye and I'm having difficulty catching my breath. The sound of the slap seems to echo round the classroom. By the time I focus, she's back in front of the class, looking at me sternly. She spits, 'No one smiles in my class.' I am completely confused. Has she made a mistake? Was I really smiling? This is Martin Newell, good boy, not usually in trouble for much. What have I done? Numb with shock, I sit there in absolute silence, trying to look like I'm paying attention. But the lesson does not begin.

Instead, still staring at me, she says, 'I think we are waiting for something.' Maybe she's going to pick on someone else. 'I am still waiting.' I'm scared now. I think I'm going to piss myself with fear. I have no idea what this woman wants. She asks my friend Steven, 'Steven, do you know what we are waiting for?'

Steve mumbles, 'Yes, Miss.'

She asks Duncan and David. They both seem to know what we are waiting for. She focuses on me again. 'Martin Newell, are you so stupid that you still don't know what we are waiting for?' In a shaky voice, I tell her that I am sorry but I really do not know. 'Tell him, Steven.'

Steven speaks up a little. 'An apology, Miss?' I am completely confused now. She's belted me full in the face, for no reason that I can think of and she wants me to apologise.

She stares at me again. 'Well?' I open my mouth but no words come, the lump in my throat feels like it will choke me. Tears course down my burning face as I try to say the required words, but nothing comes. She realises I am broken and contents herself with, 'I'll be keeping a close eye on you from now on, my lad.'

About two days later, with Mr Jones still off work, Mrs Lightfoot comes back to take us for another lesson. This time I stare attentively at the middle of her desk and press my lips tight together, in case any facial movement can be misinterpreted as a smile. When she looks at me I can see a malevolent glint in her spectacles. 'Uncross those lips, lad.' I have forgotten what to do with my face. I am terrified that whatever else I do might result in another attack. But that's all she says. In my mind, I have turned over my desk, thrown the globe of the world through the window, run out of the door, out of the school, down Kingsway and into the woods to live like a wild boy.

Sheer bewilderment and fear has dogged me through schools in Lambeth, Surrey, Cyprus, Hertfordshire, Scotland and Cheshire. Six schools in six years, and what I can mostly remember is worry, shame and fear; the lump in the throat, the urge to run, and the strange teachers, always shouting at me when I genuinely didn't understand.

Like Mr Down in Dhekelia, Cyprus, who because I didn't follow the system he'd devised for stacking the exercise books and handing them in, shouted at me, picked me up under my arms and shook me in the air, then swiped me several times in the face with my own exercise book until I left the classroom with a thin trickle of blood issuing from one nostril. I was eight years old. I never told my parents, of course. I was too ashamed and they'd probably just have said something like, 'Well you should have been paying attention.'

But of all the humiliation, random violence, slipperings, strappings or whatever I came up against in my eleven schools in ten years, it is Mrs Lightfoot's slap which wins the award. To this day, I haven't got a clue what it was that I'd done to deserve it. Maybe there was something in my eyes, some dislikeable expression on my face that marked me out as being in some way different. Certainly, most of the trouble I found myself in during those early years and much later has been something to do with perceived 'attitude', but it was Mrs Lightfoot's slap which was the last straw. I can remember thinking, 'If the world really has got it in for me, then I shan't even try to belong to it anymore.'

So, come with me and I'll take you around my eleven-year-old world. My father is a professional soldier and by the age of eleven I have lived in more houses than I am years old. I'm a lively boy – if prone to nosebleeds, hay fever, tonsillitis and various other illnesses. My family lives in the north of England, not far from Liverpool. And The Beatles come from Liverpool. Every day, I look in the mirror and shake my fringe to see if it looks any more like a Beatle fringe than it did the day before. And when it finally does, I am yanked off to the barber's shop for a six-weekly short back and sides. And then I will stop looking like a Beatle and start looking like Martin.

Martin wasn't me. Martin was the sensible, studious-looking boy pictured on the boxes of chemistry sets. That boy wore a clean school shirt, a tie, and had a short haircut with a neat fringe. He was pictured earnestly pouring the contents of one test tube into another. He wasn't making stink bombs or explosives. He was doing homework. And I hated him.

Inside this Martin, however, was another boy. He wanted to be a lone Apache, or one of Robin Hood's outlaws. He wasn't dependent upon civilization, he lived away from it, in the woods or hills, fighting off those who would tame him. He was beholden to no ruler – until the beat boom started and he wanted to be a Beatle.

I'm not exactly sure when the sixties began, but they certainly didn't begin in 1960. You might say that they began with the Cliff Richard film, *Summer Holiday*, when Cliff and his chums finally get the double-decker bus on the road and the film changes from black and white to colour. My pet theory is that the sixties commenced in the gap between the opening chord of the song 'A Hard Day's Night' and the singing coming in. The chord, which to non-guitar players sounds a little like the sound resulting from accidentally knocking over an acoustic guitar, hangs there for a brief eternity. And then Lennon's nasal drawl comes in with, 'Issbina harr dayznite.' And in that gap, for me at least, the fifties suddenly become the sixties, the world changes from black and white to colour and young Martin wakes up with a yearning and a feeling that something brilliant is happening somewhere. Somewhere else, which at present, he has no way of reaching.

I live in a dull, army-furnished house, allocated to army families and situated in a close, about a mile from the centre of Chester. Up until mid-1964 it is, to all intents and purposes, still the fifties. The cliché is I can't remember things being in colour up until this point, only monochrome. Boys of my age wear baggy shorts, or jeans with Woolworths' snake belts. We wear grey shirts and dull shoes or plimsolls with grey socks. Everyone has short hair. All women look a bit like your mum, only fatter, thinner, older, or younger, except for what my mum describes as tarty girls with beehive hair and 'far too much eye make-up'. These young women work in Woolworths or in roadside caffs.

Trains are still steam powered, apart from some in the south which are electric and green. A man wearing bicycle clips, glasses and carrying a briefcase, comes to the door once a week, the insurance man. A coalman arrives in a lorry. He wears an ex-WD, sleeveless, brown jerkin and a cap with a leather neck protector, like a samurai warrior's helmet. Once in a blue moon, a scruffy man with an old slouch hat and a horse-drawn cart clip-clops down the road shouting, 'Raggaburn! Raggaburn!' He is the rag-and-bone man. We boys often play in the street, because we can. Hardly anyone seems to have cars. You can play for half an hour before a car comes up the street.

And everything to do with heating is kindling wood, coal, newspaper and paraffin, especially paraffin. Sunday night is bath night and a paraffin heater warms the bathroom up for you before you go in. If you go to a friend's for tea, what you smell in the hall upon entering the house is paraffin and damp coats. My friend Steve's house smells like that. It is cosy and familiar.

Steve is worldly wise and has a big sister who owns a record player. She plays Ronettes records on it and has a white dressing table, which I glimpse when I pass her open bedroom door. On it stands the eye make-up, which she wears far too much of, plus all the accoutrements for the construction of her beehive hairstyle. I find her impossibly glamorous and sophisticated. Because of her, Steve knows how to do dances like the Twist and the Shake. Steve's dad also strikes me as being very modern, with his Teddy-boy haircut. They are a modern, working-class civilian family who seem far warmer and less formal than my own.

According to Steve, I talk posh. This is my mother's fault. Although from a working-class family herself, she comes from a generation who believe that you'll get on in life better, if you sound your tees and don't drop your aitches. She's always picking me up on sloppy speech and I speak reasonably clearly, unlike my younger brother, who cannily changes his accent to fit in with whatever area we've moved to. Speaking 'posh' and being good at English help to get me picked on and ridiculed in every school I attend. Except by the real posh kids, who all stick together and seem to instinctively know that I'm not one of them, so I never feel that I belong. Yet I'm not friendless. I always seem to pick up the other misfits in the school, who think that I'm alright. But I'm never in the main gang and school life is a continuous battle.

I have slightly more than my fair share of illness, with the nosebleeds and hay fever the worst. The nosebleeds sometimes go on for hours. Once or twice a doctor has to be called to wad my nostrils with gauze and stem the bleeding. On summer evenings, when other kids are out playing, I'm sometimes lying in a darkened room with burning eyes trying not to sneeze, in case another nosebleed starts. A big nosebleed leaves me feeling strange and ethereal and all sorts of fanciful ideas invade me.

But my mum and dad are army folk, not exactly hard-arsed, but not the types to encourage malingering either. So I often go into school in a sort of daze, hoping that no one's going to tax me too much. They think that I'm not paying attention and they shout 'Wake up!' at me. But I can't. I want to be a good boy. I want to fit in. Up until Mrs Lightfoot bashes me in the face. But now I realise that I can't. I'm like Peter Pan, who flew back to his parents' house one night and found that they'd locked the windows and another little boy was asleep in his bed.

I realised that my parents meant well. I think I even knew that when teachers shouted at you or struck you, it wasn't anything personal. It's just that all the other boys and girls seemed to know what to do, where to go, what to say. Even Steve, David and Duncan in the bottom of the class seemed to know that it was an apology which was required. Why didn't I? What had Mrs Lightfoot seen in my eyes that was so dangerous that it had to be chopped down with the palm of her hand before she'd even said good morning to the class?

And now, aged eleven, I realise that I am an alien orphan belonging to some other world. Maybe I've come from another time. My parents aren't really my parents; they're nothing like me. And I am ashamed of the strangeness of my thoughts. The only things that really make sense are the American comics I read: *Sinister Tales, Creepy Worlds*. And the books I read are about Red Indians and ghosts. I don't play football or cricket; I don't know what they're about. No, I'm out in the woods building dens and tree houses. I get hold of a book on archaeology and become fascinated by how defences were made with mud and stakes. I get wood and mud and try to create a smaller version of a neolithic defence post. One November evening a friend walks all the way home with me to see it. He looks at me like I'm mad and says, 'It's just wood and mud.' I tell him that all our ancestors had to build with was wood and mud. To me, it's mystical. To him it's weird.

And winter Saturdays in this version of the sixties are also black and white. The background sound is an undulating grainy mush of sport coming from the TV in the living room. The smell is that of coal, kindling and wood. Further off are the distant smells of schools with their coke-fired boilers. Only the radio will save me now, because The Beatles and The Beach Boys are about to wake me up. A jangle will spill out of the radio and cause something akin to despair in many of my parents' generation. Four pied pipers will come into my town and by the time they walk back out and over the hills, all of the town's children will have followed them. And I will be among them. Although many of the children will drift back after a few years, some of us will never return. There will be nothing to go back for. And Mrs Lightfoot's resounding slap is still hanging in the chalk dusty air... But I have already gone.

Two

Long Trousers
Chester, England, Autumn 1964

I'd failed my eleven-plus exam. I'd done alright in English, alright in Intelligence but I'd completely blown the Arithmetic. Dad had received his commission and a posting to Singapore and I was being packed off to boarding school. There were two choices. If I passed my exam I could go to Wolverstone Hall in Suffolk. My mother showed me a hideous prospectus full of short-haired Martins looking attentive in chemistry labs. There were pictures of rather more daunting-looking Clives playing rugby, lots of pictures of lots of boys canoeing, studying, playing cricket, running and so on, in fact all of the activities guaranteed to horrify me. And not a Beatle fringe in sight.

From the prospectus, it looked like the kind of school where the headmaster stood up in assembly and said things like, 'It's come to my notice that one or two elements in this school are letting the side down. It's not just a question of work. It's a question of attitude. There's far too much of the sort of slackness promoted by these pop groups nowadays, with their long hair and general disregard for authority. Therefore, in future there will be no more listening to *The Light Programme* in this school and anyone found with trouser bottoms less than twenty-two inches wide will be caned.'

The other boarding school being considered by my parents was a place near London called Crown Woods. It looked the better option and it was mixed, which I took to mean that ordinary human beings went there as well as the types of creature I'd previously encountered in other schools I'd attended. Unfortunately, just before I took my eleven-plus, we heard that I'd been refused a place there. This meant that all I had to do was fail my eleven-plus and they'd have to start from scratch again – or take me to Singapore with them. Having failed the exam, I was now looking at six weeks of summer holiday, followed (hopefully) by six or eight weeks of no school at all until we went to Singapore. After all, I reasoned, why kit me out for a local secondary in Chester when I'd only attend it for six weeks? I thought I was safe. But no. This tedious bloke from the education authority came round sometime towards the end of the summer holidays and told my mum that I would be required to attend this school, even if only for six weeks, because it was the law.

Hoole Secondary Modern in Chester didn't turn out to be so bad. For a start, my mate Steve, who knew the Twist, the Shake and by now, the Mashed Potato, also went to it. Admittedly, I got in a fight with Pollard, who arrived at the after-school rendezvous on the crossbar of A Bike With Cowhorn Handlebars (the hallmark of a hard-nut in those days). He smacked me on the nose and stuck me down, then he pinioned my shoulders with his knees. A passer-by, walking his dog, shouted, 'Everything alright, lads?'

Through tears and blood, I shakily said, 'Yeah, we're just mucking around.' Pollard gave me points for that. We became sort of friends afterwards and, later on, when Steve got the better of Pollard in a playground fight and offered me a free hit at Pollard while he was in a headlock, I refused.

The most important thing about Hoole Secondary Modern, however, was that it was there that I saw my first pop group. I can remember that autumn in Chester very well because it was the last time I saw England for two years – an age to an eleven-year old. Chester was quite well-heeled and picturesque in its centre and there were great horse chestnut trees by the side of the River Dee. The leaves turned beautiful colours once the summer was on the run and, when I later sweltered unhappily in Singapore, I thought of them often.

The first thing I knew about the pop group was a handwritten poster in a school corridor. It said, 'RECORD HOP'. I'd sort of assumed it was some kind of athletics event which we were required to attend. No, don't laugh. That's what I really thought. What a record hop actually was, was a sort of dance with a primitive kind of DJ and a live band playing. It was approaching half-term and a local pop group, The Deacons, had been booked to play at the school. There was only one problem; you had to be at least a third-year pupil to get in. Luckily, John Mead, a fellow army brat who happened to be a third year, obtained me a ticket and somehow snuck me into the darkened school hall. One of Mead's classmates said, 'Bloody hell, Mead. He's a bit young isn't he?' Mead told them I was leaving school after half-term and if I wouldn't be there as evidence, how could he be punished for bringing me in? Nevertheless, Mead told me to stay in the shadows, which I did.

The Deacons seemed ever so old – at least nineteen or so – and they were incredibly loud. When they struck up, the whole spectacle completely transfixed me. Their red electric guitars were the brightest red I'd ever seen. The drum-kit and the Vox amplifiers were the loudest things I'd ever heard. The band themselves hadn't quite made the transition to mop-top haircuts yet, but they had that peculiar early sixties halfway-house look between quiffs and Beatle fringes. Their shirts were blue and satiny, their trousers tight and their boots pointy. There were bottles of Coke down by their feet and they smoked cigarettes on stage. They just didn't care. A whole row of girls stood looking up at them, while the boys stood at the back looking slightly impressed. Me? I was gobsmacked. I just thought, 'Wow. That's the job for me.'

I don't know if The Deacons did their own songs at that time. I remember they played a song called 'Seven Golden Daffodils', a rather histrionic ballad of the time, which had been a hit for The Cherokees. But it didn't matter. I can only remember the impact of it all as I stood in the shadows: the brightness, the clothes, the Coke bottles, the admiring girls, and that huge, crashing jangly racket. I walked home afterwards with John Mead. He asked me, 'Whaddid you reckon then?' I was unable to speak.

Three

Nasi Goreng and Tears
Singapore City, Spring 1965

'Selamat pagi. Ini la Radio Malaysia.'

And good morning to you too, lady. I'm twelve years old. I live four floors up in the middle of Singapore, just off Killiney Road where meals are served in leaves from exotic-smelling food stalls. My father, second lieutenant Newell BEM, has told me I must never buy this stuff. And he's an army health expert, so he should know. Little old Chinese men sit and carve ancient-looking patterns into camphor-wood chests using curved chisels. The narrow street teems with old taxis painted bright blue with go-faster stripes. Bicycle rickshaws weave in and out of the traffic. An old Tamil trader selling comics and magazines grabs me by the arm and runs his hand over my pale skin, disbelievingly. The whole place smells of food, camphor, wet bamboo, mangoes and drains.

My brother and our friends have wandered off down to Orchard Road, Singapore's main western-style shopping street. Their destination is a large department store with the catchy name, Cold Storage. The shop's main attraction for us is its air-conditioning, a thing we'd never come across in England. I'm hanging back, however, wandering up and down Killiney Road. I have bought some very rough peanut brittle from a street vendor for five cents and I am watching an old guy finish off a pattern on a camphor-wood chest. 'Berapa?' I ask the man's apprentice. (How much?)

'Forty-fy dollah.' He replies in English. 'Chakap Melayu?' (Speak Malay?) He is surprised.

'Sekit,' I reply, meaning a little.

My dad has lent me a little book, *Teach Yourself Malay*. Some of the other army kids catch me reading it on the bus. 'Newell's learning Wog. Newell's learning Wog,' goes the racist chant. There is no love lost between my fellow army brats and me. The ones in my age group are mostly thugs, clones of their parents, or nerds. I qualify as a nerd at this point. Luckily for me, most of them live in garrisons and stay there. They go to swimming pools, play football or go shopping. We haven't got army quarters yet, so for a few months we're in a flat in the middle of Singapore. Mr Lee Kuan Yew, a man whom my mother greatly admires, is about to declare independence from Malaya. Mr Tunku Adbul Rahman, the gaffer in Kuala Lumpur, isn't best pleased about this. Tough.

Mr Lee wants to clean Singapore up, make it a successful free state and get rid of its terrible opium problem. To deal with the opium problem he enlists the help of a Doctor Chen Su Lan. Doctor Chen Su Lan lives just round the corner from us in a big, old-fashioned colonial house in St Thomas Walk. Opposite his house is a rambutan tree covered in huge red ants. He keeps two very fierce chow dogs to guard his gates. You think I'm making this up? Listen: when you spend a lot of time by yourself, cut off from the British pop explosion, something's got to lodge in that pre-teenage brain.

One day, I'm walking past Doctor Chen's house with a mongrel called Vicky, which my mum has adopted, when the two chows attack. They're both on Vicky and it's not looking good. I pick up half a paving slab and throw it onto one dog's back. The slab breaks. The dog screams and runs off. The other dog follows, barking rearguard threats at me. My heart is pumping and I'm on the verge of tears. Some Chinese boys approach me, 'You wanna see fighting spiders?' This is how I meet my first Chinese friends. They're called Ah-Tee and Ah-Tah. They have a sister called Ah-Moy. They teach me how to catch fighting spiders, to keep them in a matchbox, what to feed them on and how to make them wrestle.

Ah-Tee and Ah-Tah live along the road from me. They speak Hainanese. Their rivals are some other boys round the corner who speak Hokkien. They fight with kites. Ah-Tee shows me how to bring an opponent's kite down. You have to coat your kite strings in a special resin. First you get a piece of marble and some old glass. Then you grind the glass and the marble together to make a fine sharp dust. You mix this in a little pot with some egg white. You coat your kite strings with it. Result? String with such a sharp edge, that if a sparrow flew into it it would probably decapitate itself. When you send your kite up to meet an opponent's kite, you saw away at each other's strings in mid-air, until one or the other's kite is cut free and falls to earth. Not many English boys know this, but I do. On the other hand, I can't play football, and I don't know which department of Cold Storage to go to if I need a Fred Perry shirt or a T-bone steak.

Walking down Killiney Road, I see a man with only his upper torso pushing himself down the street on a tiny trolley with castors on it. I see an ancient Tamil woman who's been barefoot for so long, the soles of her feet are about an inch thick. I buy *Green Lantern* and *Sgt Fury* comics. And I rarely, if ever, meet any other English kids on these walks. It's great. And it's my little secret.

Mr Lee says we must all learn Malay. Alone among my fellow army brats I'm giving it a go. The Chinese kids try and teach me a bit of Chinese but it's impossible. There's Hokkien, Cantonese, Hainanese and Teochew and I don't know how many other dialects. Malay is more simple. I see a Chinese play in the street one day, loads of gongs, banging and crashing, and musical instruments I don't even know the names for. I stay up late when my parents are out and watch old Indian musicals and melodramas on a black-and-white TV. I'm going native and nobody even knows. I wear T-shirts, shorts and flip-flops. I make a lot of Airfix models, mostly World War Two planes. The Hurricane's a piece of piss but I have trouble with a Junkers JU 88 bomber and the Short Sunderland III flying boat.

But something's happening out there on the radio. On the school bus, we're going down the Bukit Timah Road during a rainstorm and I hear 'For Your Love' by The Yardbirds. It sounds all grey terraced streets and blondes with white lipstick, green electric trains and smoky Saturdays. I am homesick. I feel desperately cheated because I'm stuck on this bus with these dull brutish kids. I am forced to go to school six days a week with teachers who are bad-tempered because of the heat, who bang their desks, shout and snap their fingers in front of my face if I drift off into my own world. I want to be out of here. I periodically toy with the idea of throwing myself off one of Mr Lee Kuan Yew's brave new skyscrapers, which are shooting up at a speed that British people would find hard to believe.

Later this year, The Rolling Stones will play in Singapore. Naturally, I won't go. It's not a case of not being allowed to or anything, simply that the question wouldn't even arise. Lots of people do go however. Mainly, British teenage girls, servicemen's daughters. The theatre owners will later be forced to remove several rows of seats, after many of the girls have pissed themselves with the excitement of it all. 'Disgraceful,' scream the local papers.

Crusty old expats, sitting in colonial bamboo chairs in the Raffles Hotel, are spluttering into their Bombay Gins and firing off letters to *The Straits Times*. 'Dear sir... It is outrageous that...blah blah...when the Japanese invaded this island in 1942...blah blah...and Mr Churchill ordered us to stand firm...blah blah...that I should live to witness British children fouling themselves in front of the people we used to govern...blah blah...at a concert by these so called musicians...who all look like they need a bath and a haircut...blah blah.' (Continued until the writer blows an internal organ and melts down to a pile of sludge under a Panama hat.)

My mum and dad are similarly tight-lipped and terse about the whole incident and I sit in a back room in the flat, doing my remedial maths. I'm one of two people in my entire year who are crap at maths. I just don't get it. The reward for this is two hours every afternoon, including the holidays, struggling with graph paper and all manner of equations which, to this day, I still do not understand. The strain and injustice of this will occasionally bring me to tears. To add to my problems, I have developed a crush on Mona.

Mona is a Malay woman who's married to Bobby, a dashing, blond Brylcream boy in the RAF. They live in the block of flats opposite. Mona has a nephew called Nigel, a Eurasian boy a little younger than myself. I make friends with Nigel while he's staying with Mona during the Easter holidays. Mona is stunningly beautiful, as Malay people very often are. She's dark, slightly buxom with fathomless dark eyes. She dresses very exotically and her flat, although the same design as our own, is like a completely different world. There are bamboo curtains in the doorways, green flimsy silk drapes everywhere, carved chests, wooden elephants and brass temple ornaments. Even the sunlight, which sneaks into the flat, is changed into a jungle-glade green. Incense is burning. The whole feeling of the place is opium-dream boudoir.

When Nigel and I call in, she makes us a delicious drink from crushed limes. I've never tasted anything like it. She treats me like a young man and makes me feel handsome. In no time at all, I am completely won over. 'Let's go and see your Auntie Mona, Nigel.' It becomes the mantra of the Easter holidays. The Easter holidays finish. Nigel goes back to his parents. Bobby is posted somewhere else and Mona shutters the flat up and goes with him shortly afterwards. I am absolutely flattened by this.

One day, my parents are battering on at me about something or other: the remedial maths, my attitude, I don't know. I never did figure out what the problem was. But from what I can gather it's just a squaddie parents/oldest kid equation. They've got to get you right. After all, you're the first one. If they fuck up on this one it doesn't reflect well. We're in the army, right? We can't have order breaking down. Who knows what might happen?

All I can remember is that they would not get off my case. I can't fight them. They're bigger than me. There are two of them. In a well-practised double act, he whacks me round the head for refusing to lay the table, and then he physically throws me into my room. When I don't stop shouting and banging, she roars in, says in her Julie Andrews voice, 'I know what to do,' drags me over to the kitchen sink by my hair and runs the cold tap over me. It works. I can't deal with this. I'm subdued.

People would probably call it abuse now, and they'd be wrong. I was probably a right handful. My brother never got this treatment. I don't hold it against them as such.

Their generation grew up in a war and dragged themselves up by their bootstraps. They weren't about to give quarter to a feisty little bastard like me. And anyway, how were they to know I'd grow up and become a warped pop genius? Nah, they probably did me a favour. Private M Newell, third class reporting for duty, sir.

Anyway, one day they're battering on at me, and I find I can't stop crying. I mean I'm crying all the time. I'm not interested in anything. I keep thinking about Mona and about England. I don't feel well. I eat just about enough food to not attract their attention. But I do. 'There's something wrong with you. I'm taking you to the doctor, my boy.' She drags me to the doctor, an army doctor. Great. So he too is an emotional cripple with an imagination bypass, like everybody else in the fucking army. He gives me iron pills. They turn my poo black. Finis.

What happens? Nothing. I carry on being miserable for a while and gradually pull out of it. The teachers are still yelling at me, apart from Mr Tapper, a melancholic and kindly English teacher with a Noel Coward type of voice. He notices that I've managed to learn the whole of Browning's 'Home Thoughts From Abroad'. I recite it like a pro, with a slight tremor in my voice. He congratulates me. It's the highlight of my week so far. Yes, it's all fun and laughter in my life right now. I just keep my head down and do my bird like a good prisoner.

Four

I've been in Singapore for over a year now. We live in a big army camp called Nee Soon Garrison. Our house is called a split. That is, it looks like an elongated bungalow, with a smaller elongated bungalow right behind it, which is linked by a small covered walkway. I look out of the front door and I can see rather grander houses across a deepish valley. Senior officers live there. To the side of our split and all round the camp, are small areas of ulu or sub-jungle. Small and rather aggressive monkeys live there. The reason why all of our windows have a wide metal mesh on them is to prevent the monkeys from coming in and stealing food.

We live in the front bit of the house. The back bit would originally have been servants' quarters and utility rooms. Junior officers usually only have one servant, often a middle-aged Chinese woman called an *amah*, paid for by the army. Western women, I suppose, cannot be expected to manage all the housework in the heat and humidity. In spite of this, my mother always makes sure the house is spotless before our *amah* comes in to do her work. I never felt that my mum was particularly happy having another woman in the house, since she was so good at it herself. In

20

the past she'd had the odd letter of commendation from the WD for the immaculate condition of certain quarters we left at 'marching out' time.

Living in Nee Soon garrison, for me, isn't quite as exotic as living in the centre of Mr Lee Kuan Yew's New Singapore, but there's much more open space in the valley, storm drains and a certain amount of wilderness. The insects are huge. They don't just buzz past your ear, the noise is more like a small miniature aeroplane and you see a striped thing with a six-inch wingspan and a vicious spike taxiing past your head. Sometimes I venture into the small patches of jungle. In the afternoons, after the school bus has dropped me off, I often go down to the army library. There in binders, are copies of the previous month's *Daily Mirrors*. I spend hours reading them because I'm homesick for England. By now I've taken and passed an exam called the thirteen-plus. It's like a late eleven-plus for twelve-year olds who haven't passed the first time around. It means that I'm now effectively in another school, since I've been transferred to the grammar stream. And boy do I hate it.

There's a clay-faced, bulging-eyed maths teacher who's always on my case. Any chance he gets, he has a go at me. Again, it's not anything I've done, as he's probably perceived the same thing that Mrs Lightfoot did almost two years earlier. He writes the word 'Blockhead!' in big red letters when he marks my exercise book and when he finally catches me talking in class, he sends me straight down to the deputy head's office.

The school is a former colonial garrison with Empire-sized corridors. I'm standing in this measureless cavern, waiting for Mr Newell, my namesake and the deputy head, to cane me. He finally calls me in and asks me why I'm there. I tell him truthfully that I was talking in class, that the teacher seems to hate me and that I honestly don't know why. I have never spoken so openly to a senior master before, but I figure that if I'm going to be caned, what does it matter? Mr Newell, a rather dignified figure whom I've never come into personal contact with before, tells me that he does not see this as a caning matter as he looks at the wretched second-year pupil standing before him. He seems to know something that I don't, says words to the effect of, 'Try and stay out of his way then,' and despatches me, unpunished, back to class.

It's near the end of Christmas term 1965, and I've already decided that grammar school is even more pressure than secondary school. I deliberately do badly in all exams except English, so that when I'm sent back to England, a few months later, I'm reassessed as secondary school material, which suits me fine. Right now, Christmas is looming, however, and all thoughts centre on the very staid end-of-term class party. A record player is brought in and some of the kids bring in new singles from England. People are allowed, in the last two hours of school, not to wear their uniforms. This makes sod all difference to me because I don't have anything other than some scruffier shorts and a different-coloured short-sleeved shirt. So I don't bother.

Something's happening though. Someone has produced a copy of The Beatles' new single 'Day Tripper'. It's played over and over again, occasionally alternated with a Stones record. And this Beatles single completely lights me up, for days afterwards I can't get it out of my head. For some time I have been considering what I would do or who I would be if I were in The Beatles. Much as I like their twangy guitars and their harmonies the thing that I am most obsessed with is the drum-kit. To be Ringo, bashing away at the floor-toms like a nodding dog toy in the back of The Beatles' car. At the back of the school bus, I tap away with pencils on the top of my satchel, with the backing tracks going on in my head. I no longer notice the long bus journey from one side of the island to the other. At home, when no one is around, I get paint tins, saucepans and boxes and arrange them in a spare room at the back of the split, to try and work out how a drum-kit functions. And it's the monsoon season and the rain hammers down for hours every day.

No one does Christmas like the British abroad. There's carol singing outside the houses at the edge of the jungle. My mother has a small white plastic stagecoach with red fairy lights on it, which she places on the sideboard and leaves switched on at night. A clipped voice in my ear asks me what I want for Christmas. There's only one answer of course: I want a drum-kit. Louder? I WANT A DRUM-KIT. Well now, my dad never did like a lot of noise. He's one of these people who listens to the news with the TV or radio volume down and then spends all his time tutting and shushing if anyone so much as clears their throat. There was no way I was going to get a drum-kit. In fact, there was no way I was going to get anything that the Chinese fellow who came once a week in a van, didn't have in stock.

The Chinese man comes once a week and drives all around the garrison, bringing soap powder, food, all sorts of stuff. It is quite a small van, but he must have a catalogue of back-up stuff, or maybe the van is a Tardis. Either way, this is the source of my Christmas present. The Christmas present which changes my world but which isn't a drum-kit, costs about forty-five bucks and comes from the man in the van. It is Japanese, has six strings and smells of varnish and fresh glue. It comes in a corrugated cardboard box, which looks like a cross between an isosceles triangle and a throwaway kiddie coffin. The label inside it says Nippon Gakki. Then just underneath: Yamaha Dynamic Guitar No. 10.

So now I'm a guitarist. Oh, this will be my undoing. The guitar will take me on a long and convoluted route as I slouch bleeding-fingered through schoolrooms, streets and cities. It will be my constant companion and main friend for many confusing years, it will watch me meet and break up with girls and it will listen as I write my first songs, and it will never be idle or dusty. But right now, I'm unprepared for it. Had it been a drum-kit, I might have a rough idea. But I know no chord shapes, I can't even make any notes. I don't even know how it is tuned.

After Christmas, when school reconvened, I had only one lesson. A bearded science teacher, who'd had something to do with folk clubs back in England, offered to give half a dozen of us would-be pop stars a lesson after school. First, he taught us how to tune a guitar, then he taught us a very rudimentary, two-chord claw-hammer version of 'Bobby Shaftoe'. Lastly, he showed us all what chord-pictures looked like, and how you interpreted them for a Japanese guitar with an action like an egg-slicer. And I was away. Within two weeks, I could do a very convincing 'Satisfaction' riff, using two thumbs. I could also play an autistic version of 'Bobby Shaftoe'. I really hope that The Beatles were suitably nervous about all of this when word of it finally reached England.

The one thing it did do for me was to get kids talking to me on the bus. Before I took the guitar into school for that lesson, I think they'd always regarded me as a rather square or standoffish officer's kid who wasn't interested in pop music. The kids from the other ranks – and I'd only recently stopped being one myself – lived in another part of the garrison. It's hard to convey the situation to anyone who hasn't been the child of a military family, but when your dad gets commissioned, if he's previously been another rank – that is below the rank of second lieutenant

– you move into a slightly different world. You get parked in the corner of a posher mess with your bottle of Coke and packet of crisps, when your parents go for a Sunday lunchtime noggin. Pudding is called 'sweet', a thing that I absolutely hated. You have to learn which knives and forks to use. You're expected to behave with a bit more decorum. And through no fault of your own, you're often moved to a different part of the garrison or even a different area. Officers and other ranks don't generally hang out together. This makes it much harder for their kids, who might actually have a lot more in common with each other. It was especially hard for me, because my dad came up through the ranks, so we'd all had to adjust.

I was a strange and bookish sort of kid anyway. A bonding experience, like a game of football, was out of the question, because I wasn't interested in football. I'd taken to straying just outside of the garrison and buying secondhand paperbacks full of stories about ghosts and vampires. Occasionally, I mucked around with an old tape recorder which had come from my dad's office. I spent hours reading. I had a Swedish pen pal and I wrote to her sometimes, or I lingered around the edge of the jungle looking at the monkeys.

But the Yamaha dynamic guitar experience changes all this. Now I'm in conversation with kids from the other ranks' quarters, I'm hearing pop records bought at the night market or sent over from England, I get invited to parties, I can get signed in at the camp swimming pool without an adult. They find out I can tell jokes. I even hear that one of the girls in their crowd likes me. I'm on the cusp of adolescence and even though it's halfway through the decade, I actually feel that I'm now in the sixties, rather than the fifties. One day, I go round to my friend Pete's house and he produces a record. It's called '1-2-3' and it's by someone called Len Barry. For some reason, with the monsoon rains pissing down outside, it reminds me of England and I want to go back there. This is just as well because although I don't know it yet, within a few weeks that's exactly where I'm going to be. It's typical of my luck: just when things are getting good, it's time to move on again. And it's *selamat malam singapura*. Good night Singapore.

Five

English Alien
Harpenden, Hertfordshire, April 1966

In the heavens the gods were having an idle day of it. As they looked down their eyes lit upon a boy living in the Far East...

Thor: This boy is on the threshold of puberty, but he's not particularly interested in girls yet, however he...
He is interrupted by loud laughter from the other gods.
Odin: Silence!
Thor: However, his father is a warrior and the boy has been moved from pillar to post for most of his childhood. He has not taken to this well and is somewhat confused as to what he is and what he wants to be. His only abiding interest is the jangle of popular music that he hears all around him and the rather morbid collection of vampire and supernatural paperbacks in which he buries himself when his parents, teachers and schoolmates aren't on his case.
Freya: With respect, so what? Why should we care what happens to an anaemic and soon-to-be very spotty little oik?
Thor: Aw, I don't know, I just thought we could have a bit of fun, that's all.

Balder: Great gag moving him to the Far East, to that squaddie camp, Thor. But what next? Can you top that?

Thor takes a good slug from his drinking horn and sniggers.

Thor: Easy-peasy lemon-squeezey. We move him back to England, stick him in a secondary school somewhere off the main drag, But – and you're gonna love this – we dress him like a real nerd. I don't just mean boring normal, I mean like something from the post-war Empire: baggy trousers with turn-ups, hairy grey shirt, Bash Street-type tie, oversized serge blazer, pullover and then...

Freya: Yes?

Thor: And then...(*he restrains himself from hysterical laughter*)...we move him in with his grandfather and let the grandad choose his only pair of shoes.

Freya: You mean the round-toed ones with the buckles? Those black leather things that he must have had in the cupboard under the stairs since the thirties?

He produces the shoes with a triumphant flourish.

Thor: The same! And then we drop him right in the middle of the swinging sixties.

Balder: You're a funny guy Thor, a real funny guy.

Thor: (*Adopts Joe Pesci voice.*) Do I amuse you? Do I fuckin' amuse you, you fuckin' fuck?

The hall of the gods erupts into laughter and applause.

And so, on the freezing cold morning of 16 April 1966, a suntanned thirteen-year-old boy emerged from a Boeing 707 carrying an airline bag and a Yamaha six-string acoustic guitar and accompanied by his younger brother, Mark. They were met by a kindly uncle and taken to a smallholding in Buckinghamshire. After a day or so, the older boy was taken to a small town in Hertfordshire while his brother remained behind with the uncle. The thirteen-year old remembered his parents' only instruction to the grandparents who were now his guardians. 'Five bob a week pocket money and make sure he has a short-back-and-sides every six weeks.' Our hero now takes up his own story.

I was struck by how green the fields and the woods looked, how crisp and clean the air was and how rosy-cheeked the English children appeared after my time in the Far East. I was back at Gomshall, a three-up, two-down house in a terrace of four, in a respectable street, in a respectable town thirty miles from London. The house had been the only constant in my life. I was brought back there after I was born; I'd lived there with my mum for brief periods when my dad had been given certain postings and I'd spent short and idyllic summer holidays there. It was an ordinary English town in the Home Counties. It was the only real home I'd ever known. My grandparents who'd lived here since the thirties were much easier going than my parents. They were very different from my parents and, because they treated me so well, I became a different and probably better boy. The house and its small living room were cluttered with ornaments, the type of things which turn up at car boot sales in old market towns and which are so typical of that cosier England of all our pasts. The garden was a long flint-strewn strip with a rhubarb patch, fruit bushes and a huge conker tree that my mum had planted when she was a girl.

The town, Harpenden, was reasonably well-to-do, though not ostentatiously so. It was the kind of place that Monty Python might have satirised for its sheer respectable ordinariness. On weekday mornings, the London side of Harpenden Station was packed with bowler-hatted men carrying newspapers and umbrellas. Sainbury's had its distinctive black-and-white mosaic floors and smelt of clean sawdust and fresh bacon. Woolworths had wooden floors, girls in green coats and smelt of cheap cosmetics and Pick'n'Mix sweets. Everything about the town was as I'd remembered it from two years earlier.

Eric Morecambe, the comedian, lived there in a big house somewhere over the West Common. Occasionally, I'd see him in the newsagents on a Saturday morning. Harpenden was quietly proud of him, but no one ever pestered him. There was a tacit agreement among the townspeople that he was to be left alone. He said good morning to my grandad one morning, which rather stunned me. If anyone ever stopped him you sort of knew they weren't locals.

One day my grandad pointed out to me a strange-looking old lady on a very old-fashioned bike. She was dressed eccentrically and had headgear which I'd only ever seen in pictures of early women motorists. She had very distinctive features and, although she was old, bird-of-prey bright eyes. 'That,' said my grandad, 'is a real Russian princess. Came over here sometime during the Great War.' I asked if he'd ever spoken to her but he said that not many people had. He wasn't even sure that she spoke English.

After all that time in Singapore, I was suddenly submerged in Englishness. Patriotism and national pride didn't enter into it. What I can remember is the sheer weight of cosy familiar trivia overwhelming me until I felt like a stickleback returned to its old pond after time spent in a jar on a primary-school nature table.

What I was completely unprepared for was the pervasiveness of the pop culture. In Singapore, I'd lived in my own world with the family's tiny plastic record player, sitting in the corner listening to early Beatles LPs over and over again. For reasons that were at odds with everything I knew about him, my father went out and bought the single of 'Nineteenth Nervous Breakdown' by The Stones. So now our record collection consisted of three Beatles albums, a clutch of Broadway musicals, a Russ Conway single and one by this group of despised long-haired yobbos. You go and work it out, because I gave up trying to do it, at least twenty years ago.

Now I was back in England, I was hearing new groups on a daily basis. They made the charts too thick and fast for me to take in. My grandad, bless him, knew more about it than I did; he had the radio tuned to the BBC's *Light Programme*. *The Light Programme* was the sound of an indulgent auntie blundering about in a record shop trying to please her nephews and nieces while still attempting to placate her grumbling crusty siblings. It was like a cross between Radio Two in the seventies and a wartime broadcasting service. It was perfectly possible to hear a Mario Lanza record, followed by a Who single, followed by Max Bygraves, followed by Spencer Davis, followed by Ken Dodd. My grandad would sit and tap his feet to all of them.

'Who's this?' I'd ask him.

'The Small Faces. Not bad are they? I do wish they'd try to sing a bit more instead of shouting all the time though. Apart from that, it's quite a pleasant melody innit?'

The radio was a big Bakelite job with a huge round metal-grilled speaker. It was probably the same one through which he'd listened to Chamberlain announcing that no such undertaking had been received... One thing about that wireless was that it carried pop records really well. It had a lot of bass whoomf in it and months later stood up to Hendrix distortion much better than a transistor radio might have done.

That first month in 1966 when I was back in England, The Lovin' Spoonful were at Number One with 'Daydream', the Spencer Davis group were up there with 'Somebody Help Me' and absolutely everybody seemed to be going around whistling the tunes. The music leaked out of shop-girls' trannies, open windows, building sites and twee little boutiques. They were sung in the school playground, they went round your head all day when you were in class. Then the next week there'd be an endless supply of new ones.

The Beatles released six singles and two albums a year. To be in the second rank of bands you needed to be at least The Who, The Kinks or The Yardbirds. To be in the third rank you needed to be at least The Hollies, Dave Dee, or Spencer Davis. Then there were the one-hit wonders. I'm not trying to say the sixties were better, as such, but to a thirteen-year old returned from the Far East it was almost too much to take in. Brilliant singles were being released daily. Oh, and it has to be said, quite a lot of bad ones as well. The records which I heard when I came back from Singapore became the basis for nearly everything I subsequently did musically. If I ever get fed up with music now I go back to them and listen to them again, to try and divine, over three decades later, what it was about them that affected thousands of us so much, that for years, many of us simply refused to grow up.

In the meantime, I had to contend with secondary school. And the hairy blazer. And the grey shirts. And the round-toed, pre-war shoes with the big buckles. And the new, unashamedly racist nickname conferred on me because of my deep suntan. Meet the new boy, 'Wog'.

Six

It's a Jungle Out There
Cameron Highlands, Malaya, August 1966

Hey, I'm in the Junior Jet Club! BOAC give you these little logbooks. You get the captain of the Boeing 707 to sign it for you to attest to the fact that you've clocked up all these air miles. And then, years later, nothing happens. My brother and I are already veterans of the long-haul flight. On the way back to Malaya to visit our parents during holidays we stop at all sorts of interesting places: Frankfurt, Rome, Zurich, Istanbul, Kuwait, Bombay, Rangoon, and here comes our stop. Good evening, Kuala Lumpur. I'm thirteen and I should feel really international. Luckily, I'm wearing baggy shorts and sandals and have a short-back-and-sides haircut, so I don't. It was a close-run thing back there though. Thank God for sensible guardians.

We drive north out of Kuala Lumpur and up into the division of Perak, heading for a town called Tapah. The jungle hills are layers of deep green, deeper green, light green and finally, in the far distance, blue. After Tapah we take a long winding road that climbs and climbs into ever-steeper mountains and ever-thicker jungle. On the way up the jungle road, we don't see much apart from the odd truck and small packs of scabby, emaciated dogs called junglies. The hills are called the Cameron Highlands. They are incredibly beautiful and difficult for me to describe, short of slapping a poem on you, which I'm sure you wouldn't thank me for.

The junglies are mostly strays left behind by forces personnel. There's no dog warden in the jungle; the tigers do that job, which is why the junglies hang out in packs. At night, you can hear the tigers. They don't growl or roar; they cough, a deep throaty cough. They're very fond of dogs. In fact, shortly before we arrive, one enterprising tiger jumps a six-foot compound fence, seizes an alsatian guard dog and makes off over the fence with it. This is why it's a good idea to keep the dogs in after dark. Apart from the junglies, the tigers, the monkeys, the snakes and the insects, the other occupants of the jungle are the Sakai.

The Sakai are the indigenous jungle-hill people of Malaya. They're short and they carry little spears. They get in trouble if they attack you, so they don't, but they do sometimes stand at the side of the road and lift their loincloths up at women passengers in passing cars. This is a point of interest for my brother and I, so we spend at least part of the drive keeping an eye out for anyone waving his whanger. To our disappointment it never happens, although my mother swears that she's witnessed it. My dad informs me that the Sakai are nothing like the Dayak head-hunters of Borneo and are very shy. Consequently I never find out much more about them, let alone get a chance to run off and join them. 'British Boy Discovered Living Among Malayan Hill People, Found To Be Pop Genius.' No, none of this happens.

Instead I find myself at a place called Tanah Rata. Tanah Rata is the small town at the end of the thirty-nine-mile jungle road we've just travelled up. Its chief importance to the army is the British Military Hospital or BMH. I was never exactly sure what it was my father did up there, but I believe that when he wasn't on exercise, sleeping in a rough shelter called a basha and yelling at people, he did sterling work telling less-experienced soldiers how not to get ill in the jungle.

I learned about leptospirosis, a disease which is carried in rats' urine and which if it enters a small cut in your foot, while, say, wading a jungle river, can kill you. My dad could be highly entertaining when lecturing eight hundred soldiers on the subject of various tropical horrors and the avoidance of them. Periodically, he was asked to address a group of servicemen's wives on this subject or that. Once, when another officer had to fill in for him, back came the request from the women's group. 'May we have that nice young lieutenant with the twinkly eyes again, please?' His lectures on sweaty feet or crabs, 'mobile freckles' as he called them, were his hit numbers. As a young child, I'd stood on a freezing parade ground and watched a huge, eagle-nosed general pin a gong on my dad for something that he'd done. I'm not exactly sure what it was for, but it must have been something quite impressive.

Only once when he'd been drinking, so much so that he forgot I was only twelve and offered me a cigarette, did he talk about any action he'd been in. 'We were in the desert, in a jeep. Somebody started firing. Officer said, "That man!" I opened up. Saw him go down. Got him. Dead? Think so. That was it, didn't think about it at the time. Yup, I was scared.'

So this laconic warrior-cum-loquacious lecturer, my father, was now stationed in the Malayan highlands. There were soldiers at the hospital on rest and recuperation, one or two old veterans, some rich Chinese businessmen, a handful of tourists and expats, the shopkeepers and Inche Abdul, the genial barman in the officers' mess. Oh, and us. These were the only people in Tanah Rata that I knew about. The Japanese had occupied the place in 1942. Their officers had lived in the house that we now lived in. There were some tiny holes in one of the wooden panels in the living room. Here, my dad told me, was where the Japanese had hung a dartboard, left behind, in all probability, by their British predecessors.

The Japanese had taken the whole Malayan peninsular in 1942, by cycling down it from Thailand, two abreast, rifles on backs and not much more back-up than a bit of air support. On the road up to their former officers' mess (now our home) was a pretty colonial bungalow. The inhabitant of this *rumah* was a Miss Griff, an ancient and venerable woman who still strode arthritically down the jungle road to the town and its small parade of shops. If my brother and I ever saw her as we cycled up the road on our bikes, she'd call out to us in a voice and an accent from another century, 'Good morning to yoooo!' She'd been in Malaya for years and had served as the schoolteacher for the community until the Japanese arrived. The Japanese had been sufficiently impressed with her formidable dignity to more or less leave her to get on with it. They didn't remove her; I can't imagine they even tried. And so she'd sat out the war, a solitary old Englishwoman in the jungle, having tea at four and taking her twice-daily constitutionals. She's probably still there.

Once in a while, I'd be allowed to sit in the officers' mess, where Inche Abdul served 'big ones' to my dad and his fellow officers. His drinking mates sat and drank and swapped yarns and jokes. There was Paddy, a cheerful Irishman who told long stories, and Jack, a lean quiet man whom my dad treated with some reverence, because he'd survived the Arnhem Drop, a notorious Second World War battle that had yielded many thousand British casualties. And there was Siggi, a tough Pole who occasionally shouted 'Nasdravya!' and hurled his glass at the wall. Every once in a while, Siggi, with a weekend off would drink vodka till the small hours before going home to spruce himself up. Then he'd set off on foot down the jungle road to Tapah, spend some time in a whorehouse and walk the thirty-nine miles back. And I would sit around the mess, pretending to read my book, but really eavesdropping on these old gunslingers, whose conversation I probably understood about a quarter of.

Only now do I begin to realise how strange my childhood was in comparison with those of my friends'. I have seen the low rain clouds descend on the jungle hill opposite our house and have run up the hill to stand inside them. Having found myself in thick, drizzly mist, I've run a scant fifty yards back down the hill and found myself in bright sunshine. What would I tell my friends back in Harpenden when they asked me what I did in my holidays? 'I stood in clouds on jungle hills and listened to the tigers cough at night. I heard old warriors tell stories and was greeted by strange old women on the jungle roads.' Who would believe me?

One thing my parents have done during the summer of 1966 is to procure a copy of The Beatles' *Revolver*. Do I give the impression my parents are unhip? Well, scandalously so in some ways, and yet here is this new Beatles album, high in the jungle hills of Malaya. It gets cold at night and we have a log fire. A tiny portable record player sits in one corner of the panelled room. And I am sitting here playing *Revolver* over and over again. Coming across the track, 'Tomorrow Never Knows', my dad's considered opinion is that it's 'a bit of a bloody noise'. In his view, this is a shame, because otherwise, The Beatles write good tunes. I've brought two records out from England with me. They are Petula Clark's 'I Couldn't Live Without Your Love', which my mum adores and for my dad, Frank Sinatra's 'Strangers in the Night' which, let me tell you, I am pig-sick of by the end of the holiday. To this day I cannot hear any of these records without being reminded of the jungle, the mountains, and the huge Rajah Brooke's Birdwing butterflies which I once saw scores of by a jungle waterfall in a place called Kota Tinghi.

One drawback is that I don't have my guitar. Parents and guardians have impressed upon me the virtues of travelling without lots of clutter, and guitars qualify as clutter. Since I now know about five chords, and hard-won they were too, I have been trying to teach myself to write songs, not very successfully. But they're coming. I can hardly go straight from school to pop stardom if I don't have a guitar for six weeks at a time, upon which to write the songs, which will make my name.

In a Tanah Rata shop I come across a Chinese boy a few years older than myself. He's got an approximation of a mop-top haircut; he's wearing tight black trousers and Cuban-heeled boots. He's also carrying a semi-acoustic guitar with a cutaway. My eyes nearly pop out of my head. I ask him if I can have a go on his guitar and I play the riff for 'The Last Time' and show him my chords. He looks on, impressed. Then he takes the guitar back from me and plays The Beatles' 'Ticket To Ride'. It's perfect, riff, verses and choruses. I'm demolished, and quite envious that I've encountered this in the middle of a jungle outpost, high in the hills and thousands of miles from England. I want my guitar. There is much to do, but I can't even begin.

Seven

Here Comes the Nice
Harpenden, Spring 1967/South London, Autumn 1967

I'm at my gran's place in Harpenden somewhere at the beginning of summer term May 1967. It's *Top of the Pops* and we've just had 'Waterloo Sunset' by the Kinks. Straight on afterwards are The Who, with 'Pictures of Lily'. Going down in the charts: Pink Floyd's 'Arnold Layne'; 'Purple Haze' by Jimi Hendrix; 'Bernadette' by The Four Tops. Coming up in the charts: The Small Faces' 'Here Comes the Nice'; 'Paper Sun' by Traffic; 'Night of the Long Grass' by The Troggs. Oi! You in the baseball cap. That's right, you in the appalling sportswear. You think pop music's better in the naughty noughties do you? Get a pair of ears, Junior.

I came back from Malaya for the last time in early January of 1967, the day my baby brother Joel was born. I was in Kuala Lumpur with my other brother, Mark, and my dad. Joel was in Penang with my mum. Now we're all back together in Harpenden, for a week or two. Oh except for Mark, he's in Buckinghamshire. You get used to army life, or you don't. Now, my grandad lets me have my hair a bit longer, not inches longer, weeks longer. I'm allowed to have it three weeks longer. So the first thing my dad says upon seeing his eldest son for the first time in five months is, 'Tch! Your hair!'

Straight after *Top of the Pops*, I'm out on my bike to a village four miles away. All the songs of the time are in my head and the whole backdrop to the moment is freedom and fields of Queen Anne's lace. It is decided, since my father's new posting is in London that there's no point in dragging me out of this, my tenth school. I'll spend the rest of the summer term here and move up to London to attend my eleventh school at the end of summer. Apart from more niggling about my hair, relations with my parents are mostly cordial. Then they leave my gran's tiny house and move up to some place in Putney, South London.

How do I convey the atmosphere during this period? Well a year of living in the Home Counties with civvy kids, starting to get the odd crush on girls, reading a lot of classic ghost stories and pop magazines, then cycling anything up to thirty miles round the Chiltern villages, has done wonders for me. I'm a cheerful little sod. I rush home from school at lunchtime, wolf my dinner down, rush upstairs to struggle with the chords of 'Pictures of Lily' and pelt back to school to make it in time for afternoon registration. I finish in the afternoon, rush back upstairs and struggle with the chords for 'Pictures of Lily', come down for tea, rush back upstairs, try to write something of my own, then go out on my bike to meet my best mate, Geoff Bourne, who comes from a big family on the estate round the corner. We join some other kids and play this rough game with a football called simply, the Square.

Lately, I haven't been going round there so much. This is because on one of my many solo bike rides I've met a girl in a local village. So I hang around with her, snogging in barns and on the overgrown lawn of an empty parsonage. Girls are weird creatures. This one wears leg make-up. I don't, you know, do anything to her. I simply do not know what is allowed, or what is required, for that matter. My head is full of music and dreams, so I don't even think about it. Aren't boys thick, girls? It comes as a bit of a shock to me when my friends back on the playing field, find out about my little secret. Turns out that they know her. She and her friend are well-known little tarts who like to get their tits out on the field. Boy, has she been having a laugh about me, and anyway, she's packed me in because I didn't, you know, do anything. I'd been seeing her for all of two weeks. We were practically engaged. For ages I don't bother with girls after that.

I decide to cycle to London to see my parents since they keep asking to see me. The trip is about thirty miles, much of it along the North Circular Road. Could you imagine letting a boy of fourteen do that now? I discover that my parents live in a fairly well-appointed flat about three storeys up somewhere off the Richmond Road. All the other people who live there are army officers' families. It's OK I suppose, for London. I'd better get used to it, as I'll be living there from late July. London is sort of exciting.

Remember, this is the year of flower power. According to the papers, fashionable people are all wearing flowers and bells, growing their hair and enjoying free love. This social revolution is stoked by news of happenings in San Francisco. The Beatles are singing 'All You Need is Love', the contraceptive pill is available and everything's gone paisley and Day-Glo. Down the King's Road, Chelsea, and in Notting Hill Gate art exhibitions, alternative magazines and clothes shops are springing up. This movement is called the underground – and is not to be confused with the popular subterranean railway of that name. The members of the underground have long hair, groovy clothes and are turned on to pot smoking and LSD. They call themselves 'heads' or 'freaks'. The media calls them hippies. According to the papers and TV, the hippies are taking over the city. Only I don't recall encountering any hippies during this time, just some great songs on the radio. And again this incredible feeling that something brilliant was happening somewhere.

Sometime during August, I find that the flat has a garage round the back of the block that is allocated to it. My parents don't use it because we don't have a car. The garage has great reverb, except I don't know that it's called reverb at this point. My brother and I and a friend of ours decide to form some sort of a band. We build a drum-kit out of cardboard boxes, oil drums and biscuit tins. We build all sorts of percussion instruments and with my guitar and all of us singing start making a racket. When we're making a competent-enough racket, we throw up the garage door, find some chairs and do a gig for all the other kids in the flats. It's great. I'm squeezing the last drops out of my fractured childhood.

Shortly afterwards, I start school at a huge comprehensive in Putney. I find we're moving again, to Balham. In the middle of September we move to another block of army flats. Am I changing schools again? We have to ask the authorities. Yes? No? Yes? No. I can stay at the school I've just started. There's just a bit of a train journey, that's all: walk up Balham High Road, train to Clapham Junction, change, train to Putney, then a walk up Putney Hill. Mad. And I'm not the only one. Kids come from Raynes Park, Stockwell, Battersea and Fulham.

Within a month or two however, I'm already in a band, with an extremely long-haired friend called Barry. Barry knows a drummer, Woodsy, and we rehearse once a week in a run-down two-car showroom on Lavender Hill. And all the West Indian kids stand outside and listen to it. It's quite a convincing racket when we do 'All Or Nothing'. Barry gets kicked out of school for refusing to have his hair cut, or it might have been waving his dick at a teacher, I can't remember exactly. He was a working lad after that, so I didn't see him for a bit.

I also meet my mate Dave, who's huge. He introduced himself to me on the first day by lobbing a regulation school bar of soap at the back of my head. I felt dizzy and threw up most of the afternoon. He didn't own up to it until about a year later. He and his mate Gary are like giants compared to most of the boys. It's strange the disparity in physical development when you're fourteen. It all comes out in the changing room. Some boys have deep voices, muscles like men and great bushes with huge whangers. Then some of us are sort of lean with a few watch-springs round the cricket set. Then there's the C-team with high piping voices and willies like cooked, peeled baby prawns. You all just get thrown in together, the nipple twisting the wet-towel cracking and the brutal jokes. And that's just in religious instruction.

The school hasn't got its own playing fields. For sports, they bus everybody out to various sports grounds and playing fields. You can do ice-skating, which everybody wants to do. This is why I volunteer for cross-country running. Only three of us in the whole year do it. Rejected ice-skaters get put into football or rugby. I'm alright, as I volunteered for cross-country. This kind of lateral thinking will ensure that I never play any sort of a team sport after my third year, and never play many team sports ever. While the rest of the year gets in a coach to go off to Raynes Park playing fields for football and rugby, two other boys and I get changed in an empty changing room. A master gives us a map. We're to run over Putney Heath, over Wimbledon common, drone, blah, etc. What we actually do is run dutifully out of sight of the school, and then stroll to a pub called the Windmill. Because he looks old enough, my mate Milton buys some beer. I take the ten cigarettes out of my sock and then we have a leisurely stroll back and a theological discussion, or something. Of course, we splatter a bit of mud on ourselves to make it look good. Once back in sight of the school we start running. We report to the teacher in his office and tell him that we think our timing's getting better. He marks our reports, and we're already strolling out of the gates early, before the other kids have even got back off the coaches. This is possibly why our school makes such a dismal showing in the London cross-country races.

In this, my eleventh school, I have learned the lessons of the past and have reinvented myself. No one knows where I come from or where I've been. I listen carefully to the accent and imitate it exactly. I tell jokes and I bring my guitar to school and play Small Faces and Who songs in the toilets. If I'm not actually one of the lads I'm to be left alone because of my entertainment value. I try not to show off in English or history, although I actually love the subjects. I've done a great job of disguising myself, or so I think.

I am highly flattered when I'm befriended by Phil, a hard-nut and junior terrace thug, who tells me all about his running battles as a Fulham supporter on Saturdays. Phil wants a favour. He's mad about this girl called Georgia, pronounced Jorjah. She is indeed a beautiful young girl, and very posh. She lives in a big house somewhere near Barnes Common. He wants to ask her out, to a football match. He wants me to write her a letter expressing his interest and extending the invitation to her. I ask Phil why he thinks I can help him. 'Well, Mart...you're like her. You know? Posh.' How do kids work stuff like this out? I'm speaking perfect Sarflundn. I've got the slouch. I hang out with the boys and Phil thinks I'm posh. Why? He's noticed I write a lot during English lessons. He's noticed that when

I'm asked to read a passage out in front of a class, that I can do so without difficulty. This, apparently, is what has given me away.

So I concoct the letter for Phil. He copies it out and gets an intermediary to pass it to his intended. And whaddya know? She buys it. So Georgia goes out on the terraces with Phil a couple of Saturdays later. And then he takes her to a Wimpy Bar. She writes him a letter back, a little while later, saying, thanks for taking her to the football match and look, it's been great but... And Phil never forgets this talent of mine, so periodically, whenever he's adapting the words of current pop hits to turn into obscene terrace chants for Saturday afternoons, it is yours truly here who Phil pesters, to give the words a bit of a nip and a tuck. Well there you go, my tiny part in sixties' football hooligan culture.

Now it's autumn half-term. The leaves turn on Wandsworth Common, and at the back of the huddled terraces, seen from the trains as I come home to Balham, the lights go on early. There's a faint smell of coal, kindling and burning leaves, the occasional bang of a firework in the denim dusk. There's bluebeat and ska music leaking from the windows in Bedford Hill. I come down Atkins Road with my guitar trying to figure out the opening bit of 'The Burning of the Midnight Lamp'. And at home, there's Andy Williams on Radio Two and the smell of ironing and tea. I've become a London kid.

On wet Saturdays I go into Watkins Electric Music at the bottom of Balham High Road. Here, I play the guitars, pretending that I'm going to buy one, and Charlie Watkins, pretending that he believes me, allows me to. This shop is the home of famous WEM musical equipment, much used by sixties' English rockers, and Charlie is the inventor of the WEM Copikat echo unit. Even though, to me, he's an old gaffer, he knows all the pop groups.

Everyone comes in here. Even Keith Moon has occasionally popped in for drumsticks. I ask Charlie who he reckons is a good band; 'That Crazy World of Arthur Brown, they're good. They're gonna do alright.' And sure enough, Arthur Brown's at number one, a few months later. Charlie's two brothers invented the Watkins Rapier, everybody's first electric guitar, bright red or bright blue, with twin cutaways and umpteen pick-ups.

Over the road is a groovy-gear boutique called Take Five. The guy in there has got long hair and plays in a band. I hang around talking with him too. His band is supporting another band called The Gods, whose members include Ken Hensley, soon to be of Uriah Heep and one Mick Taylor who will later join The Rolling Stones. A group van is parked around the corner. It belongs to a band called The Bees. They'll change their name to The Pyramids and have a hit soon with 'Last Train to Rainbow City'. And from windows above newsagents, from run-down old church halls and from the bedrooms of the grimy back-street terraces, music spills: guitars, drumbeats, over-driven organs. I can't wait to grow up and get in a band myself.

I take a train back to Harpenden to spend a few days with my gran. On the last night there I decide my fringe needs shaping. I take the scissors to make it a bit more like McCartney's. I do it skewiff. I take a bit more off, and a bit more off. It now looks like a Frankenstein hack, done by a barber with advanced Parkinson's disease. When I get home, my mum takes one look at it and sends me straight off to a brutal Polish barber in a market arcade. He just shaves the lot off. I go back to school and even the cropped mods go, 'Faackin' 'ell! Wot 'appened ter you?' I promise myself something there and then, after this, I am growing my hair, as long as I want, and if anyone wants me to cut it, they'll have to kill me first.

Eight

Yer in the army now
Yer not behind a plough
Yer'll never get rich
By diggin' a ditch
Yer in the army now.
(Traditional, as sung by my mother)

I was not in the army. But I sometimes felt like I was. Dad was in the army, Infantry then Medics. His brother had been in the army, his dad had been in the army, both big wars and several smaller ones. From what I've heard of my father's father I wouldn't be surprised to learn that he'd started a few modest ones of his own: fought at Mons; wounded and decorated at Salonika; re-enlisted as soon as the Second World War started. Even my mum was in the army ATS. It's how she met my dad. Her sister married a soldier. When he died, she married another one. Their dad had been in the army during the First World War. I even had a great uncle who was a trooper at the Battle of Omdurman, under Kitchener.

For most of the last century, wherever there was trouble in the world, there was probably a Newell there. The list of their postings sounds like a playlist for *Now That's What I Call War Volumes One and Two*: South Africa, France, Libya, Suez, the North West Frontier, Germany, Malaya, Cyprus, Northern Ireland. It goes on and on and all the dates of postings match all the troubles. When they're not fighting wars, they're fighting anyone who'll fight with them: other soldiers, civilians, the military police and occasionally each other.

And yet, like all good Saxon hotheads, they settle down with girls, the hormones calm down and they become solid old dads with good stories, a love of gardening and a respect for nature. They nurture a robust scepticism about politicians, and the political views they hold tend to be reasonable and fair-minded. There's a grid reference on the political map where anarchism with a small A and conservatism with a small C converge, and my family, like so many families of our type tend to squat right on it. They don't want any trouble because they know what trouble is worth, what a broken head feels like, what newly orphaned children sound like when they cry. And when some prat of a politician, or would-be politician starts upping the stakes, it is with a certain insight and experience that they visualise the eventual outcome of any possible conflagrations. But when there is trouble, there they are.

And while they are still in the army, the people in my family are full-on. 'I am a professional,' was one phrase I often heard. 'You are a second generation barrack rat,' I was told. Barrack rat. Son of a soldier. We were pretty much yeoman class. Not the 'pot-bellied, snobby, chinless wonders' my dad disparaged so much. We worked for it, every inch of it.

But I am fifteen. I live in an army flat in Balham, South London, and I am determined not to have anything to do with the army. I fight it with every bit of resistance I can muster. And anyway I'm a weed. I want to have long hair and be in a pop group. It's all I can think about. My brother has pictures of Chelsea football players all over his wall. I have Pete Townshend, The Small Faces and The Kinks on mine. At my big comprehensive school in Putney I'm the guitar star of the school bogs. The previous ten schools I've attended have at last taught me my lesson. If you can't fight, you must sing songs and tell stories. You become a sort of sacred cow. No one wants to beat the cabaret up.

I can play The Move's 'Fire Brigade' – even the twiddly bits in the middle eight. The thugs are in awe of me and give me cigarettes at break. I'm also a good dinner-ticket forger. To stop a black-market trade in school dinner tickets, the school issues a different colour batch each week. If you build up a big enough collection of unused ones, you wait for a week when a colour reoccurs and sell them. But the authorities have thought of that. And halfway through term they put the headmaster's signature on the back. So if you have a collection the right colour, you still need the signature on it. A week's practice and I've got it down to a fine art. The dinner-ticket black marketeers have to come to me, the forger, to make their dinner tickets legal. I do it for cigarettes or cash. I also forge the odd report, but this is a lot more dangerous so I'm wary of doing it. My other source of revenue, apart from a paper round, is stolen film posters. I've learned that, if I peel the edge of a film poster on a railway station and then give it a good yank in the right direction, it comes off in one. Best to do this just before the train pulls out. Then I stick it under my blazer, take it to school next day and swop it for money or cigarettes. I remember the poster for Shalako was popular because it had a big picture of Brigitte Bardot on it. I got about five of them. Anything with Clint Eastwood was easy to shift too.

My friends are a smart bunch of misfits. Over there is Robert, with his long black hair and Jagger fixation, full of cynical jokes about the teachers. Sparking up a sly Number Six in the corner is Hedley, an Arabic-looking French boy, who's so devastatingly good-looking even some of the younger female teaching staff are rumoured to be in love with him. Twanging Mavis' bra strap and getting a fearful smack in the face for it, is Joe Robinson who looks and acts like a young Lee Marvin and can do brilliant impersonations of both film stars and teachers. Dave and Gary, two young Battersea mods who look almost grown-up, are taking the piss out of the middle-class sixth formers while they talk about going down to Chelsea Bridge this weekend to have a go at the rockers. Barry Collier, my guitar-strumming mate, is in the bogs, playing a song about wanking. Barry was the first bloke I ever met who took a picture of his own dick and managed to get it developed somehow, by convincing the people in Boots the Chemist that it was some other part of his body. There's a quiet, handsome guy hanging around with us all, and smiling. He wears a smart blazer and always has the right pens. What we used to call 'well-turned out'. Everybody likes him. He's called Irish. Because that's what he is. The world knows him better by his real name now. Brosnan. Pierce Brosnan. And somewhere, running around among all the little second-year oiks two years below us is Chris Miller, who will later become a punk rock drummer called Rat Scabies in a band called The Damned.

Just released and being played on the radio is Manfred Mann's 'My Name Is Jack'. Going down is Reparata and The Delrons' 'This Is the Captain of Your Ship'. And coming out any minute now is 'Jumpin' Jack Flash' by the Rolling Stones. Every one of these songs measuring the gap between my childhood and what happens next. And Miss Nostalgia... Can you get your hand off my thigh now?

Look. I've told you, I don't want to go out with you any more. OK, just once more then. But don't break my heart again.

Back at the old homestead, mum listens to Jimmy Young. Andy Williams is never off the radio and life goes on much as it always does in an army flat. The old man's doing some kind of a desk job at Chelsea Barracks, which isn't quite exciting enough for him by the looks of things, so he goes off to the Brecon Beacons, or somewhere like it at weekends, to teach the Territorial Army how the pros do it. On these weekends, Camp Newell can stand at ease awhile and I can strum my guitar at all hours of the day and night. Sometime on Sunday, however, the Jack Russell's yapping and a kick on my bedroom door will signal that the CO's back from exercise and it's time to, 'Stop plunking that bloody banjo'.

I once heard my mother remonstrating with him in the kitchen, 'But he's composing, dear.'

'I don't care if he's decomposing. He can still stop plunking that bloody banjo,' came his now famous retort.

I'm not saying the man wasn't funny at times but his way of coming to grips with the effete young stag rapidly growing up in front of him was to treat me as a new conscript who needed to be broken. As a long-term army man, I suppose it was the only way he could deal with it. There was just one flaw in all this. I was made of more or less the same material as him, maybe a bit flimsier, maybe with a pretty paisley pattern on it. But if he pushed one way, then I pushed the other. The repartee got pretty nasty on occasions and I learned to stay out of his way when he came back from army exercises and got stuck into the whisky.

His own dad, who was by all accounts, a pretty fearsome old sweat, was probably the same with his sons. I once asked my dad what kind of treatment he'd received from him. He mulled it over for a few seconds, before answering, 'Oh, I was tolerated. I was tolerated.' Years later, when I was long out of drug-taking but now drinking rather heavily instead, I came home one day, having made my peace with him to ask his advice on something. I found him reading his paper in the living room.

Me: Dad, I need to ask your advice on something.
    Father: What's that boy?
    Me: Dad... I think I'm becoming an alcoholic.
    Father: Rubbish. You're not trying hard enough.
    Me: What? Do you have to try then?
    Father: No, that's the whole bloody point, boy. You don't have to try at all.
    Counselling session ends. Exit baffled son to kitchen.

Dad's solution to most of my problems when I am fifteen is to join the army. 'SAS. You'd be good at that.' A bit later on, 'Military police, you'd make a good military policeman. And so would your brother.' I tell him I want to be a professional pop musician. 'You're one of millions. The army's got musicians too, military bandsmen. Sign on for three years. When you come out, you'll be able to read music and play several instruments. And you'll be able to work anywhere.' Yeah, right. Cheers dad.

As for the length of my hair, this is one of the biggest bones of contention of all. It's about the length of a mid-period Brian Jones-style hairstyle. It's mousy blonde and covers my ears. And it's very, very controversial. This is south London 1968, but you would think, from all the fuss it causes, that I was wearing a pink Mohican. From reasoning with me, to threatening to try and cut my hair while I'm asleep, my parents never get off my case over it. My mother even tries clumsy psychology, 'I see from this

article in the paper, that long hair's on its way out now.'
(No it's not.)

And my father says, 'Yes, a lot of them are wearing it
short again now.' (No they're not.)

People shout at me from cars, 'Are you a boy or a girl?'
To which the standard reply becomes, 'Why dontcha
suck my cock and find out?'

People serving in shops sometimes ask, 'Can I help you
madam?' The most common taunt is of course, 'Getcher
'air cut, you bleedin' poof.' But it goes on and on and on.
I never did find out why people, especially older men,
found it such a threat. The treatment I receive, however,
will only have the effect of buttressing my rebel stance,
making it stronger. For the charmed denizens of London's
hippie underground movement, swanning around
Chelsea, Kensington and Ladbroke Grove, there's some sort
of strength in numbers. For the rest of us, living off the
main drag, there's just a daily gauntlet of insults mitigated
by the occasional excitement of sprinting through side
streets pursued by first-wave skinheads intent on teaching
us a lesson.

So I begin to read underground magazines like *IT* and *Oz*
and I kid myself that I understand half of the
gobbledegook that I find therein. And of course, I imagine
that the underground really does include me and that one
day we'll all rise up, have The Fun Revolution, and I'll meet
a groovy chick, be in a pop group and my whole life will be
a bit like The Beatles' film, *Help*.

I am living in something of a golden age of daft
psychedelic singles. After headway made by The Beatles,
Traffic and Pink Floyd a few months earlier, every tin-pot
band in the land has gone psychedelic. Bands with names
like Tintern Abbey, Turquoise, Amazing Crocheted
Doughnut Ring, are making the most baroque and strange
singles. Backward cymbals and sub-Hendrix guitar solos

proliferate, as does Lewis Carroll imagery, odd time changes and obligatory sitar parts, even among bands that were previously straight pop groups. Everyone now has some sort of a concept in mind. And incredibly enough, the recently formed Radio One is playing the discs. Years later some of these records will still sound endearing. Most will just sound bloody silly. But then, isn't that what pop's all about?

So it's a reasonably happy, if slightly perplexed schoolboy who comes home on Friday nights to watch *Do Not Adjust Your Set*, eat his beans on toast, and struggle straight afterwards with the chords of 'Armenia City in the Sky'; the best song that Pete Townshend never wrote. Somewhere out there, something brilliant is going on, but he just doesn't know how to get there yet.

And in that happy land, which is only just over the blurred blue hills, there is no school or army. No one tries to kick your head in as you walk down the tree-lined avenues in your pop-star finery. Virginity has been lost and jangly electric guitars play all day long. And in a tower by a lake, a girl with daisies painted on her face and wearing a medieval dress comes softly up the spiral staircase by candlelight to whisper that the unicorn has been delivered. A million dragonflies shimmer up from the still waters below. And as the painted drawbridge is let down, there's an almighty crash and a cry of, 'Stop plunking that bloody banjo!' Very good, sergeant major.

Nine

Being Beaten
South London, May 1969

A man who's had some training in the manly art of boxing will hit you in a quite different way to an ordinary scrapper. He'll take a short jab, marshal his whole weight behind it and turn his body into it, so that at the moment of impact, as the arm extends, the punch delivers strength of arm plus body weight. All the better too, if the person who delivers the punch takes a ten-pace run up to the target from a nearby parked van. In this way, a properly trained thirteen-stone man can do a fair amount of damage to a sixteen-year old weighing about nine and a half stone. When the sixteen-year old has spun round and lies semi-conscious on the pavement, he's far less likely to attempt to rise, as two or three of the man's friends kick his prone body in the back and ribs for a minute or so. At least this has been my experience of such matters...

Pete, Rob and the hippy girl are dragging me along Swinburne Road, Putney. I can't walk but I'm just about conscious. I can feel the toes of my Chelsea boots scuffing on the pavement and I'm aware that I'm being dragged quite fast. I can't see because my eyes are full of blood from the wound above my right eye. My legs aren't working. The door of Rob's house is open and his sister Sharon is screaming at the sight of me. I've been professionally done over and the effects of it will reverberate through my life for a long time afterwards.

It was not the best of times. I'd left school a few months earlier and taken a dead-end job so that I could buy the amplifier and better guitar I needed for chart stardom. The job was in Farringdon Road, logging, grading, and filing old GPO telegrams with a forty-column punch-card system. I'm not even going to go into it but my problem wasn't with the job itself, so much as the slavish adherence to normality of my colleagues whose common mantra seemed to be, 'You got to getcha money. Intcha?'

My first band had just folded before we'd really even done a proper gig. Dave, Hedley and I had done our best with the gear we had and the scant talent we possessed between us, but finally we'd had to sell the drum-kit. To add insult to injury, when Dave and Hedley were carting the kit over Putney Bridge, they'd stopped halfway for a break, to smoke their last cigarette. As they turned out of the wind to light the thing, they'd heard Boom Boom Boom on one of the tom-toms. A passing pigeon had shat on it. Rigor Mortis, as we'd schoolboyishly called ourselves, had been untogether for nearly a year, since we were all still at school in fact. But now we didn't even exist. It had been my main reason for living. Rigor Mortis was dead.

In addition to this, I really had fallen quite madly in love with a blonde girl called Sue. I must have been seeing her for all of two weekends. Only kissing and stuff. I went to call for her one Friday night and her mum told me she'd disappeared. She seemed worried about her. I made it my mission to track Sue down. I spent nearly the whole weekend asking everybody in Balham where she was. Some people seemed to think a past boyfriend, an older foreign guy, had abducted her.

Through sheer adolescent obsession, after two days I finally found her, in a dingy flat in an old Victorian building up the road in Tooting Bec. She was with the foreign bloke. 'Hallo,' she said. 'I didn't think I'd ever see you again.' I stood in the hall and asked in whispers if she needed rescuing. She laughed at me. 'No, I wanna marry him but my mum said I'm not her daughter if I marry a foreigner.' She told me that she was going to have a baby. She kissed me on the cheek and told me I was 'sweet' to worry. I left. I don't remember walking home. I don't remember most of the week at work: my horrible job, my lost pop group, and my lovely girlfriend.

So. Let's recap on this, shall we? I'm sixteen, living in London with my parents, having left school. I'm in a dead-end job. My band has broken up and I've lost my girlfriend. So I've started hanging around in Putney with my mate Rob from school, and his mate Pete. Reader, these are strange times. Four protesting students have recently been gunned down by state troopers in America, Vietnam's in full whack. Music has stopped being pop and started being progressive. Hair has got longer, at least for Rob, Pete and myself, though not so for legions of other young men in our respective areas of London. Hair has got shorter for them. Boots have got bigger.

Journalists on fashionable magazines, both then and now, may talk all the toss they wish about underground London, long hair, revolution and hippies. But out here in the suburbs, young blades are shaving their heads, listening to reggae, going to football and having a go at anything that doesn't conform to their sartorial or racial ideas of normality. Boys I once played football with, who called me Shirley Temple because of the length of my hair, are now skinheads. I'm alright on my own turf, on the estates of Balham, Clapham or Putney, but anywhere off this territory can be dangerous for me.

It doesn't help that I wear a Hendrix-type guardsman's jacket with yellow epaulettes, gold frogging and a yellow-trimmed red collar. It doesn't help that I wear a shocking-pink shirt with white collar and cuffs, or that I wear grey chalk-stripe hipster bell-bottom trousers, a lacy scarf and Chelsea boots with ankle zips. My attempted Brian Jones hairstyle doesn't help. The guitar I often wear on my back doesn't help. But what the hell. Rob and Pete have even longer hair and wear crushed-velvet trousers and grandad vests. It's the end of the sixties and no one knows exactly what's going to happen.

So Pete, Rob, the hippy girl from round the corner whom we've just met and myself are walking up Dover House Road. We're going to Pete's to listen to discs by The Small Faces, Led Zeppelin and The Moody Blues. And then argue about it. It's a beautiful late May evening. We're not stoned or anything, not yet. We're just into music, clothes and teen bickering. Suddenly a white van passes us, heading up towards Roehampton. We can hear jeering and banging from inside it. As it drifts slowly past, V-signs can be observed in the back windows. I casually flick a V-sign back. I know most of the people round here. After all I used to go to school with them. They're probably just some idiots from school. The van backs down the road and two of the occupants leap out to confront us, or rather, to confront me. One of them I recognise. He's a thug from school, two or so years older than me. He was also known as a prize runner. They're after me now, but I'm faster. Not only that, but I'm hurdling hedges with great ability. Half a mile on, I've outrun them. The van can't follow the route I've taken, since much of it is across gardens.

We meet up back at Pete's house, have a cup of tea, listen to some records and after two hours prepare to walk back down the road. The girl will go home to her bedsit in Richmond Road and I will walk to Putney Station to get a train back to Balham. On the corner of Dover House Road and Swinburne Road there is a squeal of brakes. It is over two hours since my hurdling race. Jackson, the prize runner I succeeded in outrunning, is standing with his arm stretched across my chest, to prevent me walking any further. Pete, Rob and the girl are standing back. Quite right too. No point in all of us getting our clothes ruined.

I really wonder sometimes whether there ought to be some kind of Government Ministry for The Prevention Of Boredom In The Very Thick. It could find things for them to do like counting their legs, painting bicycles interesting colours or something. Perhaps then they wouldn't derive such excitement from going around in teams having a go at anyone who is different to them. These men, reader, waited for over two hours in a hot van on a beautiful summer evening just to injure one sixteen-year old who didn't even fight back.

Supposing I'd gone the other way home, down Putney Hill? They might have been there for days, years even. Something should be done. Televised football and boxing is simply not enough. Huge sections of the population have suffered too much for too long. Or can't we just give them electric guitars and wah-wah pedals, then dose them with very strong hallucinogens? Call me an old psychedelic bigot if you like but it never did me any harm.

With Jackson's arm in front of me, I scarcely noticed the running footsteps behind me. For a minute I thought I'd piss myself with fear. I thought the attack would come from the front. As I turned round I heard a shout, and saw a bulldog of a bloke flying through the air. I heard my own

59

voice moan, as the punch hit me. Then semi-blackout. I felt the boots going into my ribs and back, but it didn't hurt. That was the weird thing. It didn't hurt. It felt like empty boxing gloves being thrown at me. Then a voice, 'That's for running away from us.' Well let that be a lesson to me then. I should have stayed for the seminar, and hands-on workshop with discussion groups afterwards, accessing further essential info on a need-to-know basis. More blackout, more running. Are they coming back? No. The van starts and squeals off.

In Rob's living room, Rob's mum and sister are trying to clean me up. There's blood everywhere. Nothing hurts as I'm in shock. I didn't know the guy who hit me. They do. He's called Colin. He's a boxer. The others laid into me with their boots. When I wasn't moving they got scared and ran. I'm a mess. Near midnight I insist on walking the mile or so to Putney Station. Change at Clapham Junction. Train to Balham. Another mile or so back home. No one in the train wants to sit near me. I come home and put myself to bed.

In the morning, I'm almost unrecognizable. I can't open one eye and my whole face is swollen. My mum seems concerned. I tell her I was beaten up. My dad, who I'm not getting on too well with at present, sees me in the corridor. I hear him ask my mum what happened. She explains that I was beaten up. I hear him mumble, 'It was because he had long hair.' That's all.

At work, the androids either laugh at me or they say, 'Well that's what you get if you go around looking like that. Bound to happen sooner or later.' Let that be a lesson to me then. Round about lunchtime I start to feel dizzy. My ribs and back hurt a lot. I'm sent home. My mum insists on taking me to the hospital. I've got badly bruised ribs and some damage to a nerve centre over my right eye, and bits of my face feel dead. They prod me around a bit and send me home.

I spend the weekend in my room reading. I wonder if it would be any easier for me if I cut my hair, wore normal clothes, played the game. But I know it wouldn't. The thing about the androids is they don't even like each other. And anyway, unorthodoxy is in the eyes. In fact, I think they can even smell it on you. May as well stay weird. But I feel safe now, because I'm such a mess that no one's going to do it to me again for, ooh...at least a week. But as I remark elsewhere in this tale, these are not the best of times for our young hero...

Ten

Leaving London
London, Autumn 1969-1970

I lived in London for just over three years. When I'd arrived in the summer of 1967, aged fourteen, it was a rather magical place. By the winter of that year, I'd got to know it so well that I was happily wandering round Soho watching buskers, staring in windows and looking at the exotic people. I saw Pete Townshend, once, in a station underpass at St Pancras. He was wearing an old raincoat and walking along, deep in conversation with someone else. In the West End I saw David McCallum, who played Illya Kuryakin on the *The Man From Uncle* TV series. I stared at him and, for a moment, he looked back at me. Walking up Wardour Street, I once saw the singer from a band called Rare Bird who'd had a big hit with an organ-driven song called 'Sympathy'. It was weird to me that I might see all these people, just walking around. The only famous people I'd seen before we lived in London had been Eric Morecambe and Harry H Corbett. Before this I was beginning to develop a theory that no famous people really existed. I was becoming rather like those nutters who believe that men never walked on the moon and that it had all been staged in a TV studio.

In early 1969, the Post Office, whom I worked for at the time, briefly sent me on a day-release scheme to Kingsway Day College near King's Cross. Apart from my fellow working lads, there were lots of hip young London long-hairs at the place, art students, the type of people who made inserts in their bell-bottoms out of tapestry curtain material. Sophisticated. Anyway, one of them told me that this band called something something Corner were playing at the college, that very Friday evening. I thought, 'Ooh, must be Amen Corner. Bit famous for a little college gig.' I mean, they've just had a number one disc with 'Half As Nice'. So on a snowy Friday night I travelled from Balham to King's Cross to see Amen Corner, but when I arrived at the gig, there were only two people up on the stage. It wasn't Amen Corner. One of the men was an old geezer in his thirties, playing guitar. And the other one was this curtain-haired bass player, whose face I couldn't see. There was something about the guitarist though: he had an authentic blues sound, and this way of playing the notes. The duo played some Willie Dixon numbers and generally jammed quite coherently for ages. After they came off stage, fifteen-year-old prat face here, goes up to the guitarist and starts asking him fascinating stuff like, 'Oh er, what gauge strings do you use, mister?' Well, the guitarist was very patient and kindly to your boy and spoke with him for some time. He had a voice that sounded like about sixty fags a day and he was the first man who ever called me Baby.

Who was he? I wasn't exactly sure, until Brian Jones died about five months later. They interviewed a lot of people about the dead Rolling Stone, but the guy who gave the most articulate interviews on television, the guy who had known and helped encourage Jones and the other Stones from the very beginning, was the same man who'd answered all my dumb questions about guitars, and called me Baby. His name was Alexis Korner.

I saw the Stones in Hyde Park. That's me under the tree there, with the heavy nosebleed and serious heat-headache. The thing I was most impressed with was the rockers in their studded jackets and the rather more serious-looking Hell's Angels. I'd never seen so many all in one place. The Stones were a bit ragged, as I remember. King Crimson were good, and so were Family, but the band who really suffered was poor old Pete Brown's Battered Ornaments. Pete Brown was a hero of mine. He was a poet, who'd written most of The Cream's lyrics. Along with Roger McGough, for me, he was a sort of logical link between lyric writing and poetry. The wonderful peace-loving hippy crowd wanted to see the Stones though, and from where I was sitting, the bastards were giving The Battered Ornaments quite a bad time. It was a shame.

One misty autumn Saturday in October of 1969, having nothing else to do, I took a bus from Putney up to the West End. Wearing my military jacket with yellow epaulettes, with my guitar slung over my shoulder, I met a young rocker on the bus. He told me that he was going up to the Dilly to hang out with his big mates in the Hell's Angels. The Angels were getting quite a lot of press at the time. They and some hippies had occupied 144 Piccadilly, a huge empty bit of very expensive real estate. We hooked up with these dangerous-looking men outside a place called the Pronto Café, by Piccadilly Circus. One of the Angels asked me if I could play the guitar I was carrying. I said I could. He said, 'Play the fucker then. We'll collect some money for you.'

More out of nerves than anything else, I began playing The Who's 'The Kids Are Alright'. I followed it up with

Donovan's 'Universal Soldier'. The bikers began holding out their chain-festooned peaked caps and a Nazi helmet, and shaking down passers-by who were rather too intimidated not to contribute. Within minutes, we had a few quid. We went and had coffee and cakes and they split the remains of the take, giving me about ten bob. I spent the rest of the day wandering around the West End with them.

On the corner of Carnaby Street we saw John Lennon and Yoko Ono dressed all in white. Yoko was wearing her pith-helmet hat. John had his lion's mane and a Jesus beard. A Hell's Angel from Hull shouted over at them, in broad Yorkshire, 'Hey mister! Are you John Lennon?'

The John Lennon figure replied in a BBC accent, 'I'm terribly sorry. I'm afraid I'm not.'

None of us were sure if it really was them or not. Not even the Angels wanted to pursue it. I've always rather liked Hells Angels, after that day I spent with them. I was only a kid but they looked after me.

I wandered around London by myself, sometimes with mates, just looking or mucking around. Sometimes I hung around with a streetwise mate called Gerald who'd lived in children's homes. At school he didn't care what he said to the teachers. They'd quite often have to drag him out of a classroom by his hair, with him still giving them lip. We were in Rupert Street one day and he met this chubby Indian bloke, Ranji, whom Gerald seemed to know well. He told me that the Indian bloke was a psychic. While the man went into a shop to buy some cigarettes, Gerald warned me that the bloke 'liked boys' and to watch out. But he also said he was a good race-tipster. I knew nothing about horses.

Gerald asked, 'Whatcha got Ranji?'

Ranji said, 'Purple Haze. Favourite. Two-thirty. Sandown.' Ranji grabbed my arm and he looked at me.

'You will be a great singer. One day you will write many great songs – maybe not successful here, maybe America. Somewhere. Not now. Long, long time in the future.'

I replied, 'That shows what you know. I'm not even a singer. I play the guitar.'

Gerald told me to take Ranji seriously, that he did know what he was talking about. We said goodbye to Ranji. Gerald looked at his watch.

Gerald demanded, 'Gimme a quid!'

We ran into a betting shop. I gave Gerald a quid, no small sum for me then. He matched it and we put it on Purple Haze. Purple Haze romped in. We now had about six quid each. My only ever trip to a bookies and I won.

Gerald and I went to Frith Street. A muscly looking dwarf in a monkey suit shouted, 'Come een, boys! Feefteen larvly girls. All naked. Only a queed!'

We coughed up and went down some rickety stairs. A huge bonehead at the bottom of the stairs asked us how old we were. We added two years to our ages and told him we were eighteen.

He looked at us, 'Members?'

We shook our heads, forked up another quid each and went in. A tinny old record player started up and amidst lots of coughing, rustling and stifled groans from the old men and foreigners occupying the club's creaky, church-hall chairs, the show began. A rather sorry parade of bored, knackered-looking girls, not much older than Gerald and I, came out to strut their stuff: a bit of bum, a bit of nipple and a flash of bush, before lights out and the next girl.

At no point did I find this situation erotic. Neither did Gerald.

'Didn't like that much,' I said to him, when we came up on the street.

'Naah. 'Orrible innit?' he replied.

I asked him why we'd gone in there. He told me that everyone should go once, and anyway, it 'hadn't cost nuthin', had it? Won it on an 'orse.' Easy come easy go. Perhaps I was a late developer or something, but I actually preferred playing the pinball machines in the arcade at Clapham Junction Station. I never knew what happened to Gerald, but wherever he is, I really wish him the best. He was a good bloke.

One sunny Saturday afternoon in the summer of 1970, I was walking across Clapham Common. I came to the bandstand, where a long-haired bloke was up on stage reading out poetry. Two other long-haired blokes were sitting in the rows of empty chairs. They applauded when he finished. They were the only people watching. One of them got up and stood on the stand and the one who'd been reading sat down to watch. I sat down a few chairs away and listened. They were reading quite improvisational stuff. It was much more like the Liverpool Poets than, say, anything I'd learned in school. I began applauding too. When they'd all read, I went over to talk to them. They were three friends from Tulse Hill. They explained that they did this sort of thing every couple of weeks and that they wanted to be poets. I was quite mystified and impressed by them. I went to see them a few times and there was never anybody else there. After a while I lost touch with them, but my meeting them had sort of planted a seed. I took a lot more interest in poetry after that.

Later that summer, my parents announced that they were moving to Essex. I didn't fancy the idea much. I started looking around for a bedsit and found one right away. I was very lucky to get a large room, with its own kitchen and landing about three floors up, in a lovely old house off Nightingale Lane for four pounds and ten shillings a week. It was one of those old-fashioned London town houses with harlequin tiles in the hallway, an elephant's-foot umbrella stand and a stag's-antlers coat stand. It was only a bit run-down, all things considered. In early August I scrubbed the bedsit out and moved my four cardboard boxes of books, records and pop-star clothes in. The old lady whose house it was didn't seem to mind musicians. Apart from her and her even more elderly mother, who occupied two floors below me, the only other tenants were two pop musicians from The New Overlanders, a one-hit-wonder band on its way down.

When I say the band was on the way down, it's true. The two musicians, however, weren't. They were boys not much older than me, who'd been drafted in after some of the original members had left, and they soon went on to better things. The drummer, Graham, later joined John Entwistle of The Who's band, The Ox. Mike the bass-player, joined Caravan. They were very kind blokes and both excellent musicians. Mike, who lived on the top floor, even had a piano up there, on which he would belt out a very convincing version of McCartney's 'Maybe I'm Amazed' in the small hours. They took me under their wing. I used to go up to Mike's room most nights and just sit around listening to all these older musicians, talking shop and jamming.

I'd smoked a bit of dope before and had done since I was fifteen, but these blokes got me so smashed that I actually fell off my chair one night while listening to some Mothers of Invention tracks. Two of them had to lift me back upright. I had never been so stoned before. There was never any drink. Nobody drank. There was just music and dope. Occasionally, in his very civilised way, Mike would make cocoa for everybody at the end of the night, the end of the night frequently being three or four in the morning. I played Mike my early efforts at song writing and he'd go, 'Hmm, yes. Quite Who-like, Martin.' Or, 'Hmm. A bit Syd

Barrett, that, young Martin.' In the end, I wrote something completely off-the-wall, to see what he'd say. He told me, 'That's more like it! That's original. Do more of that.'

I was going out with a young woman, whom we shall call Gina. She looked a lot like a young Billie Whitelaw, who let me tell you, was right in the top five of Newell's screen goddesses at that time. Now, Gina was quite a straight young woman and very prone to fits of moodiness and temper. The wrong record put on the turntable might elicit a contemptuous, 'Oh God!' spat between clenched teeth. It was even worse if she was in a bad mood. One day she brought round a record by a band called Bread. It was called 'Make It With You'. I hated it then and I hate it now. It sparked a huge argument and Gina left. I was too proud to ask her to come back. End of story. Hello heartbreak.

Mike and Graham went out on tour. On a cruise ship, I seem to recall. I was very upset that Gina had gone, so upset that I spent the weekend crying. When autumn came, it rained a lot. I took some time off work and went down to Harpenden to see my friend Aero, thinking that it would be great to get out of London.

I'd known Aero since I was eight years old. He was a dark-eyed, skinny little Jewish kid whose family lived round the corner from my gran's. When I'd come back for holidays I'd seen him. He was an imaginative, artistic kid who, like me, tended to be an outsider at school. His interests had always run roughly parallel to my own, right from the days of tree houses and toy soldiers, to the current time of girls, guitars and two-quid dope deals. The good thing about Aero was that he was always doing something interesting. But he was also vulnerable. He had the look of a deer startled in a forest. And he was awkward like a foal learning to run. Young women found him impossibly cute. They wanted to look after him, so there were always lots of girls around. His dad had died when he was thirteen and his rather eccentric mum never minded me being around. My friendship with Aero was the only one from childhood that had survived into adulthood.

Round about early October, I had a party in my bedsit to which I invited a few people I knew from the Temple club, my mates Robert and Pete from Putney and Aero. I took a couple of blues for the first time, stayed up all Friday night, and then on Saturday, with a slight speed comedown and the beginnings of a nasty little flu bug, I left London and moved in with Aero and his mum, into the old house which I'd known since we were kids.

It turned out to be one of the best autumns ever. Most of the time, Aero and I had the run of the whole house. We knew all kinds of interesting kids of our own age but nothing sordid was happening, except maybe a little bit of smokery. As far as sex was concerned, it was down to a bit of snogging and heavy petting. What I remember was the frosty clean mornings and the turning of the leaves, as I shambled up the lane, less and less frequently, to go to London and the job I was just about to be sacked from. In those days, when I did make it to the station and catch the commuter train, there were still orderly battalions of men with bowler hats, pinstripe suits and umbrellas crowding the neat platforms. It was 1970, but it may as well still have been the sixties. England was indeed still dreaming.

Aero and I had that feeling of freedom, the feeling that something brilliant was about to happen. I remember the languid young women we used to bump into in the High Street on still-grey Saturday mornings, and the records people brought round on rainy week-nights. If a girl left a scarf behind on the bannisters, it would always be with a sense of wonderment that Aero or I would pick it up and think, 'Wow! Don't girls smell brilliant?' That autumn was the end of innocence for us all, because within a short two years, the game would have moved on up the field and several of us would be in deep shit.

Eleven

I am riding a Moulton Mark III through the freezing wet Essex lanes at six-thirty in the morning. Bicycle spotters will remember that the Moulton was developed in the sixties as a round-the-town sort of conveyance. Chiefly distinguishable by its tiny fourteen-inch wheels and strange compensatory suspense system, earlier models had a drum brake on the back wheel, which was a bastard to fix if it went wrong. The Mark I was highly fashionable in the mid-sixties and pictures in the newspapers of the time featured folk as diverse as Ringo Starr and Quintin Hogg, the then Lord Hailsham, perched demurely upon it. The Moulton finally devolved into the much inferior and universally despised Shopper Bike during the late seventies, which was a shame as the Moulton was a beautiful thing and another great British design idea which should have received far greater acclaim and support than it did. I occasionally hear that it's made something of a comeback but I haven't seen one for years. Damn the mountain bike. Damn the mountain bike.

Right now, however, I am two months away from my eighteenth birthday and I cannot find Mr Crabbe's farm. Before pop music began to lure me onto the rocks, I'd vaguely wanted to be a farmer. Now, eight years later, here is my big chance. In a fine drizzle, on a freezing dark February morning, I am cycling through Little Horkesley trying to find the lane, which will lead me to the track, which will lead me to the pig farm where I am engaged as a labourer.

How did this happen? How did our would-be rock guitarist come to be dressed in old jeans, wellies, a baggy old biscuit-coloured jumper and a borrowed, oversized gabardine mac? Come closer now. It is tedious to go into, but for three months, due to unfortunate circumstances, I am back in Essex and temporarily living at my mum's in a small terraced house in Colchester. After an indolent month of reading I have consumed almost everything that Ian Fleming ever wrote, as well as lots of ghost stories and two Jackie Collins books. During this time, my mother has approached me with monotonous regularity, brandishing a copy of the local paper with various Situations Vacant circled in red ballpoint. I have capitulated. Meet Pig Boy.

Let me say right from the start, I don't like Mr Crabbe, the farmer. When I arrive at two minutes past seven in the morning, the first thing he does is come storming across the concrete yard yelling at me, 'When Oi tell yew ter git here at seven a fuck'n clock, Oi mean seven a fuck'n clock. Not two minutes fuck'n paast!' Mr Crabbe is an old-fashioned East Anglian farmer. If you can recall Carl Giles' cartoons in *The Express*, you may also remember that he often used to depict farmers wearing battered old macs tied up with baler twine, a flat cap, Argyle gumboots and a thunderous face like a smacked arse with a permanent deep scowl on it. Here then, is our man. His habit of yelling had come, I later gathered, from years in the Royal Navy as a chief petty officer. His chief pig man intimated to me that Mr Crabbe had left the service under rather a cloud.

Even though I'm not averse to hard work and muck and have done manual labour before, Mr Crabbe treats me like I am the most lily-handed city milksop he's ever met. My duties include shifting tons of pig shit around low-ceilinged concrete bunkers with a giant squeegee and a hose, fetching endless bales of straw from a Dutch barn to other parts of the farm, feeding the different pigs their nuts and pellets, opening sacks, sweeping the yard, being shouted at and, apparently, testing the electric fence.

Upon my second morning I am in trouble. I am not late. I am early. My problem is that I've arrived at the front door of the farmhouse, instead of the back door. Cue yelling, 'When yew come here in the morn'n, yew come ter the back door. Yew dun't come ter the front door. Cause if yew do, moi woife's jist as likely to point a shotgun out o' the top fuck'n winder at yer. Gottit?' Yes Mr Crabbe. An hour later, he's at it again. I have apparently given the wrong pigs the wrong pellets. The bigger pigs have got some of the pellets meant for the smaller pigs. It's not harmful, it's just a bit more expensive that's all. He's in fine fettle now, I'm standing there with my hair blowing back in the gale of his fury which he caps neatly with, 'Now goo and test the 'lectric fence.'

Electric fences on farms carry about six volts, which surge through the wire about every one and a half seconds. It's a chastening sort of belt should you ever receive it but it does no harm and helps to discourage farm animals from straying from their fields and pens. On this morning however, I am not keen. A few months earlier, while trying to fix an amplifier, I had forgotten to turn the juice off and had received a whack that had thrown me against a wall. It's given me a bit of an aversion to electric shocks at the moment. This is why Mr Crabbe finds me gingerly touching the wire and swiftly moving my hand away again.

'Whatever are you fuck'n doin'?'

He bids me take my glove orf. He bids me take my other glove orf. He bids me kneel down and put one hand in the dew-soaked grass. With his own fully-gloved hand, he holds my bare hand onto the electric fence wire. The belts rack through me for about ten seconds: Kazunk. Kazunk. Kazunk. Kazunk. Kazunk. I feel slightly sick and tears spring to my eyes. 'That,' yells Mr Crabbe, 'is how you test an electric fence. Yew fuck'n outsiders. And yew call us, fuck'n country bumpkins!' I explain to him about the belt from the amplifier. My voice is shaking and a tear is rolling down my face. 'Roight,' he says. 'Now before we go any further, is there anythin' else you're scared of?'

I am so pissed off by now I don't care what happens. I throw my gloves down, turn to face him, wave my fist in his face and scream, 'Well I'm not fucking scared of you!'

To my complete surprise, he steps back, looking vaguely hurt and says, 'Well there's no need to get nasty about it.'

At this point, I realise that I'm dealing with either a nutter, or someone with the people skills of Idi Amin. He puts me to work shifting more straw.

I begin to take to the work. He still yells at me, but no more than my dad might have. This is actually a fair amount when I add it all up. One afternoon I'm out by myself on top of the straw bales in the Dutch barn when I see the crows fly out across the setting sun. The sky is blue. There's a smell of smoke in the air and a feeling of very early spring. I'm happy. I can do this job. Maybe go to agricultural college and get a smallholding of my own some day...

There's great excitement round the yard. The vet has arrived. I must accompany Mr Crabbe and hold the piglets while the vet shoves a thermometer up their arses, getting covered in junior pig shit while he's at it. This is not the

cause of the excitement however. Today is the day that Mr
Crabbe's top sow is to be mated with Farmer Thorogood's
prize boar. A huge lorry arrives mid-morning and
Thorogood and three labourers build a pen from hurdles.
Intimidating noises come from within the lorry. When the
ramp comes down I see why. A monster of a boar, grunting,
shoving and generally looking pretty evil is persuaded
down the ramp. He's not happy. He's testosteroned up and
all observers accord him a respectful distance.

The huge boar is ushered into the pen with the sow. He
seems pleased about this. Crabbe's wife comes out to have
a look. She is gorgeous in a counties way: headscarf,
expensive tweed jacket and skirt, black shiny boots, honey-
blonde hair, patrician face and posh voice. She looks like
Honor Blackman but chunkier. How on earth did he pull
that? Later, I find out that she's the one with the money
and the land. Very strange. But she's country through and
through, as I am just about to discover.

The boar makes a charge for the sow. There's much
grunting and a deafening squealing as he mounts her. He's
off-centre though and his huge corkscrew whanger is
sliding all over the place as the beast tries to hit the target
and fails. He slides off her and seems to be in even more of
a rage. The pig's scrotum stands out from his hindquarters
like an overblown football as his unemployed dong waves
up and down like a giant admonishing finger. He goes in
for a second charge but misses again. This time he's puffing
and grunting but still aboard the sow. None of the men
want to interfere, but I sense a general concern that all is
not going to plan.

At this point, Crabbe's wife takes over. In an exasperated
voice she hisses, 'Oh for God's sake!' She removes her
jacket, hitches her skirt up to her thighs and climbs into
the pen. She marches over to the struggling honeymoon
couple, and grabs the boar firmly by the shaft of his

whanger. She then yanks the boar a foot backwards, at which substantial squealing is heard, and then with a firm tug forwards again, she shoves the pig's dong right into the sow's vagina. She's got mud on her blouse, her hair's ruffled, her skirt's rucked up and then she hitches it up again and climbs back over the hurdle, exposing even more thigh. She looks crossly at the helpless men, picks up her jacket and marches back to the farmhouse. I don't know about the pig, but even I've got the bloody horn by now.

The pigs don't spend long at it. With a bit more squealing and grunting, the boar disengages as a teacup's worth of pigs-jism spills out of the sow and over the concrete floor of the pen. It is a much more co-operative boar which is ushered back up the ramp into the lorry and a hip flask is passed between the two farmers in celebration of another job well done. I set to work putting the hurdles back and lashing the hose to the yard broom in order to clean up the yard.

I have nearly forgotten about rock and roll for the moment. I say nearly. Not quite. While scanning the small ads in *Melody Maker*, I read that a lyricist needs someone to put music to his words. Your hero is just about to begin his long association with Tin Pan Alley, Denmark Street, London. With my farm-labourer's wages I pay for a ticket to London where I meet a well-dressed long-hair with a Zapata moustache. He's much older than me, say about twenty-five years old and seems ever so worldly.

We meet in The Giacconda Café in Denmark Street. Reader, if I had a pound for every time I've sat there, talking with musicians, managers, writers, and other professional bullshitters about how my songs would take the world by storm, I'd probably have over seventy-six quid by now. The Giacconda was the café where everybody went to broker deals, moan about deals, take a break from the studio, do post-mortems on gigs or simply have a tuna and mayo on white and a cappuccino, please. It was a perfectly ordinary, well-run London Italian café of the type that may be found all over the West End. Its sheer proximity to the rat-run studios, rehearsal rooms, publishers and music shops that make up Denmark Street is what gave it its immortality. It wasn't a star hangout as such, more like a canteen for people on the shop floor. You'd never go star-spotting there. But if you sat there for a week, and were observant enough, you'd probably spot more famous rock stars and music-biz movers than you would at a glittery award ceremony. It has another name now, The Barino, but it's still the same place and probably functions much the same as it ever did.

In 1971, though, I am sitting here with Chris, who wants me to play Elton John to his Bernie Taupin. His lyrics don't particularly start my moped, but I spend a week or two putting them to my peculiar downbeat and slightly depressing adolescent tunes and return to meet him at the café. From there we do the rounds of the record companies, with him doing the pitch and me playing the songs on my battered old Yamaha. At one point we meet Fritz, an A&R man for Chrysalis. Previously, Fritz had enjoyed a brief pop stardom in the sixties with The Four Pennies, who'd had a number one with 'Juliet'. I'm impressed.

Contrary to everything I know about the coldness of the music biz, Fritz sits us down, gets us tea and listens to our wares. He's kindly and constructive in his comments but doesn't think we're ready for stardom yet. We meet lots of record-company guys, and although no one's interested, for me, aged seventeen and a farm labourer, it's all quite exciting. The long and short of it is that Chris and his folder of lyrics and I with my battered guitar will part company not long afterwards. He's in London and I'm in north Essex. We're different ages. He has a moustache. I don't. But we've given it a shot at least. Armed with this, I go back to Mr Crabbe's farm.

Mr Crabbe is being as difficult as ever. I like the work. I can even put up with the yelling. What I don't like is the lack of thanks I get when I work really hard and begin to get the job right. One Saturday morning, a half-witted Saturday boy of about my own age begins talking to me about how he's going to work on a farm all his life. I ask him about what kind of pop music he likes. He isn't sure. I tell him I can play a guitar a bit and that I want to end up in a group. He looks at me gormlessly and drawls, 'Oi expect yew think yore gonna be on Toppa the Pops then dun'tcha?' He starts laughing, a low, stupid, hopeless laugh. This is the kind of bloke whose idea of entertainment is pointing at the moon. A wave of despondency washes over me. It's Saturday lunchtime, and I'm standing in a wet farmyard with this prat, covered in pig shit and waiting for the farmer to give me my twelve-quid wages.

Meanwhile, the whole summer is stretching out in front of me. All my friends back in Hertfordshire are listening to Stray, Hendrix and Uriah Heep, getting stoned, meeting lovely hippy girls, forming bands, playing guitars, wandering around the wooded hills at the edge of the Chilterns, tripping, dreaming. What the fuck am I doing here in these flat muddy fields? With this bad-tempered, mean farmer and his idiot Saturday boy? Why aren't I in a band? Why haven't I got a girlfriend? What the fuck am I doing? I'm seventeen for Christ's sake. I get my wages. I walk out of the yard, I get on my Moulton Mark III and I cycle off Mr Crabbe's land. I am never going back.

Twelve

In Painful Employment
Hertfordshire/Soho, May-June 1971

I have woken up on the living room floor of the Seven Rooms on a sunny spring morning in early May of 1971. Although I'm living in this house, I'm not really living in it. Let me clarify this: I'm just eighteen, I've left Essex and farm labouring and I've come to stay with my childhood friend and fellow boy-run-wild, Aero. His mum owns the house but she's not always here, because she's a chronic depressive and what used to be referred to as neurasthenic, so she's often in hospital. Aero and I and various other wayward boys and girls hang out here, in Harpenden. The place is full of books and paintings and gives the impression of artistic gentility gone rather threadbare.

I've known the house since childhood, when Aero's dad, a top-notch Jewish intellectual, once on Hitler's hit list, was still alive. Aero's mum is divided in her opinion of me. On one hand she thinks I'm noisy, inane and with 'the sense of humour of an SS officer.' On the other hand, she tells me I am a loyal friend to Aero, that I'm honest and, most importantly, a hard worker. When I lived at the place the previous autumn, I was useful for getting Aero out of bed to go to college. I could also cook a bit, so she'd occasionally get me to make sure he ate. Mainly though, I was good at cleaning the house.

When I arrive back from Essex, almost broke, except for a few quid I'd saved up, she lets me doss where I may, providing I do the housework. I am surprised to find myself on the floor this merry morning though. I normally sleep in the bath, or fall asleep in Aero's room after getting too stoned to stand up, or sleep in Grizzly the biker's room when he's over at his mum's place. Oh, I forgot about the bikers. They're good lads, a bit crazy maybe. It's a marriage of convenience with the bikers and the hippies but we all hate the skinheads though. We recognise each other's outlaw status. We take drugs. They get in fights.

On this particular May morning, I feel a little strange. I've had half a tab of acid and a couple of Dexedrine the previous evening – and four hours' sleep. Next to me is a girl whom we shall call Amandrax. There's nothing going on between us, we just happen to have woken up together, that's all. I draw the curtains, go upstairs, wash and shave my bum-fluff off. I have no money, not a penny. I am ruminating on this when something strange happens. I think, 'I've got to get a job.' I have a bowl of the landlady's cornflakes and then, from a plastic bag in the cupboard under the stairs, I exhume the Only Suit I Will Ever Own. I put the suit on, brush my shoulder-length hair, polish my black Chelsea boots and I walk out of the house.

My conditioning has kicked in. I have done all I can over the years to be a true, card-carrying bohemian layabout. I have taken the drugs, woken up looking at the wrong wallpaper, played in the dodgiest bands and generally fucked up. But the one bit of programming I could never rid myself of was the urge to work, to pay my own way, to be able to look the society I hated in the eye and say, yes, I may be a deviant. I may be a scumbag. I may be a flub on the fabric of society, but at least I paid for it myself.

When I slouched out of my eleventh school one December afternoon in 1968, never to return, my mother said to me, 'You will work for your living, my boy.' Those words still ring in my ears. Over the years I have been accused of being a traitor to my kind, for the simple sin of not signing on. Clever people have argued with me and told me that my country owes me the money. Well I don't want it. If I don't take it, my country has no right to tell me how to live my life. That's not to say I'm against other people signing on. I'm quite happy to pay my taxes and subsidise people, many of who I believe to be psychologically or aesthetically unfit for painful employment. But the day I take their shilling is the day I've lost the game.

Anyway, bees out of bonnets and on with the story... I go round to the Labour Exchange and they make me fill in all these forms. Then they tell me I'm not entitled to any money. I tell them that I don't want any money; I want a job. The middle-aged woman who's interviewing me, looks suitably puzzled then her tone softens. She asks me if I've got any A-levels? Nope. Any O-levels? Nope. Any qualifications at all? Nope. It doesn't look hopeful. She produces a plastic box with a load of cards in and she pulls the first card out. It's a washing-up job on the other side of Redbourn, a village four miles away. It's split shift, badly paid with no prospects at all. I ask, 'Is that it?' She nods pityingly. 'I'll take it.' She asks me if I'm sure. Yep. I take the card, saying that I'd better start walking. She's so impressed that she lends me the bus fare to Redbourn out of her own purse.

So I turn up in a suit for the washing-up job at this very posh country hotel. The manager asks me how I will get back at nights. I'm not sure. We do a deal. If I wash up six days a week, ten till four, I've got the job at thirteen quid a week. In the blazing hot May sunshine I walk down the country lane in my suit. I'm a working lad again. I get back to the Seven Rooms and some piss-taking goes on because I'm going straight. A job is to be viewed with suspicion. I point out that I'm only kitchen-portering and that it hardly prises me off the human scrap heap. My transgression is overlooked for the time being.

A day later, I am welcomed into the bosom of the catering trade. It will be a long association with that worthy group of people. It will be interrupted by artistic success only occasionally over the ensuing years. What I don't realise on this, the fifth of May 1971, is that I won't finally hang up my washing-up scourers until almost the same date in 1986, a mere fifteen years later. Surely the world will not see a genius of my calibre washing the plates of the bourgeoisie for so very long, will it? It transpires that the world is only too happy to watch me engaged in this pursuit for as long as I wish. The world doesn't give a toss.

The first thing I'm greeted by when I enter the enormous kitchen is the Fawltyesque sight of a large, bearded head chef, bawling oaths and hurling a metal ladle at a cowering Spanish waiter who is pleading for mercy. A kindly head porter named Domingo shows me how to operate a dishwasher. Then I am on my own. It is lunchtime and everyone is screaming: chefs at waiters, waiters at commis waiters, commis chefs at each other, wine waiter at waitresses and everyone at me. This is normal in any good working kitchen. But I work my little arse off trying to keep up with it all and at the end of the day the fearsome head chef approaches me. He's an ex-Navy man with a terrible stutter. He looks me up and down like I am something blocking the garbage disposal and walks around my workspace, inspecting the shelves as if we are on a ship. Then he says, 'N-n-not bad. N-n-nowmopthefloorandfuckoff.' The second chef later tells me that this means I've done well. And I should keep it up, because good kitchen porters are hard to come by.

Within a few short weeks I've become a good kitchen porter. Domingo goes back to Spain. Two students arrive for holiday work. The head chef has a row with somebody too high up in the hotel hierarchy to jangle with. His head rolls. Second chef is now head chef, while I am top porter, in charge of the two students. Aero's mum comes out of hospital, and when Grizzly the biker leaves, I get his room as a rent-paying tenant. Because I've got money, I put away a couple of quid a week in the Post Office, my 'bust and eviction money'. Not only do I buy some new clothes at Kensington Market, I go to a London cellar club, watch bands and take loads of speed. Early summer finds me an independent working lad. Life in the fast lane, huh?

While I'm washing up, I think about what it's all come down to. It hadn't been what I'd intended. How many jobs have I had? I started work January 1969, punch-card operator for the GPO, till I got bored. Next I changed to office runner and coffee-machine cleaner for a Swedish travel firm in EC3 for eight months, till I got bored. Then I was window cleaning with a mate from school for a month, till I realised we weren't making the money. After this I worked in a sawmill in Bermondsey for a few weeks in 1970, till I saw how many of the older guys had fingers and hands missing. Briefly, I was a cloth examiner, warp, weft and flub spotting for two weeks in the Tottenham Court Road, till they found out that I'd lied about my age, in order to get a man's wages. This was followed by work as an office-boy-cum-carpet-fitter for a couple of brilliant Jewish wide boys in the Charing Cross Road for a few weeks, till they had to skedaddle. The following job was office runner and whipping boy for a tea centre in Regent Street for five months until November 1970, till they sacked me for answering back and coming in late. For a few weeks I lived on spare cash, till it ran out and I went back to Essex for Christmas. Finally I got a job as a labourer on Mr Crabbe's pig farm for a while, till I got pissed off with Mr Crabbe and came back to be with my mates in Harpenden in late March 1971, with whom I spent a month or so getting stoned and tripping, till the money ran out. Now this: suds a go-go, the Prince of the Sinks.

This is actually the lowest I've come so far. I wash up dishes. I have no qualifications, no job prospects, no band, no girlfriend, but it's as good as it gets. For the first time in my life, no one is on my case. No one expects anything of me. No one's asking me what I'm going to do, or what I'm going to be. I'm renting a very cheap room. I don't drink, but I get stoned at night, taking speed and acid whenever they're about. I listen to The Pink Fairies and Stray. I read underground comics and Norse legends. And I don't give a fuck. Do you want to know what my mother's last words to me were, as I left Essex with a bag of clothes, a bottle of Cougar aftershave and my electric guitar? 'You may be my son, but I don't like you.' In the mornings, I get up, have a yoghurt and some cornflakes, smoke a roll-up, get on a bus and go to work. I have reclaimed my youth. It is one of the best times in my life.

And I'm still a virgin, not even thinking about sex very much. I'm too into drugs. I sometimes think a girlfriend would be nice but they're always hassling, and the girls we know are mostly middle-class sixth-form types or art students, very well-spoken and from good homes. Aero and I fascinate them, of course. We're the wasters with long hair and exotic clothes who never do anything but what we like. But if you go out with one of these girls, you end up having to meet the parents, who ask searching questions about job prospects and what you intend to do, and you cannot help yourself but bristle and say something inappropriate to them.

Then you can't see the girls anymore, but the girls come round anyway, followed by their dads. Being all angry middle class, look here sonny, I'm in the rugby club and I'm dead tough, and everything. Then you have to go to all the trouble of getting the bikers involved, because the last thing the dynamic daddy wants, is a herd of rockers driving bikes around his lawn in the small hours. So he goes away, but then the police come. You just don't want the arse-ache really, do you?

The parents of one girl I used to see, referred to me as 'the youth with the gap'. For some while now, I've had a huge gap in my teeth, one front incisor missing. A bottle hurled at me in a silly game with the bikers had chipped it. And then an abscess caused by amphetamine abuse had worked its magic. A dentist took the rest of it out for me. I had to completely relearn how to say 'fuck off'. When I first lost the tooth, it came out as 'vuck ov'. The gap will be with me for almost two years. This is how I eventually get my nickname, Zap the Gap. But right now, when I go round to call for Claire, mum or dad answers and it's, 'Oh, Claire... It's the youth with the gap at the door again.'

So the virginity? Aero and I often attend an all-night club in the West End. It's a scuzzy little place called the Temple, but it has great DJs and good bands, Edgar Broughton, The Pink Fairies, Stray. The people who go there are the tough little brothers and sisters of the London mods who frequented the Pink Flamingo a few years earlier. That's right. The Temple used to be the Pink Flamingo, downstairs from the Whisky a Go Go, which is now the Wag Club. These kids are the very earliest glam-rock speedsters, all feather-cuts, long black cardies, tight trousers and mascara, mingled in with young latter-day hippies. The club, which smells of patchouli and disinfectant, is all black, punctuated with ultra-violet and strobes. Friday nights are the best. A handful of blues at ten a quid and you're away, chewing gum, drinking Coca Cola and verballing all night. London belongs to us.

One night I meet Lorraine, who's a couple of years older than me. She plays bass in a band, was married at sixteen, and has two kids. When she split up with her husband, he got the kids. We're talking all night until the club kicks us out at six in the morning. After a wash in the toilets of Charing Cross Station (speed freaks can be very fastidious), we go to Hyde Park to watch the free concert. On the stage are Heads, Hands and Feet, Humble Pie and Grand Funk Railroad. We watch the concert and say goodbye. The next week I see her again, and the week after, but nothing happens. We talk all night, take pills and kiss goodbye. Sex doesn't come into it. When I'm really pilled-up, we're talking button mushroom in the trouser department. Anyway, most Saturdays I have to go back to Redbourn to do my washing-up shift on a speed comedown, or actually speeding, if I haven't had the willpower not to down all my pills.

But one weekend it all gets really strange. Back at the hotel there's a new commis chef started, who becomes my best friend at work. He's called Taff, and he is straight up from the Welsh valleys and a smashing bloke about my own age. This is one cheerful sod, always singing. I go back to his chalet with him, where he plays me his Black Sabbath and Uriah Heep records. He knows I go to the Temple at weekends and he's begging me to take him with me as he gets Friday night off. The new second chef, who's a miserable, tough bastard from Crewe, and always digging at my appearance and nicking my fags, corners me, 'I know what you get up to in London, sunshine. I know what you're on. Taff's doing lunchtime tomorrow, and I'm holding you personally responsible. I want him back in one piece. If anything happens to him, you're dead meat. Alright?' I nod gravely and he lets go of my shirt.

Oh brilliant. I'm going to London and I'm in charge of the cheerful but completely innocent Taff. We get on the train to St Pancras, and when we get off we hit the West End and, just for once, I don't buy any pills. I see Lorraine, tell her the score, that I'm working tomorrow and that I've got to get Taff back for his shift or I'm dead. She says no problem and that she'll come and see me on Saturday evening. About three in the morning I'm watching the band, when Taff comes up to me and tells me that a friendly hippy has sold him a pill. I ask him what kind of a pill, precisely. We go to see the hippy concerned. The hippy has just given him a tab of Strawberry Fields, a fairly strong, brand-leader reality-dissolver, lysergic acid. And Taff's taken it. I mean, even I don't take acid at the Temple. Now we're in deep shit.

Five o'clock in the morning and I'm up on the street with Taff, opposite Gerrard Street. And Taff's gone completely loopy loo. He's giggling and roaring at people that he's a farmer. And there's a copper walking up Wardour Street towards us. Suddenly Taff goes tearing off up the street towards Shaftesbury Avenue making high-pitched shrieking noises. The copper doesn't even appear to notice. Taff eventually completes his circuit and comes haring back into sight from the Leicester Square end of Wardour Street. I am really glad I haven't had any drugs right now because, if I had done, I would be freaking out.

Two of the regulars grab Taff and haul him into the doorway. Steve, a blonde Stevie Marriott lookalike, offers to run round to the all-night chemists in Piccadilly and get Taff some glucose tabs and some Vitamin B13 to bring him down to earth. We feed Taff the vitamins and the glucose and hope for the best. Come six o'clock the Temple kicks out and Taff is peaking on the trip. He's gone all quiet and pliable. There's too much going on in his head right now for him to even speak. Steve gives me three or four blues to keep me alert for when I try to get Taff back to St Pancras. Somehow I manage to get Taff onto a tube train and then onto a train back to Hertfordshire, then onto a bus back to the hotel. We get to the hotel at nine in the morning. I dollop the pills down and start work. Taff goes off to his chalet to try and get some kip before lunchtime.

All through lunch, Taff is singing as usual, only not his usual songs. He's singing these weird, moaning noises, but he's getting through the shift. The second chef is giving me absolute daggers every time I look up. He shakes his fist every once in a while. Since I'm so poker-faced, with just enough pills in me to keep me going, I get away with it. That afternoon, I'm coming down off the speed, waiting miserably for a bus in the lane, when a car slows down on the other side of the road. The driver pulls a pistol out and points it at me. I just stand there, not believing that it's happening. Suddenly he shouts, 'Bang!' Then he laughs hysterically and drives off. I don't like cars slowing down near me anyway, because that was the prelude to the epic kicking I'd received two years earlier, but the gun really does it. I'm a nervous wreck when the bus arrives. Who was it? I haven't the foggiest, although it was probably some prankster. He just picked the wrong day, that's all.

Now I'm feeling really washed out, and I have to meet Lorraine at the station. I go into a chemist shop, buy some Pro-Plus and some Do-Dos to keep me awake, then go and sit on a station bench. When she arrives, I'm rattling with tiredness, nasty pills and comedown. I notice she's had her hair cut like mine, spiked and feathered. We look like a couple of Bowie clones, all pale and shaky. We get to the Seven Rooms and we find that it's empty. Everyone's gone off to a festival, except for Bob, who is always hanging around. He's not a biker and he's not a hippy, but he's got one brother who's a biker and another who's an old mod. He hangs around with us because there's nowhere else for him and his high-powered air rifle to hang out. Did I say air rifle? Yeah. Bob likes to muck around with guns.

So I've made a cup of tea and I'm showing Lorraine around the place, when there's a crashing at the door and lots of shouting, for it is on this evening, this very evening of all evenings that the skinheads from the estate down the road have decided to mount an attack on the house. With the bikers and everyone away, I guess we're fair game. To say that I am freaked out is an understatement. I look for the piece of wood which I barricade the door of my room with, the door having no lock on it. I'm not thinking of fighting back. I'm thinking of barricading myself in my room until they all go away. As my dad was fond of saying, 'Cowards run in our family.' I'm about the fastest.

Bob has run up the stairs too. I gesture to him to come into my room with Lorraine and me. Bob is not having any of it. A windowpane on the front door smashes. Bob calmly sits down on the stairs, loads his gun and fires at the first arm reaching towards the door lock. Then he reloads very rapidly indeed, and fires. There's a shout. He's reloading and firing, and reloading and firing. There's a sound of boots retreating, and a strange silence. Bob shouts, 'I think I got a couple of 'em.' I am shaking so much I need to hold my fag with two hands. Bob asks me if it's all right if he stays the night, in case they come back. Absolutely fine with me, Bob. I try and tell Lorraine, that it's not normally like this round here. I'd painted her a picture of this groovy pad where everyone ate flowers and loved one another. Lorraine just smiles and makes a cup of tea for the three of us.

After the tea, she takes me into my room. She pulls all of my clothes off, except for an orange tie-dye grandad shirt. She takes my virginity quite vigorously, and again later on in the night, again in the small hours, first thing the next morning too, and then most of Sunday. Then she goes to the station and goes home. Having left the hotel on Saturday afternoon a boy, I return on Monday morning, not a man but at least a boy with an extremely sore dick and a back which looks like a peak-season ski run, and strangely wobbly legs, and this wild, knowing look in my eyes every time I pass a mirror. I never told her that I was a virgin, but I think she knew and I think the little house knew too.

Thirteen

Dawn of the 'Aicd Wag'
Hertfordshire, July 1971-April 1972

It had been a great summer at the Seven Rooms. Aero's mum had been away for weeks and weeks getting herself sorted out in hospital. An academic in her fifties, she sometimes needed to go back into the unit to reduce her drug dependency and avail herself of the cures on offer for her severe depression. These included all sorts of strange early antidepressants, occupational therapy and electroconvulsive therapy. As fucked-up boys of seventeen and eighteen respectively, I don't think either Aero or I really understood how serious her situation was, or how we were supposed to help. Sufficient to say that when she was well she could be fun, witty and kind – she actually liked having all these wacky teenage boys around most of the time. She wasn't conventional and, as she was fond of telling us, 'In my younger days, I was considered something of a "hot piece".'

Having Aero and his friends around meant there was always someone to run to the shops, clean the house and do any number of other chores beyond the capability of a neurasthenic. However, when she got an idea into her head that things had to change, she could be a real pain. Such and such a youth would be banned from the house and we'd have to try sneaking him in, or hide him if she was about. Aero and his mum had a love-hate relationship and when they were at war, both would marshal troops. Our practical jokes on her verged on cruelty and she would take terrible revenge by dropping one or the other of us in serious shit with the authorities. The things that happened in that house would ideally warrant a separate book, if not a sitcom series. With the benefit of three decades' hindsight, however, Aero's mum was definitely a force for good. Out of respect for her and Aero, I will draw a veil over the details of her life.

Later, when she was away, Aero and I, as captain and lieutenant of this strange house, got ourselves into all sorts of trouble, but that summer was a good one. I was the cleaner-in-chief. I reasoned that if we were going to run the house ourselves we should show the outside world that we weren't a bunch of tramps. One bloke, whose personal hygiene wasn't great, had his room trashed by us. A group of us smashed out of our skulls nailed his socks up all over the walls of his room. We labelled them: 1952-1954, 1956-1960, etc. He responded by beating Aero up. While he was out the bikers held a firing squad against his French windows, using a mixture of rifles and shotguns, the front rank kneeling, the back rank standing, they stood out in the garden and blasted his windows out.

The bikers could be a pain in the arse, or they could be hilarious. One afternoon, Spider, Grizzly, Dave, Aero and I were sitting down to some beans on toast. We had been tidying the joint up and sorting the garden out, so we figured we'd earned some food. What we didn't count on was a visit from Chopper Saunders. Chopper was well endowed and could do a number of amusing tricks with his organ. Lately, however, he'd had something wrong with it, so he hadn't been flashing it around as much.

Chopper came stomping into the breakfast room in his motorcycle gear and Spider asked, 'How's the old dapper then?'

Chopper said, 'I've just been up the quack's, as a matter of fact. It was peeling a bit, round the helmet, so I thought I'd better get it sorted out.' With that, he whipped it out and slapped it on the table where we were eating our food. All eight and a half inches of it, peeling helmet too. One or two of us recoiled, and Aero actually left the table. Chopper said, 'It's alright, it's not VD or anything. The doctor just told me to wash my hands first if I've been taking me bike apart. He thinks it's some sort of impetigo.'

We never had too many problems with Jehovah's Witnesses either. I used to answer the front door and be incredibly helpful and interested – in the nude. Another useful thing about that house was that the bathroom was above the front door and it had a sash window. The top pane was clear glass, but the bottom pane was frosted glass. If I happened to be in the bath when a stranger called at the front door, I'd stand up in the bath and haul the frosted pane up to the top. Although this obscured me from the face up, it revealed a naked torso to the caller and anyone passing in the street. I'd then shout, 'Who's that? Who's that? I'm terribly sorry. I'm in the bath. There's something wrong with this bloody window!' Exit caller.

In spite of these teenage shenanigans there was never any shortage of young women arriving at the house to spend an afternoon or evening watching what we did. This only encouraged us to ever-greater heights of stupidity. Rarely did these young women stay to sleep with us; they were mostly high-school sixth formers. I believe that Aero had a higher score than me. He was a very pretty dark-haired teenager, painfully skinny with seal-pup eyes, quieter and more mystical. For girls, I was probably one step beyond: Marty Feldman with a rock-star haircut and bad skin. My idea of an introduction when the girls arrived was to roll down the stairs in my underpants, like a stuntman, locked in a fight with a dressmaker's dummy that I hacked at frantically with a six-inch knife. Landing in a heap at their feet I'd say, 'Hello ladies. It's been a funny sort of day, hasn't it?' We all grow up sometime.

Certainly Aero won the August 1971 Stained Bedspread Competition. I'd only recently lost my virginity, although I like to think I'd caught up quite well. We were neck and neck in the pointless activities stakes. I woke up one morning, still tripping on acid, to find that Aero and another friend, T, had arranged all the garden equipment in the branches of the apple tree outside my bedroom window. T was a former mod who had become one of our inner circle. Although older than us, a tab of acid generally brought him down to our level and he could come up with some very surreal ideas. It's certainly very odd to see a Ransome motor mower hanging in a tree next to hoes and spades. I reciprocated by scattering a shredded loaf of Mother's Pride bread all over the living room in an Internal Feeding of Birds Event. Several of us were involved in Outdoor Housework, vacuuming the garden, or playing chess on manhole covers with apples as the morning rush hour went past us. We'd been up all night tripping and it seemed to make sense at the time.

Early that autumn some particularly strong acid came through. Little Pete, a prankster after my own heart, didn't like getting too far out, so we'd only take half a tab each and sit on the kitchen floor all night making stupid jokes, often at Muttley's expense. Muttley was a sort of greaser and a good bloke, but he often took himself quite seriously. One of the best things about Muttley was that he'd decided to boost his image as a hard-man by having BORN TO

RAISE HELL tattooed on his arm. Then he'd fainted while it was being done.

When Muttley had gone, Pete and I went upstairs to see how Aero and T had been getting on with the full dose. Both of them swore that they'd been to the moon. They pointed at the full yellow autumn moon. 'You won't believe this, man. We've just been there.' Talk got round to the local beauty spot, Dunstable Downs. Aero and T wanted to go there immediately. It was decided that at five in the morning we'd steal Muttley's van, which he'd left parked outside. T insisted that we should show the world who we were. This involved painting the words ACID WAGON on the side of the little white van.

Aero found some paint somewhere and T started painting our message to the world. Unfortunately, his co-ordination wasn't too good and when we came out to admire his handiwork, what he'd actually written was AICD WAG. After the hysteria had subsided, we christened the vehicle the Aicd Wag. T was actually a brilliant driver and fully capable of out-running any pursuers, even when tripping. His navigation wasn't quite as good though, so we had a confusing and paranoid twenty minutes or so when we were hopelessly lost and parked in a back street in central Luton. After this false start, it was plain sailing to a psychedelic dawn on Dunstable Downs. I stood in the long grass by the side of the road, wrapped in a white blanket, which scared a passing motorist. Afterwards, Muttley wasn't ecstatic to learn about his van being defaced, but since the Aicd Wag hadn't come to any harm and we had a whip-round for the petrol we'd used, it all ended reasonably amicably.

Summer nights were often spent on the lawn, getting stoned and drinking Earl Grey tea, which to this day I still hate. I had an old pedal harmonium, which got brought out into the garden, where I'd sit, frantically pedalling away at the bellows and playing ghastly chords, or doing bad Keith Emerson impressions. The harmonium was the type of thing that you'd find in a Sally Army hall, being played by some formidable woman, while the down and outs ate their soup. It made a dreadful clumping noise and it puffed and wheezed almost as loudly as the chords that came out of it. One evening I got too stoned to bring it in from the garden and it rained overnight. When I next went to play it half of the black keys fell off. I couldn't afford to buy any glue so I stuck them down with some ancient honey that I found in the kitchen. It worked fine until it rained again. I'm sure the neighbours loved us.

If I look back on it all now, every town in England must have had a house like the Seven Rooms. I'm not a great one for analysing why people turn out like they do and I can't think of any one thing that we had in common, apart from the fact that we were all, in our warped way, quite creative. Television, the hated Radio One and the mainstream music industry hadn't got anything that we wanted. We wanted a medium that was ours alone. We wanted a place in which to do it. The idea of a career seemed pointless. Our thinking was that if you had to do a job, best to do a dead-end job so that they didn't steal your brain. Politicians, figures in authority and serious-minded people seemed completely irrelevant. What did they know about anything? What we actually needed was a kind of adventure playground. In the end we made our own.

The amount of drug-taking that I was doing was bound to have a payback sometime. Given that most pharmaceuticals are like an overdraft on one's own health and happiness – an overdraft paid back at a high rate of interest – I was bound to come a cropper. After a great summer when the parties got wilder and the drugs got stronger, the autumn just seemed to sneak quietly in though the back door like an uninvited guest. He also brought his two mates, Mr Depression and Mr Junior Psychosis. To cut a long story short, I wasn't in great nick. The comedowns were getting worse and lasting longer, and I'd split up with Lorraine, who'd introduced me to sex, and started hanging out with Patti, who was very cute, very skinny, a beast for sex and a heroin user. I'd also started swallowing Methedrine capsules. This was speed for boys in long trousers. Two capsules would keep me up for three days. Only an interruption in supply stopped me from becoming a basket case. By the middle of October I was confused and depressed and I was seeing faces at the window and was convinced that someone was out to get me. They didn't have things like drug-counselling units in those days so I had to muddle through by myself.

In the end, and with Patti's help, it was decided that I should move myself completely away from the area and all my old haunts, in order to sort myself out. I ended up in a house in Woolwich with some of Patti's friends. The other occupants of the house were Steve, a guitarist with a good glam-rock band called Silverhead, his girlfriend, Shelley, who was a rock promoter, and Ginger, a likeable Australian rock drummer who'd come over to the UK to look for work. These people were older and wiser than me and were very kind to me. They didn't use drugs – apart from the odd joint, which Ginger used to stoke up after tea.

I slept on the living room floor in a sleeping bag. I had terrible trouble sleeping and used to dream about speed. I also itched like crazy. Over a few days the itching became intolerable and I went to a run-down surgery in the Woolwich back streets to get myself looked at. A very grumpy doctor informed me that I had caught scabies. He more or less told me I was filthy, which I wasn't, and issued me with some medicated soap and a brutal emulsion called Benzyl Benzoate. They don't use this stuff anymore, it's considered too crude. After scrubbing myself in a hot bath with the soap, I coated every crevice of my body from the neck down with the emulsion. Within ten minutes I was hunched over the edge of the bath and moaning due to the burning sensation. I had to do it all over again the next day. My clothes and sleeping bag were cleaned and the dreaded itching went. The whole experience did wonders for my morale.

After a couple of weeks I began to think more clearly. I suggested to Shelley that maybe I could find some way of contributing to the household expenses. She came up with the inspired idea of getting me to do some support slots for the main bands at her promotions. That was how I found myself as the opening act for Spring Offensive and Good Habit at Bowes Lyon House, Stevenage, a big rock venue at the time. I went on by myself, armed only with my old Hofner guitar and played a handful of my songs to a sit-down audience of several hundred people. I was astonished when the applause came back. After I did a couple of other gigs for Shelley, I really should have twigged that that was what I was cut out to do. But I didn't, I packed up and went back to Hertfordshire. I'll always remember what Steve said to me just before I left. 'Martin, if you ever decide to go into this game, it doesn't matter what bullshit happens with the drugs, the girls and the money, always keep the music together, because that's what it's all about. If you forget the music, everything else goes down the pan too.' Unfortunately, this message would take another two years to sink in.

It was coming up to Christmas when I got back, only to find that Aero's mum had banned me from the Seven Rooms. Trying to stay on the straight and narrow, I got myself another job as a kitchen porter and started renting the little boxroom I'd slept in as a kid at my grandmother's house. I don't remember much about Christmas or the next two months. I lived quietly, read a lot of books and tried to get another job after the Hotel laid me off.

There was a bit of a dope famine, it was midwinter and I had no money. In February I was introduced to heroin. A 'friend' jacked me up on two occasions. I remember coming out of the second fix and thinking how great it was. This was followed by a massive wave of guilt and common sense, which dictated that I've never knowingly had it since. It was a salient lesson to me, that even at my lowest ebb, I still had a strong streak of self-preservation.

I did an interview for the Post Office and secured myself a job as a postman. I took it as seriously as I could, and by early April I was trained and out doing rounds on a bike, my long straw-coloured hair bushing out under the peaked cap. I should have stuck at it, I was good at it, but now I had money again. And guess what I spent it on? By the end of April I would be headed for the worst twelve months of my life.

Fourteen

Burning the Works
Hertfordshire, Mid-May 1972

We're in a yellow Mini. It's sometime after midnight, midsummer-ish and we're somewhere on the A5 between Town A and Town B. I'm stoned, really stoned. A friend of my girlfriend came back from India with about an ounce of Nepalese Blue in her honeyed cleft. This stuff is just about recognizable as the dope we know and love but is veined with white stuff and looks like Stilton cheese in negative. Two puffs of it is enough to strand your average teen user out on Planet Wibble with not much hope of a rescue mission for several hours.

I did not plan this jaunt. I had intended to stay in this night. There are good reasons for this. One, I've been busted for possession of dope and am due up in court soon. Two, after tripping all night a month or so back, in the middle of his second delivery, your very own psychedelic postman here managed to crash his post-bike into a parked vehicle, in the middle of a particularly colourful acid-flashback. The postmaster, already suspicious of me, is having me watched at the moment. For these two reasons I am trying to be a good boy.

Fred, however, has other plans. Whatever happened to Fred? Fred the skinhead turned Clockwork Orange glam-kid? Fred is my big friend right now. With our spiky Faces haircuts, our mascara and speed teeth, we even look a bit like each other. But Fred is something of a street fighter. There's a complete air of danger about him. He does grown-up stuff like going up to London and scoring huge bags of pills. He's fearless and doesn't care what he does. Women can't say no to him. Like so many villains I've known, he seems to like me because I make wild jokes the whole time and I can play the songs he likes on my guitar. And I'm not scared to get wrecked with him. But I am really. He's crazy, man.

Fred wants company. He's going out on some kind of a sortie. No one else wants to go. Fred's in a weird mood, maybe it's something to do with a girl, or his ex-wife. Everyone else is scared to go with him, whereas I'm scared not to go. Stoned as a rose I agree to go. He borrows Aero's mum's car. Naturally she doesn't know about this. It's because she's upstairs laid out with a cocktail of cheap Scotch and chloral hydrate. She nearly always is by nine in the evening. Chloral hydrate? The original Micky Finn, which was slipped into drinks to lay people out in gangster movies. She drinks it voluntarily. Has done since her husband died and her only boy went wild.

We've been to a pub. We've had one drink, maybe one or two more. Oh yeah, and Fred's scored some heroin. And banged it up. I haven't. He's been flirting with it though, and he wanted company. So now we're in the car, he's had a fix, I'm stoned and we're driving at twenty miles an hour down a deserted A5 back to our town. He keeps bumping the kerb. It lets him know that he's not in the correct bit of the road. And me? I am terrified. I don't even care about being busted anymore. I just want to live. The journey seems to be taking all night. I can't recall seeing another single vehicle on that whole nightmare ride.

Fred's driving with his eyes half shut, sometimes fully shut and groaning things like, 'Fuck me, Mart, this shit's really strong.' Even more disconcerting is the way he keeps asking me if we're nearly home yet. I'm reasoning with him and suggesting we just abandon the car and walk, but nothing doing. I can feel my hair turning grey. I'm seeing headlines in the local paper like 'Nineteen-Year-Old Postman Found Dead of Old Age in Stolen Drugs Car'. And then we're there, home. Back in the Seven Rooms Of Gloom, the landlady still asleep upstairs, everyone else still out somewhere. This is where it gets worse.

There's another tenant called Wretch. He doesn't wash and he's one of life's misfits. People take the piss out of him. His room stinks, but he ministers to the landlady and creeps around her. He cooks for her and cleans the house to pay his rent. It keeps her quiet while all this other stuff is going down. So nobody hassles him too much. But nobody trusts him either. He's a necessary evil. I'm not living in the Seven Rooms at the moment. I'm still around the corner back at my gran's. All my friends live here and I spend all my time here, so now I'm not banned anymore I may as well be a permanent resident.

Anyway, for some strange reason, Fred decides to bang up some more Henry. He decides two other things as well: one, he's going to do it in Wretch's room, as Wretch is out, and two, he wants me to keep an eye on him while he does it. No amount of reasoning will dissuade him from this course of action. He bangs up the shit. Within seconds he's in trouble. He moans and gasps, and then keels over on the stinking mattress where he was sitting, the tie still round his arm. He's gone a really horrible concrete colour and there's dribble on one side of his mouth. He's now silent. I can still hear him breathing so I know he's not dead but I really don't know what to do next.

If I call an ambulance, we'll get the police too. If I don't call an ambulance he might die. If I call an ambulance and he survives, I'm dead after he comes out of it. If I don't call an ambulance and he dies, I'm in even deeper shit. I'm strangely calm. The Nepalese Blue has settled down from paranoia into a leaden mental fug. I wait. Ten minutes later Fred starts to rally a bit, except that now, he's panicking. He thinks he might die. Do I call an ambulance?

'Naa. Naa. D'nt call 'n ambulance.'

'What am I gonna do, Fred. What d'you want me to do, Fred?'

'Ah, God. Burn the works, Mart. Burn the works. Burn the fuckin' works! You gotta burn the fuckin' works.'

I search around and find a big ornamental blue-glass ashtray. It's Wretch's pride and joy, his seventies bachelor-pad ashtray. I put the syringe in it and start a small fire with a pile of old matches and some cigarette packets. At last, the plastic syringe starts to burn. Toxic smoke stinks the room out as the works melts and flares. It settles down into a small black molten lump with a blue flame on it.

'Have you done it, Mart?'

'Yeah Fred, I did it.'

'Good boy.'

I'm just about to ask Fred if he wants some water or something, when there's a big bang. Wretch's beloved ashtray has shattered into pieces from the heat of the burning works. Fred flakes out again. But this time he's snoring. His breathing seems to be regular. There's a shadow over me. Wretch has come back from the pub. I explain to him what's happened. Then I tell him about the ashtray. He's pissed off of course, but he's also terrified of Fred. He slopes off to the kitchen for a cup of tea. People begin to return to the house. At about two in the morning the psychedelic postman goes home to get two hours' kip before his next delivery.

How did this happen? How did your sparkly little pop boy get himself into this sketch? Well it's got to get worse before it can get better. This, as we shall see, is nearly, though not quite as bad as it does eventually get.

Fifteen

Most Certainly Not Valhalla
Hertfordshire, June 1972

Version One:

Recently I got talking with a friend of mine over a few drinks. Like me, he is the son of an old soldier. Also like me, he rebelled big time, when he was younger, albeit differently. As we stumbled together over the minefield of our encroaching middle age, we found ourselves examining not our own lives, but those of our parents, the wartime generation. As the drinks sank in, on a humid August evening, we began to admit to each other that our parent generation was tougher, more resourceful and in most ways, better than our own. As we talked about the privations, conflicts and losses our parents faced up to, looked at the freedoms we ourselves had received, mostly as a result of their courage and tenacity, we had to concede feelings of uneasiness if not actual contrition about our own behaviour as younger people.

We, the so-called baby boomers, are the last link to that hardy generation. The generation growing up now doesn't even know as much as we know. As I observe young guys rampaging down provincial high streets, scarfing down beer and pills like lemonade and Smarties at a kids-party-gone-wrong, I am alarmed. My generation helped to set this scene. As I look at overweight twenty-year olds driving to the shop down the road, buying their thrills on video and spending an absolute fortune on sports clothes, I am alarmed. When I think about an advertising-led society that measures its citizens not by what they do, or what they know but by what they own, their ability to consume, I am alarmed.

When the Berlin Wall came down and communism collapsed, it was almost touching to see the glow on the faces of the concerned classes as they yattered excitedly about how our Iron-Curtain cousins would now have the freedom to make films, write music and books. All kinds of fancy foreign words peppered the breathless articles in their journals. How baffled and disappointed they were when it transpired that our benighted communist cousins actually wanted microwaves, toasters and new cars. I'd been in one or two communist countries before and had sort of suspected that people might hold shopping as first priority if the guards ever left the towers.

As the pundits gushed and twittered with each crumbling piece of masonry that was torn down, old soldiers such as my dad and my friend's dad looked at the television, shook their heads and tut-tutted, with a certain knowledge that things weren't going to turn out quite as rosy as perhaps some of our happy columnists thought. I do not know what has happened to us all. I do not know what will happen to us, not now that everyone expects to own everything all the time. I am beginning to think that a few restrictions might actually benefit us as a people. Perhaps if we really want to excel, we need a cage to be brilliant in. Total and absolute freedom really doesn't seem to work. Perhaps, as my mother used to say, we need 'an occasional clip round the ear'. Walk around any shopping street in Britain. Never have so many people been able to buy such a huge choice of so many things seven days a week, twenty-four hours a day. Do the people look happy? Are their eyes shining? No. They look anxious. They look stressed. They look slightly cross. Theirs are the faces of people who feel they haven't quite got all that they deserve yet, or quite enough time in which to buy it all.

I don't think it's a just a case of us getting soft and decadent, like the late Roman Empire, although we probably are. I don't fear that a fit race of barbarians are going to swarm in and conquer us, while we're stoned out of our skulls and piling on weight in front of the telly with takeaway pizzas. I think that it is we who are the barbarians. The barbarians aren't at the gate. They are already among us. They are thronging the shopping malls and discos. The only way to escape them is to go into a second-hand bookshop. It is our own fault. Actually, it's probably all my fault as usual...

Brought up by doughty, austere parents, who came home from the war to a land fit for zeros, my compatriots and I have helped turn the place into a land fit for Neros. The trains don't run on time and it's almost impossible to see a doctor but hey, let's dance and then go shopping! In my own defence, I have to say that having such Spartan forbears did make me feel slightly inadequate. Brought up with tales of heroism and general derring-do and being told how lucky I was, did make me feel like having a war all of my own. And so I did. I fought it in my own head, against myself. And I lost.

In a climate of off-the-peg rebellion, purchased for the cover price of any number of airhead magazines, I can at least say to callow teenagers, 'In my day we made our own rebellion and dress-codes. Not like today.' The truth is though, that whatever the day, sometimes it just all goes wrong. Now read on…

I'm in a hospital bed somewhere in the Home Counties. There's a drip of some kind in my arm, another tube somewhere nearby. My head feels like cotton wool. There's this really loud whining whooshing sound in my ears, which won't go away. When a doctor comes and asks me how I feel, my voice isn't working properly. It's a kind of whisper. I tell him about the noise in my ears. He says it's called tinnitus. It's what happens when you have a dangerous amount of aspirin in your bloodstream.

A Catholic priest comes round and leans over the bed. He asks me if I believe in God. I try to shout 'fuck off' at him, but it comes out as a whisper. He tells me that the sun will shine again and moves swiftly on. A middle-aged man called Michael Twenty-one wheels his wheelchair over to my bed. He's in the same ward as me and is recovering from a stroke. He just happens to be a senior Samaritan. I don't mind him and so I ask him where I am. He tells me that I'm in intensive care and that I've been here for two days. It's the summer of 1972 and I am a nineteen-year-old postman. I have bungee-jumped over eternity instead of diving into it.

When things used to upset me, I buried myself in a big old children's book about Norse mythology. It was a book from the twenties with lovely colour plates and it must have been expensive in its day. Eventually, I decided that it would be nice to go to the place it depicted. So I bought five bottles of barley-wine, a couple of Mandrax and a hundred aspirins. I was in Harpenden High Street on a bench, under a big tree. I drank four of the barley-wines, and took a Mandrax. Then I walked to the public toilets and began to down the aspirins, washing them down with the remaining barley-wine. I got about three-quarters of the aspirins down me and flushed the rest. I sat in the cubicle reading the graffiti as the Mandrax kicked in.

The idea was that the booze would give me the courage, the Mandys would put me out and the aspirins would give me a haemorrhage and kill me while I was out of it. Good theory. What actually happened, however, was that I'd already drunk too much and I wasn't used to drinking. The Mandrax and the booze combined too quickly and made me violently sick. I threw up most of the aspirins and staggered upstairs to the street and sat on the bench for a while, till I stopped feeling so sick. Then I went to the phone box and told my girlfriend, whom I'd just had a row with, that I was sorry. She said she was sorry too and why didn't I come round?

I got myself on a bus to the next town and staggered over to her house on a council estate. I didn't tell her anything, and she didn't ask me anything. She was used to me being in every kind of state. We had some salad and bread to eat, but I wasn't feeling great so I went to bed. She came to bed later. Sometime in the early morning I woke up and I crawled to the bathroom. I was spewing some very interesting colours. When it was green I started to get a bit bothered. When it was red I knew I was in trouble. My girlfriend was going to call an ambulance, but I told her not to do it. Because I'd been busted, I didn't want the police involved. They'd probably use it against me in court and they might even search her place. I held out for a bit but it was getting bad. Sometime later that morning she got me a taxi.

At the hospital it was too late to pump me. I'd already done an efficient job of that myself. They took blood samples and they found the high levels of aspirin. I don't know what they actually did with me in the end, as I wasn't there. Only my girlfriend came to visit me, and some young well-scrubbed, hippy Christians. They told me they knew a place where I could stay when the hospital let me out, and they said they'd help me, and we'd all pray together. I was so fucked up for a while I nearly took them up on their offer. I reckon these people must study the form in intensive care wards, and then go in while people are depleted to try and recruit them. That's pretty cynical garbage, isn't it?

Towards the end of my brief stay, I had one more visitor in the form of my mother. I hadn't seen much of her for about eighteen months. What was I going to do when I got out? Same as I ever did. You could see she was upset about it. What was she doing there? I suppose the hospital had contacted her. She'd driven about seventy miles to see me, and she hated driving. She'd smoothed things out with my grandparents, whom I'd been temporarily staying with. She'd told them it was food poisoning or something. They were very gentle with me when they finally saw me again. My mother dropped me off at my girlfriend's place. It was the only way the hospital was going to release me. My druggie mates ruffled my hair, called me a silly bastard and asked me where I'd been. I don't know what actually happened. Even the gruff postmaster back at my depot was being kind to me. Why was everybody being kind to me? Nobody knew what I'd been up to, did they? Was I ashamed? Yeah, really.

I promised myself that in the future, if I ever found myself with a suicidal urge, I would go to an organization that helped people worse off than myself and say, 'Hi. My name is Martin. I'm young and fit and have loads of energy.

111

Perhaps you would like to make use of my life, because I no longer feel that I have any use for it myself.'

Version Two:

This part of the story was not easy for me to write. What damaged vanity, despair or confusion could lead a nineteen-year old to become unbalanced enough to even toy with suicide, let alone attempt it? Having written down what actually occurred, without I hope, being so inconsiderate as to bleed all over the reader, I concluded that I'd only shown half the film. I asked myself, if Martin Scorcese had been directing this film, what would he have done? The answer, I decided, was that he'd have told the story again, possibly beginning the story earlier, to give details of the events leading up to the events. He'd have used a different camera angle and another voice to narrate the story. He'd have moved round the assembled characters in a circle noting their facial ticks and speech mannerisms. Well, I'm not Martin Scorcese; I'm Martin Newell. But I couldn't think of a better way of telling this particular tale. So, you in the back seats, stop rustling that popcorn, sit up straight and watch.

There had been power cuts during February. Things had got a bit strange at the Seven Rooms, and I'd moved in with my grandparents round the corner. I'd got myself a job as a postman. There was a fortnight before I started training, when I was at a loose end, and my friend Noreen and I embarked upon a project. I'd read a half-arsed article in an underground magazine, probably written by an acid-casualty, about alternative time zones. The article said that, if we really wanted to be alternative and revolutionary and all that, the alternative society would operate in all the hours that straight society didn't. For instance, we'd sleep through the day, rise and have breakfast at six in the evening and then work through the night doing creative things, party during the small hours, finally hitting the sack round about ten in the morning. If enough of us did it, we'd have alternative-time-zone shops, cafés and jobs, and we wouldn't have to have anything to do with the straight society any longer. I believed it. And Noreen thought it was worth a try. We had time on our hands and so, hey ho, off we went.

The power cuts made it even more exciting. For hours at a time, the streets of our town were bathed in total blackness. The two of us were an exclusive little sect with our own support group. We'd ring each other up at seven in the evening and ask, 'How did you sleep today?' We'd go walking around in the blackness talking about important stuff like how we could change the world. It has to be said, we did feel extraordinarily weird most of the time. I think we lasted about two weeks. Then I started training as a postman.

The trouble with being a postman is that you have to start at 4.30 a.m. But if you're nineteen and want to stay up taking acid with your mates, you're not going to even try to go to bed until at least midnight. And then with the curtains melting in front of you, your grandparents looking pretty strange, speaking in slowed-down voices and then glittering fairy castles in your head every time you close your eyes, you get pretty weirded out to say the least. And it doesn't help when some bulldog of a postmaster is breathing Horlicks tablets and halitosis in your face and getting at you while you're trying to sort your round out. The hallucinations don't help when you're riding a bike in semi-darkness either. But when you're nineteen, things like food and sleep seem like so many unnecessary luxuries.

That spring I'd started going out with a smoky-eyed, stoned hippy princess called Miriam. Some of Miriam's friends were junkies. They were artsy bohemian people a little older than us and they were into reading William Burroughs books and listening to The Velvet Underground. They didn't take to my constant speed-tripping zaniness very much – too much work for them. They were pretty laid-back. So much so, that one of them once nodded out in front of us with a lit cigarette in his hand and burned a deep hole in his leg. When they were awake they tried to make me feel uncool, although I thought that they were precious and slothful. Miriam thought they were lovely, whereas I'd known junkies before. Hobbyists or full on, they were a pain in the arse.

It has to be said I was very struck on Miriam. She had a *trompe l'oeil* painting in her room and she listened to some pretty exotic records. She was a nice person in a bombed-out Annie Hall sort of way. She could be very kind, always making cups of tea and snacks and looking after people. She looked after lame ducks and they all loved her for it. I suppose I wasn't the lamest duck in her lexicon really. I couldn't compete with well-spoken, well-read, doomed junkies, could I? Either way, we began to fragment after a while. I was desperately trying to hang on to her, believing that we might be A Forever Thing. Now there's nothing like that for putting a girl off, is there chaps? The more I tried to hang on to her, the more she gave me the why-can't-we-just-be-friends shtick. I was taking more and more acid – and then I got busted. But that's another story for another day...

What happens when the person you tell all your problems to becomes the problem? What happens when you're becoming such a liability that your friends are starting to get at you? What happens when the boss at work is making you feel like you're the world's most incompetent person ever? Add some strongish acid administered about three times a week, subtract quite a lot of sleep, multiply it all with a few questions pertaining to what have I managed to achieve up until now? And don't talk about it to anyone because they couldn't possibly understand. Is it therefore any wonder that a 1920s children's book about Norse gods and Valhalla begins to look not only more attractive than real life, but actually attainable?

The afternoon that I formulated my little reality-hopping cocktail, a bloke I knew only from parties came and sat down on the bench beside me for a few minutes while I was getting started on the barley-wines. His name was Dennis. Dennis thought I was a funny guy, wacky, different and always up for a lark. He asked me what I was doing. I told him about the Norse gods and about how sad and pissed off I was and said that I was going to kill myself. I think he just thought I was doing one of my many party sketches. He said words to the effect of me being one crazy fellow and whatever next? Then he walked away chuckling.

Well no change there then. As for Miriam, why would she care? In fact I might even expose her cool junkie friends for the charlatans that they were if I upped the stakes. My parents? Yeah well, they shouldn't have pushed me. They should have let me build those dens. They shouldn't have made me go to those schools, should they? What about my trippy, speedy mates? They'd get over it. And anyway, they'd see me again during their trips. My employers? Ha! This would show them that I wasn't interested in their rules, bonuses and pensions. The police who'd busted me? The straight society who hounded me and despised me because I didn't want to consume or conform? The politicians who would govern me or imprison me as they saw fit? Their jail wasn't strong enough to hold me. I was out of here. I was going to escape into that book. Someone would open the pages one day and find my face there among the heroes. I was going back where I truly belonged. And no one would ever be able to hurt me or tell me I was useless again. So remember kids: don't fuck with Norse mythology. And don't do drugs.

Sixteen

Postman Carried Drug as 'Act of Chivalry'
Hertfordshire, May-July 1972

There's a hamlet in Hertfordshire called Peter's Green, near a beautiful village called Ayot St Lawrence, just north of Wheathampstead. There used to be a pub there named the Tin Pot, where Dick Turpin the highwayman is reputed to have once stayed. When I was a kid, my grandad would take me out there and park me on a pub bench with a bottle of ginger beer and a bag of crisps with a little blue twist of salt. Near Wheathampstead is Nomansland Common, where they made a film called *The Wicked Lady* starring Margaret Lockwood. It was based on a true story about a real highwaywoman and local people such as my grandad were sort of quietly proud that it was made there.

I knew this countryside as I cycled all around it when I was a boy. When I was a slightly bigger boy, I'd wander round here out of my bonce, whenever I was feeling wounded by anything. There were ancient earthworks nearby, left over from some huge battle between the Romans and the Celts. I didn't know much about it, but I do remember that there was a legend that in certain atmospheric conditions, the ghostly forms of the old warriors were to be seen and the cries of the dying heard.

Near the village of Ayot St Lawrence was an old silk farm. There was also Shaw's Corner, the house where George Bernard Shaw used to live. The ruined church had a graveyard whose tombs had been desecrated, allegedly by people practising black magic. The Brocket Arms, Ayot's local pub, was reputed to be very haunted. In fact, the whole place was steeped in magic for me, and had been ever since I was about ten years old. Best of all though, and not visible from the road, was a church which looked like a small Greek temple. If you wanted to see this strange folly, which I believe was built in the late eighteenth century, you had to walk up a short lane and through a gate, and there, in a small English meadow was the strange and incongruous sight of a Greek temple.

The odd thing was that even many of the people in the surrounding towns of Harpenden, St Albans and Welwyn Garden City didn't seem to know about it. In all the times I went there, I don't remember ever meeting any other visitors. Maybe our increasingly twee heritage industry has changed all that now and there are brown signs, posts with blue arrows and leaflets left in visitor centres to tell you how to get there. At the time, however, it was one of my little secrets. It was a great weapon to have on your side if you were nineteen and wanted to impress someone, say, erm…a girl.

I was pretty crazy about Princess Miriam, the stoned, rescuer-of-lame-ducks. I'd been going out with her for a couple of months, but the path of love is strewn with great yawning, saw-toothed bear-traps. And I had stumbled into one. I was beginning to sense that she was going off me. I mean, I think women can smell desperation on you, and then you are really stuffed. For no matter how much you may try to cover it up – with Devil-May-Care lotion, Cavalier body spray, or Nonchalance's So What? – you will still end up stinking of a cheesy little fragrance called Please Don't Leave Me.

On this day, a sunny Saturday, with Miriam's hymn sheet reading those well-known dirges: No. 104, Perhaps We Shouldn't See Each Other Quite So Often; No. 65, Maybe We Could Just Be Really Good Friends; No. 33, No Don't. Not Here; and worst of all, the hated No. 114, Ken Plays The Guitar Really Nicely, it's not looking too good. I've got to pull something very special out of the bag. I've got to show her that I'm not just this noisy guy who turns out gags every minute and takes the piss out of her friends. I must convince her that maybe I could even get to like Cat Stevens, a little bit. Take her somewhere nice that she's never been, and listen to her, as well as talk at her.

So I take Miriam to Ayot St Lawrence, show her the church, which looks like a classical temple and walk in relative quietness through the lanes with her, where the sun strobes through the trees. It's great for a while. Framed against the wheat fields, with her long dress and long auburn hair she looks like a Sunsilk shampoo commercial, if not actually a Flake chocolate commercial. Then she mentions India, and I go up like napalm. Because every dopey girl I ever fell for always wanted to go to India, or Morocco, and get dysentery and hepatitis, and come home via the London School Of Undiagnosable Tropical Lurgies talking absolute rubbish. Afterwards they meet 'really lovely guys' who meditate and are cool, and wise. 'Like Mark's really, really wise, you know? He doesn't often say anything. But when he does…'

We had that Mark round at ours once, this little nut-brown Dylan-haired, twinkly-eyed hippy, and he sat down on the floor, cross-legged and assumed a beatific smile. I'd been warned about how cool and wise he was. 'Hey, better not try any of your ego-tripping joke routines when Mark's here, Martin. I mean, he's really, really wise. He's been to India and he'll suss you out.' Golly. I'm really scared. What's he gonna do? Tell me my karma just ran over his dogma? I already know that. Anyway, Mark eats all the food. Mark smokes all the dope. The chicks are sitting round him, waiting for him to distribute his pearls of wisdom. But he doesn't say anything, not all night. Until he leaves, then he says, 'Really nice, maan.' He leaves, and everyone goes, 'Wow!'

I have a fundamental fault here. I do not like travel. I have done travel. I have been forced to do travel, and I have met interesting people, but all of my life I've just wanted to stay in one place. I couldn't, because my dad was in the forces and then, later, I was in travelling rock bands. Naturally I don't want to travel. What's the point of falling in love with some young woman, only to find she wants to go and travel? I just found it very unsettling, that's all. Being a young and emotionally inarticulate young man, whenever I heard the dread phrase, 'I want to travel and meet people,' it would light a touch-paper. I never used to think why a young woman wouldn't want to travel, I just saw the whole business as an utter threat, which I couldn't even explain to myself, let alone the young woman.

All these girls want to travel and meet guys like Mark, but what they actually do is meet a bearded Genesis fan called Geoffrey, take their teacher-training and become teachers. A while after that, Geoffrey shaves his beard off and becomes a very well-paid systems analyst. Then they get married, have three children all called Emily and go and live in a big house in St Albans and eat polenta or some rubbish like that. When that breaks up, she rediscovers her Irish roots, changes her name to something I can't even spell and becomes a Tai-Chi aromatherapist. Geoffrey spends the next ten years drinking, wanking and paying for two houses, and then he marries another teacher who looks like his first wife but, crucially, is not as good-looking.

And Mark? Mark makes a fortune importing Indian rugs and furniture and buys some luxury pad on the non-ravey side of Ibiza. Then he settles down with a top-notch Brazilian bird called Conchita, who's half his age, and lives happily ever after with two pairs of leather trousers, a bomber jacket and the profits from a disco bar he owns. You think none of this is true? Prove it, and I'll buy you lager all night.

Miriam mentions India just once and I get all insecure and angsty. Mister Wacky Cynical pops his vermilion head over the pyjama-elastic of courtly love and the golden afternoon begins to disintegrate. When we get to a main road, she gets on one bus while I get on another. I'm not cool. I'm not mature. I talk too much. She's not seeing me for the rest of the weekend. I'm seething and I've been defeated by my own stupidity. I hate all girls forever, and I want to smash something up. Where can I score some acid?

So, ladies and gentlemen, the long and short of it is, one afternoon, only days later, I'm walking in St Albans with Aero, when we get pulled in by two drug-squad guys. Aero and I aren't bothered as such. I've had a half-tab of acid, so I sort of wish that they weren't searching me in the street, makes me feel self-conscious. Aero is as clean as a whistle. They've nearly finished with me when they open my tobacco tin and they pull out a packet of green cigarette papers. They rip open the packet and inside is a small crumb, a blim, as we in the trade call it, of dope. That's nine miligramms of Afghani Black cannabis resin, to you, not even enough to get you stoned.

I do not believe this. For a start, the one thing I haven't been doing is getting stoned. For another thing, I haven't bought any dope for weeks, just acid. For a third thing, these are not my papers. I ran out of papers. I picked them up off Miriam's dressing table, earlier on this week, after we'd patched up our differences. The crumb of dope does look like the same stuff that Miriam and her friends have been smoking recently. DCs Rix and Hibbertson of the local drug squad intend to nail me over it. Great. I'm being pulled in and I'm going to be interrogated while I'm tripping, and then they're going to bust me. Perfect.

I deny that it's my dope. Whose was it? An ex-girfriend's. Who is she? An American hitchhiker. She went this week. I don't know where. I'm winging it. This is spurious. They're going to bust me for nine milligrams of dope that I couldn't even get stoned on, and it isn't even mine. There's worse. I admit to carrying the dope. Who for? Whaddya mean who for? Give me a break. I'm tripped out. Who for? For the vanishing hitchhiker, of course. Why? Out of a misplaced chivalry, I suppose. Occupation? Postman. Savings? None. They turn me out.

I telephone Release, the organization that helps people who've been busted for drugs. They get me a great lawyer. In court, the prosecution briefly try to hint that I habitually carry cannabis for people. I am freaked and my barrister is furious. He gets it overturned. I am convicted of possession and I am ordered to pay thirty-two pounds and am given two years' probation. My earlier Mandrax, booze and aspirin overdose, which they've somehow turned up, is mentioned and referred to as item four, even though it has absolutely nothing to do with this case. The psychiatric report says that I am intelligent and sane but 'an extremely mixed-up young man'. The only positive things said about me are that I am in full employment and that I 'have acquired some skill on the guitar'.

A day or so later I go to buy the local paper. This is one headline I don't need. It's huge. Across the top of the page it reads, 'Postman Carried Drug as "Act Of Chivalry" '. The report of the casual way I spoke to the police and the headline have my friends in hysterics. They think it makes me sound really cool. The truth of the matter is that I'm feeling pissed off, persecuted and maybe a little ashamed. There's more.

I'm with a friend and his girlfriend, and as I cross the road from the newsagent's and begin to walk up the lane to go home, out of nowhere, a car swoops on us and out jump DCs Rix and Hibbertson, and a woman constable they've brought with them so they can search the girl with us, too. They go through my tobacco tin again. This time I don't even have any papers. I've got that paranoid, I'm poncing them off other people for the time being. The two officers tell me that they think I've got off lightly on this occasion, and that they'll be paying close attention to me in future. I'm totally freaked-out and very, very puzzled. Who do they think I am? What do they think I'm up to? Why are they wasting all this time on a pill head who's only been found with a crumb of gear on him?

The other big problem that I've got is that I'm renting a tiny boxroom off my grandparents. They must not see the local newspaper's headline. I decide to ambush the paper boy and I lie in wait for him at the top of the street. As soon as I see him coming, I walk across the road. 'Number twenty-seven mate? Yeah, s'alright, I'll take it. Save you the job.' I take the paper and make it disappear. By the time they get to the newsagent's to pay the bill on Saturday, there won't be any copies left. Unfortunately, Mrs Summers, their next-door neighbour and award-winning busybody, goes marching into my grandparents' house brandishing her copy of the paper and says, 'Here, Mrs

Wright, have you seen this article about your grandson?'
Fucking cosmic.

Well that really puts the tin hat on it. They remember
the overdose incident, which they weren't supposed to
know about, and they put two and two together. My gran,
God rest her soul, doughty old Edwardian that she was, just
sort of says, 'Well, best be on your best behaviour from
now on, I suppose.' My grandad, who never did me a
wrong turn in his life and coloured my broken childhood
with great stories and homespun wit, is...disappointed isn't
the word. He's stopped talking. I have brought disgrace on
his small blameless household, the household which
always earned its shilling, did its bit, put up evacuees
during the war, never broke the law or hurt anybody ever.

He says one thing only, 'You've broken my bloody 'eart,
boy.' Then he goes out to walk the dog, and he doesn't
speak to me for weeks. That was the worst punishment of
all.

Princess Miriam and I are all but over now. She's got more
into her artsy, junkie friends and I'm treated more or less as
a social liability, to be pitied and treated warily. I do not
know my own strength when I bring my bitter mile-a-
minute comedy skits to their laid-back living rooms. When
Kerouac or Burroughs, neither of whom I am interested in,
are offered to me for my consideration, I merely say,
'Frankly, I think we are wanking in the sleeping bag of
doubt, here.' Naturally, such an attitude is unwelcome
among these serious and thoughtful people but I am so
bored. I do not want to sit around in stoned silence for
hours listening to George Harrison's 'All Things Must Pass'.
I want action. I have had it up to here with this, so I cut my
hair like a Clockwork Orange droog, I take to wearing ice-
blue Levi's Sta-prests and braces for a while. We've got to
bust out of this hippy torpor.

One evening, I'm in turmoil, I get an American friend with a car to take me over to Miriam's for one last go at winning her back. He waits outside in the car and wishes me luck. I walk in to find dope, incense, gentle sounds, and candles. Everyone's sitting around blissed out. I have a brave stab at, 'Hi, I was passing and...' I even try, 'I was wondering if...' But there's nothing. It's like The Tasmanian Devil's trying to get a gig as a meditation instructor. They look at me like I'm a grenade that's rolled onto the carpet. In the end I go quietly. As I walk out of there I hear someone say, 'Too fuckin' much, maan.' Keith's in the car.

I put my shades on to disguise what's in my eyes and in his kind, Yank voice, Keith says, 'Let's go home, Martin.'

After this, because it is July now, I spend the rest of the summer getting up early for work as a postman, trying to write songs and listening to Stray, The Pink Fairies, Hawkwind, Family and the B-side of Pink Floyd's *Atom Heart Mother*. I go out to Ayot St Lawrence by myself and wonder how one man can get it all so wrong. I want to make it all better, I really do, but that's not going to happen just yet.

The postmaster comes up to me breathing Horlicks and halitosis and informs me that my drug misdemeanours have been noted but that no action will be taken. Oh yes it will. As soon as I have paid off my fine, I quit the job and go and get another one as an industrial contract cleaner. I spend a wretched two weeks with a misery-guts called Joe cleaning about 300 windows of an empty public school in Gerrards Cross. Then in the autumn, I go and get a job with my friend Fred and the boys at the dust factory. And I am headed for disaster again.

Seventeen

A Town Like Acid
Hertfordshire, October 1972

It's the autumn and it's gorgeous. The sunlight's gone rusty and sprawls like a golden squatter on bare boards. Down the lane the oaks and the birches drip leaves like ingots. I'm walking up the road from my job at the dust factory. Starlings sit on wires like bad music on shaky staves. Aero, dark-eyed hippy princeling and favourite of flaxen-haired girls, and me have taken a walk round to Clarendon Terrace. Here we meet Minty, a cool, high-cheekboned, middle-class kid who knocks out a bit of this and that – not really a drug dealer as such, more a young gentleman hobbyist.

Minty's got a problem. He's bought a batch of green, microdot, acid tabs, and they've turned out to be very strong indeed. His friends have all been having rather too hairy a time of it, so he calls Aero and offloads them on us for twenty-five pence each. What are Aero and I going to do with sixty strong microdots? We are going to have ourselves an acid-taking contest. I'm not as seasoned a space traveller as Aero, but I reckon that if I take some amphetamines at the same time as the acid, I'll at least be able to reduce the hallucinations to a manageable level.

Here are the rules: thirty tabs each, starting Saturday night and ending the following Saturday night. The contestant who is the least fucked up wins the competition. On your marks, get set, trip. And it's Aero with two in one go, Newell starting after midnight with five blues, a joint and one of the green microdots. Aero's well away. He goes up to his room to listen to Quintessence. Newell's down in the rumpus room, with Fred, Little Pete and three young women, listening to Led Zeppelin. Nothing's happening. After half an hour, he whacks down another two. Whoa! No sooner has he done this, than the first one comes up to hit him. How's Aero doing? Your correspondent has no idea. This is because your correspondent is watching the carpet melt, listening to cosmic winds and trying to understand what his friends are saying. They appear to be speaking Saturnian, in slowed-down voices.

Hours dissolve. Dawn breaks. Through the French windows, I can see that the autumn winds are coloured, the shrubbery is dancing, my companions' faces have changed. Some of them look like foxes or beautiful sea lions. There is a deep, low pounding on the door. Fred deals with it. It's the landlady. She is also speaking in slowed-down Saturnian. This task is beyond comprehension; I can barely understand what is required. Fred, who is speeding, comes to help and talks me through it. It seems to take hours. She is asking if I can help her move a heavy armchair from downstairs to upstairs. The cosmic fun goes on until late afternoon, when I am found in a nearby garden, wrapped in a blanket and repeatedly moaning the words of a Pink Fairies' song called 'Marilyn'. Aero has tripped, come down and crashed out.

Because I have a factory job, I only nibble away at the pills during the week, a half here, and a half there. My strategy of building up constant-use tolerance is beginning to pay off. Although events get a bit much in the factory one afternoon and I have to take a few hours off from work in order to regain my mental balance. By Thursday night, almost out of a sense of duty, I'm knocking the microdots back in twos and finding that they don't have anywhere near the mental maelstrom effect of Saturday night's brain cabaret. Things, however, are becoming a bit of a strain. When I move my hands through the air, coloured after-images follow them. I think, 'My God. I'm so bored with the lack of normality. I just want it to stop. Make the tracers go away!'

Aero, meanwhile, has been steadily tripping. With no job, he's been able to sleep whenever he wants. It's the next Saturday evening and I still have eight pills left. I eat them all in one go and attend a soirée in the nearby town. To my relief, the eight pills hit me no stronger than a half-tab. Aero is as cool as a cucumber. Sitting in a candle-lit room after midnight, I burst into tears of exhaustion and ask a friend to take me to a mental hospital. The friend makes me a cup of tea and bids me sleep. Aero, with a smug, cosmic smile on his face, is declared the winner of the Autumn 1972 Acid-Taking Contest. I am awarded my brain back as a consolation prize. This story is not an exaggeration. It actually happened. Don't try it at home. In fact, don't try it.

Around this time, Fred notices that we earn much more if we do overtime in the factory. The work is arduous, hot and slightly dangerous. We come out of the place every night exhausted and covered in either white or black dust. Fred has a solution to this fatigue/work interface problem. Speed. Drinamyl pills bought wholesale from a man in Islington. The foreman, a tough old first-generation mod has taken a shine to Fred. Jacko the foreman has noticed what a real mean team he's got. We work like no other team in the factory. One day, Fred tells Jacko exactly why it is that we work so hard, and so well.

We expect Jacko to be shocked. Instead he says, 'Blues eh? Can you get me some?' As Jacko's wife is in hospital with some complications of the something-or-other, Jacko is on the loose with nothing to go home for. Soon Jacko is driving Fred up to Islington and bringing back bags of doobs, as he calls them. Any time that any of our team of six begins to flag, a trip to the shot-blast cupboard with Jacko rectifies the matter within twenty minutes. We have become the A-team at the factory. Our workmates look upon us with amazement. They sense that something is going on but they're all so thick and straight, that they don't know what it is. Our output has reflected well on Jacko. His boss gives him the keys of the factory. We go in at six in the morning. We knock off at seven or eight in the evening. We're all on about ten or fifteen blues a day and extras on Fridays. Jacko takes the pill money out of our overtime. Which is huge. I make seventy-five quid one week. My normal wage would be about twenty. The lads are breaking production records.

Fred has pushed it one step further. Before the nine-to-fivers arrive and after they leave, he and Jacko set up a big stereo near our workstation and blast out anything from soul music to The Pink Fairies and Led Zeppelin. The rest of the idiots have to put up with Radio Two. On Friday nights, Jacko and Fred take us juniors to the pub. I don't drink beer, so I'm on whisky or brandy. For one of our team, it's all too much. He goes into a sort of open-eyed coma and we can't shake him out of it. Luckily, Jacko knows what to do. He runs a cold bath into which we lower the naked boy and amazingly he comes round. It's November now and we've been pushing this particular scam too far. Even our girlfriends don't think it's funny. In fact, none of us have girlfriends anymore. We're losing it.

People are beginning to get frayed around the edges. The team is falling apart. One day, a senior management man finds Jacko talking to himself in the shot-blast cupboard. This is wrongly interpreted as strain caused by work and by Jacko's home life. Jacko is given some leave and we get a new foreman. One or two guys on the team are weeded out. It's the end of the game, the end of the scam, the end of the pills and the end of the money.

For reasons that I genuinely can't remember, a team of boys smash up our headquarters, the Seven Rooms. I'm supposed to be there, but I'm not. I'm in another town drinking several barley-wines because I can't find any pills. barley-wines were the strongest beer you could get before they invented 'spesh'. On the train home, I remember that I have to check in at the police station. I've been asked to come in as a witness to an assault. Don't even ask. I give the statement and I walk round to the Seven Rooms. The place has been trashed. There's only one person there, a girl. I waltz drunkenly around the wreckage with her. I've no idea what's happened? Now there's nothing left to wreck. I half-heartedly throw a table down the stairs, kiss her good night and go home.

The next evening the police accuse me of wrecking the entire house and arrest me. I am as baffled as anyone else as to why this is. Someone has set me up. Luckily another policeman comes to my rescue. He tells the arresting officer that, since the damage must have taken some time to do, I couldn't have done it. I simply didn't have time. He works out what time I left the police station the previous night. He works out how long it would have taken me to walk there. He finds out what time I got home. And he concludes that I wouldn't have had time to do that much damage. I put my hand up to throwing the table down the stairs. It had woodworm. Value? Three quid.

So who did it? I honestly never knew. I never found out. One final injustice, somebody has named names and people are being pulled in. I'm supposed to be the one who named names, so now there are people after me. Did they ever do anyone for it? Yes. Me, but only for the table. I am now beginning to think that someone is out to get me. When the probation officer comes up with a deal, whereby I move out of town and they waive breach of probation, I'm too exhausted to resist. I'm sick of pills, sick of the backstabbing and sick of being picked up by the police. We used to be a bunch of boys taking a few pills and having a good time. We wanted to get a band together, stage strange events, and generally turn the place into a merry pranksters' house.

Eighteen months later, two of us have been busted; a knife-wielding girlfriend who's pawned his ring for skag has chased Aero. There's been heroin. The bikers have split up into different factions. There's been a slow descent into violence-tinged low life. We've all had too much of everything for far too long. The more sensible, creative, fun people have drifted away, leaving the hardcore drug hooligans and the problem people, and I am becoming one of them.

A local newspaper editor, a kind, open-minded fellow, who had invited me into his house on numerous occasions when I was in all sorts of fucked-up states, gives it to me straight. One evening after I've regaled him with a long acid-fuelled conspiracy theory relating to subliminal advertising, I ask him what he thinks. He looks at me steadily and says, 'Do you really want to know what I think, Martin? I think, that if you carry on like this, you will end up being institutionalised.'

They were his exact words. I giggle awkwardly, but the words echo in my head. A couple of days later, I ring home. I don't say goodbye to anyone, I just say that I am going away for a while, to straighten myself out. I tell my probation officer, I inform the police. I pack a few boxes of clothes and books, and I leave.

I don't know what kind of picture I presented to my mum, when I turned up in the village. I hadn't seen much of her for months. But, you know, she's a tough old army wife. She never gives much away. I owe her.

Eighteen

Ghost Mode
Goldhanger, Essex, December 1972-Early March 1973

I'm in Essex. I'm not in Essex because I want to be but
because I am in trouble on several fronts. I'm on probation,
I'm teetering on the brink of amphetamine addiction and
I have bronchitis. Some people back in my last town aren't
pleased with me because they think I'm responsible for
flooding their flat. Some other people are still after me
because they smashed up the Seven Rooms and they think
that it was me who spilled the beans to the police. The
police actually think that it was me who smashed up the
house and are still considering charging me with it. All of
these people have made a mistake. And I'm nearly
innocent, OK?

So let's just recap on that. I'm broke; I have no girlfriend
and no job. I'm ill, overfond of drugs, in trouble with the
police, people are after me and the probation authorities
have advised me to go and live with my parents in a tiny
Essex village where I don't know anyone. Am I
downhearted? Well, no actually. The whole thing is a
massive relief. I want to make a fresh start. I needed a kick
up the arse and I'm getting one. Things are about to
change for the better. Not straight away. We've got a bit to
get through first but it's going to happen. One day soon,

spring will come sashaying into the meadows, the sun will come out and I'll join a proper pop group. Right now though, it's early winter. I am nineteen.

I immediately like Essex. The early winter is clear and cold and I spend vast amounts of time by myself walking the sea walls and the lanes around Goldhanger and Tolleshunt D'Arcy. Occasionally I play my guitar and write down bits of gobbledegook and song lyrics. Sometimes I walk the three miles into Maldon and drink a couple of barley-wines in the pub. I walk the lanes by moonlight and gaze across the weird flat fields. I have reverted into ghost mode. At night I dream of taking Drinamyl, the blue amphetamine pills I'd become so fond of. Years later I learn that this is not uncommon in people who stop taking drugs.

I'm not exactly dressed for the cold weather and walking in the country. I'm one of the young dudes that David Bowie wrote about. I have long spiky layered hair, I often wear mascara and my clothes are ridiculously flimsy and pop star-like. I wear white Levi's flares, a white glam-rock jacket and high-heeled boots. The locals look at me strangely. I must be one of those weirdoes from London. My favourite jacket is a maroon, herringbone double-breasted highwayman thing, three-quarter length with long side vents. I should be in a pop group but I'm not.

My parents, to give them full credit, go easy on me at this time. They seem to realise that I've had a rough time. My mum makes only the gentlest noises about me getting a job. And I do. I march straight into Maldon the next day and secure myself a position as a paint-sprayer in a local factory. I can start straight after Christmas. One night the police turn up and I find that I'm only going to be charged with damaging the table. My court appearance is in February. I sign a form. They go away. Breach of probation is waived.

One day, while hanging out in Maldon, I go and talk to some long-haired kids of about my own age. A dark-haired, chunky girl who is with the group invites me to the pub that night. They're trying to get a band together. They don't need a guitarist but they ask me if I can play a keyboard. I tell them that I can only play a harmonium, a type of pedal-organ, and that I do actually own one. We arrange a jam. The girl is a brilliant singer. She's sixteen and she can do Janis Joplin covers, note-for-note, scream-for-scream. Her name is Helen Terry. She will later become Boy George's main backing vocalist and will feature on most of his biggest hits. Right now however, she has Martin Newell as her keyboard player.

After one midnight walk back from Maldon, I wake up and realise something isn't right. I have a fever and my chest feels like it has steel bands round it. I can barely get out of bed. The doctor is called. He tells my mum that I have bronchitis. My chickens have come home to roost: the night I fell asleep in the freezing rain after a party in St Albans a few weeks earlier; the constant feeling of weakness which never went away; taking drugs; coming down; living on yoghurt and cornflakes for months; walking around in mid-winter dressed like Mick Ronson, David Bowie's lead guitarist; smoking all the cigarettes and joints that I could. Teenage Superprat. He's back, and this time he can't even get out of bed.

Coming up to Christmas, I'm well enough to start walking around the lanes again. I go into Maldon and meet my new friends. The band hardly ever practises. They party and go to pubs. I manage to locate small quantities of Dexedrine and acid from time to time. I wash it all down with barley-wine and pretty soon I'm roaring around talking gibberish again. One night I'm tripping and watching some crap on telly and laughing at it hysterically when my dad starts to look at me suspiciously. It's the *Six O'Clock News*. Oops. Incorrect response. Better skedaddle.

So I walk round to the village pub. On the way round there, I'm walking up the lane, when I notice a red glow and loads of smoke coming from a cottage chimney. It's on fire. Should I tell them? I take my courage in my hands and knock on the door. A slightly startled-looking woman answers the door.

'Excuse me. I live down the road and er... I was just walking past when I noticed your chimney's kind of glowing and there seems to be a lot of smoke.'

She appraises the wild-eyed weirdo at the door and comes out on the front path to get a better look at things. She looks at me again. 'Well, it doesn't seem to be smoking any more than usual.'

'Oh... I'm sorry. I just thought...maybe...better check it y'know.'

'Yes, of course. Thank you. But I'm sure it's alright.' I stutter another apology and start walking away. She calls me back. 'Erm... I have just put a pair of my husband's old slippers on the fire.'

'Right. That's probably what it was then. Good night.'

I hear her door shut as I walk to the pub. The pub appears to be very brightly lit, and such a strange lighting scheme. The landlord and a handful of regulars seem to be peering at me. Things feel edgy. What am I doing here, by myself, tripped out in a village pub? What the hell am I doing here? What time is it? How long have I been gone? I drink two barley-wines and wander back to the house. In the kitchen I apologise to my mum for being gone so long. It seems like three hours. I've been about forty minutes. For the next two days I am ill again. I fear we have a little way to go yet before we're completely out of the woods.

My dad says that I ought to get the gap in my teeth fixed. This is a big gap. My front incisor has been missing since a Herfordshire dentist dragged the remnants of it out in June of 1971. It makes me look even more low-life than I actually am. I go and see Mr Kruger in Maldon.

English rock musicians are renowned for their bad teeth. There are reasons for this. If you spend all your life sitting in the back of a Transit van taking speed, eating crisps and Mars bars and nobody ever pays you enough or gives you enough time to eat properly, your teeth are the first thing to suffer. If enough of the back molars are removed however, it does give you a great bone structure. People in LA pay perfectly good money to have their back teeth taken out for better cheekbones, whereas English musicians don't need to.

When you get a gold disc or an award, you can tell the record company, within reason, how many you want sprayed up. Then you can have copies to give your mum, your manager, the recording engineers, etc. But the people who really deserve the gold discs are the dentists. Dentists don't get enough good press. Mr Kruger fixed me up with a false tooth on a plate that changed my life. I was able to smile again and not look like some junkie pirate. My new tooth probably helped to get me the job in the band; this in turn saved me.

I dedicated my last collection of poetry to my current dentist. When you're on tour and stuck in some god-forsaken quarter of the former Eastern Bloc, the last thing you need is toothache. Only your dentist stands between you and this abject misery. Salute him. Or her.

It's early 1973 and I've got a pretty mouth again. Only now do I realise how much the gap in my teeth had subconsciously affected me. The previous summer, when

I'd sat in the Release lawyer's office in Stevenage, after being busted, he'd asked me, 'Doesn't that gap in your teeth bother you, Martin?'

I'd brazened it out with, 'No. It sets me apart. Shows people that I'm not conforming to anyone's standards.'

He'd studied me for a while before he asked me, 'Why do you keep covering your mouth with your hand then, every time you smile?' Yeah, lawyers should get gold discs too maybe. He'd started the ball rolling. Geoffrey Clapp, wherever you are now, call in. Martin Newell owes you a gold disc.

And now, with a full mouth of teeth again, I can safely attend the Hertfordshire magistrates' court, knowing that if they do make an example of me for my vandalism, that it certainly won't have anything to do with my teeth. The day dawns, and I brush my hair as tidily as it will go and attend court in a pair of horrible blue flares, which I've only ever worn for that purpose. As promised, no breach of probation is mentioned, the magistrates barely glance up at me before administering a fine and I say, 'Thank you, sirs,' and walk out. The only person who's attended the trial with me is Dave from the Seven Rooms. He's made friends with the previous defendant, a very nervous, slightly neurotic, middle-class housewife who has been done for accidental shoplifting. The three of us repair to a pub for a sandwich and a glass of beer. This poor woman was obviously very distressed and ashamed and, odd as our company must have seemed to her, I think she was very grateful for it.

Later that drizzly, February afternoon, I head back to Essex, and I think myself reasonably lucky. But I haven't quite learned my lesson yet. I'm still nineteen and mad. Not bad. I just have a bit of waking up to do, that's all.

Nineteen

What a Bunch of Sweeties
Colchester, Essex, Early March 1973

In a separate case, Martin Newell nineteen, of Goldhanger, Essex, formerly of Harpenden, was found guilty of damage to property and was fined thirteen pounds.

That's that out of the way then. I'd got over my bronchitis and I'd started work as a paint dipper and sprayer in Maldon. It was piecework. Providing I worked like a Trojan from Wednesday through Friday, I could use Monday to come back from St Albans, recover from my speed comedown on Tuesday, then work the last three days to earn enough money, enough money to get myself out of this backwater, sneak back to St Albans, fill myself up with pills on Friday and Saturday, spend Sunday tripping and shagging and stumble back to Essex on Mondays. There was also this leggy posh girl called Sooz who liked dressing me up in women's clothes when I was out of it, but you know how it is. For a few weeks after my court case, once the breach of probation on the earlier drug-bust was waived, that's all I did. It was all I was interested in doing, and I might very well have continued to do it until I got myself into more trouble, had it not been for my parents.

I was just past my twentieth birthday. I was sitting on the sofa with the chemical equivalent of a slow-motion car crash going on in my head when my dad started with, 'Yes but what are you going to do? You don't seem to be going anywhere. You aren't interested in anything,' and so on, until I told him that I was only interested in music. He began to tell me that I didn't show much sign of being any good at that, either. Had I made a record? Was I in a band? When was it, precisely, that I'd last performed in front of any kind of an audience? He was hitting me where it hurt now. I stormed out.

But it had planted a seed. The next morning, still in a rage, I remembered reading an article about a local band, Plod, who were from Colchester, the nearest large town. They'd got loads of work, lots of publicity and locally, they were beginning to get well known. Their singer, who'd been the bloke who started the band, had left them. They were real glam-rockers, make-up, stack heels, loud stomping music, the lot. My mum had pointed the article out to me. I didn't go into work that day. I got on a bus and went into Colchester. You're going to think this next bit is like something out of a bad pop B-movie.

I walked into a music shop called Harper's, marched straight up to a bunch of long-hairs who were standing around discussing equipment and asked, 'Do any of you guys know how I can get in contact with a band called Plod?' The oldest of the group started laughing, and asking why I'd want to hang out with a terrible band like that. Then a young guy of about sixteen told me that I was talking to three of the members of Plod, and asked me what I wanted. I said, 'I heard you needed a singer.' They told me that they'd got a singer for the time being but that they didn't know whether he'd be permanent, not only that, but he had bad tonsillitis. I replied, 'Maybe you should try me, cos I'm better.' I remember hearing the words coming out of my mouth and not believing I was being so cocky. I wasn't even a singer. The most I'd been was a second guitarist doing back-up vocals, and then a few dodgy solo gigs supporting bigger acts at venues in Hertfordshire. What I was, up until this time, was a painfully unconfident singer-songwriter with a terrible reputation for letting people down, because of my drug-taking. My father had been absolutely right and it hurt, but the anger his attack had generated, had worked like a defibrillator on my drug-damaged ego.

The older guy who'd first spoken to me was a blues guitarist called Bill, who was trying to get a band together with a bass player, Mick Hutton. Mick later became a very well-regarded jazzer. The other three guys, who introduced themselves as Stix, Jack and Paul, were none other than the band I'd been looking for. They took me to their headquarters, their roadie, Big Nik's flat on Hangover Hill (as I'd later come to know it). They were interested in me because they wanted someone who was prepared to give total commitment and, more importantly, leap around a lot and wear the make-up and silly clothes. I might be that very prat. Their founding singer, Steve, had been a Bolanesque character, very charismatic. He'd got the whole band going by firing them with his own enthusiasm. He'd also been a brilliant self-publicist, but then he'd left. I told them that I lived for nothing else but pop. I had no other ties, and when could we set up an audition? They gave me a telephone number and told me to ring up in a couple of days. It wouldn't be too long, because they had gigs set up.

I went home with a mission. I was going to clean myself up, miss out on the pills that weekend and buy some clothes. I didn't say anything to my parents. I quietly phoned the number I'd been given. The band said they still had to fix a rehearsal room. They gave me a list of chart numbers they'd be doing: 'Jean Genie', 'Gudbye T'Jane', stuff like that. A week later when I still hadn't heard from them, my confidence was beginning to flag. Summoning up my last bit of cockiness, I rang them and said, 'Are we doing this thing or not? Because I have to go for an audition in London, otherwise.' Jack, the bassist, told me they'd had a bit of bother lining things up and would I be available for Tuesday? Goal.

The audition was in Great Horkesley village hall. They played, I sang and shouted and jumped about a lot. At the end of the session, they went into a scrum. Then they told me, 'You're in,' and they dropped me off in Colchester after the session. It was a warm spring afternoon. The blossom was out on the cherry trees. On a bus full of noisy schoolchildren, I sat looking out of the window, with my mind somewhere else completely. I had twenty-four sets of lyrics to learn, in just under two weeks. And then it was going to be the real thing. I got back to Goldhanger and walked into the house. My mum asked me how I'd got on. I told her I'd got the job. I was a singer in a working band. I told my dad. Were they pleased? I think relieved is more the word. It was early days.

My dad wasn't in the army any more, hadn't been for two or three years. We'd only lived in two houses since he'd come out. So guess what? It was time for one more move, this time to a village on the Clacton side of Colchester, about twenty miles away. I'd been back at the parental home for about four months, under the probation officer's advice. My new probation officer would be in Clacton. I went to see her in her office and she said that she wanted to do a home visit. I think she was trying to make sure that I actually was where I said I was. She was pleased that I was in a band too. Although, like my parents, she was vaguely concerned that I'd just given up my job at the factory. Given it up? They were glad to see me go. They'd hardly known me. It had been punch-clock time keeping. You put your card into the clock and if you were late, it was red. If you were on time, it was blue. I used to deliberately get mine red/blue/red/blue/red/blue. The foreman asked me why that was. I told him that I thought that it looked prettier at the end of the month. He gave me a funny look. What with moving house and joining a band, the Friday that I left, I skipped out of that factory. I knew that the band might not make me a lot of money but I could always get some kind of a cleaning job, where I wouldn't be missed if I went off to a gig. My probation officer asked how she would find my house. I told her that it was the one with loads of girls trying to climb up the drainpipes. 'Really?' she asked.

What I didn't know at the time was that within a couple of months, I was going to get myself in one more serious bit of trouble. That, however, is a story for another day. Meanwhile, having moved to the new village, I had to get on with the serious business of learning the pop set, the rock and roll set and all the moves and chops with which I and the other members of Colchester's finest were going to set the world on fire.

I soon realised that the members of The Mighty Plod were chaps after my own heart. Instead of the vaguely hippy-dippy people I'd known, or the rather harder drug hooligans I'd hung out with, they were cheerful and rude Colcestrians. Two of them had Polish surnames. Jack and Stix would later become the feared and sceptical rhythm section or the 'Polish Engine Room', as they sometimes referred to themselves. Paul, the guitarist, was slightly quieter, but he looked every inch the rock star. Thin as a pin, he wore clinging satin trousers, skimpy glittery tops and stack-heeled boots. On stage, he threw himself and his guitar around like a veteran. He was probably the best musician at that time and capable of peeling off very good rock and roll solos for as long as was required. Just as impressive however, were their roadies Big Nik and Sav.

Big Nik was a belligerent, hotheaded but extremely shrewd and funny bloke. He dressed more like a rock star than the rest of us and was a daring, if slightly dangerous, driver who got us out of trouble more often than he got us into it. He acted like the band manager and made his flat, his van and almost everything else he had available to the members of the band. Sav, with his long blonde hair was Big Nik's number two. A quiet country lad, he'd acquired his name, The Horkesley Savage, through his occasional habit of firing a gun at sundry wildlife from the open door of a moving van on the way home from gigs.

Big Nik had a wicked repartee and a sharp tongue on him, as anyone who argued with him discovered. Once, after a fierce argument about Sav's loyalties, someone had said, 'Sav would say that. He thinks the sun shines out of Nik's arse.'

Big Nik immediately replied, 'That's why I have to get up early every morning.'

On another occasion when Big Nik was berating me about my drinking and general *louche*-ness, I shouted at him, 'You should have been on the Mayflower with the other fucking puritans.'

Big Nik shot back with, 'They already had a Captain.'

The three members of my new band and their roadies were also forever grabbing at each other's dicks and arses, using the foulest language and generally horsing around. They were rude, sexist, boorish and only interested in matters relating to the band. They were a team. And with forty-odd gigs already under their belts, they seemed to be headed nowhere but up. It was with the greatest of ease and excitement that I fell into their company. It was Stix whom

I first became friends with. He was very intelligent in a hard-headed way, with a cruel sense of humour. Like me, he was not a snob about the kind of music he listened too. Back in those days, there was a great deal of elitism among the long-haired and bearded ones over what music was acceptable. The critics in the increasingly precious rock press of the time fostered this.

Stix liked to listen to John Barry, The Carpenters, old Thunderbirds soundtracks and Dave Brubeck. He didn't consider David Bowie to be any more important than The Sweet. I went one further than that. I actually preferred The Sweet. So we had that much in common. The whole idea that pop was better than rock pervaded the band ethos. We were concerned about selling out; we wanted to do it. How much better, we thought, to be on *Top of the Pops* than *The Old Grey Whistle Test*. Sod the idolatry of the music critics, we wanted the screaming chicks. This attitude, well established in the band before I joined, managed to get the members of The Mighty Plod banned from almost every cool party in Colchester. And they couldn't have given a fuck. To upset the parent generation by rebelling is human. To piss off your own generation is divine. Which, I suppose, is why punk eventually happened. Pity we were four years too early for it.

Twenty

Reader, I Carried Him
Colchester, Essex, April-June 1973

What makes silly boys join pop groups? With me, it certainly wasn't the money; although it would have been welcome enough if I'd ever made any. No, I think I was just looking for a way out of mundanity, or a way to find a girlfriend. Although joining a band may be a good way of finding a girlfriend, it's certainly the worst place to try and hang on to one. I was obsessed with music, of course. I had lots of energy, and if I'm really honest, I wanted to leap about a lot and have people look at me. Mummy, you're not watching me.

I didn't expect to be a singer, either. I wanted to be a guitarist who jangled and did harmonies. I also wanted to be the songwriter, more Townshend than Daltrey, more Ray Davies than Eric Clapton, more Keith Richards than Brian Jones, more Callard than Bowser, more Spencer than Marks, more Stratton than Briggs. I'd watched quite a few bands, and the jangly baroque way of playing a guitar was out of fashion. You now needed to know lots of widdly-widdly solo stuff. A faux reverence for virtuosity had sprung up among the greatcoats and Zapata moustaches. I thought it was boring, unless Jimi Hendrix or Jimmy Page was doing it. I wanted to be in a pop group not a string quartet. I wasn't interested in art. I wanted to make a racket. I'd noticed it looked like good fun being a singer as you weren't tied down to a guitar and amp, but you could run all over the stage, climbing things and mucking about.

I think it was seeing Rod Stewart with The Faces that sold the idea to me, no standing still with this bloke. He had a top haircut, great clothes and a working-lad approach which countered the general self-important I-am-an-artist vogue of the time. A less well-known role model of mine was the singer of Stray, Steve Gadd. No, you may not have heard of Stray. But for thousands of young blades in the early seventies, the members of Stray were, potentially at least, the new Led Zeppelin. They had a cool lead singer with a defiant adenoidal voice. They had a drummer who wasn't far off Keith Moon, a bassist who played with the power of a rocker but the precision of a jazzer, and best of all, they had in Del Bromham, a guitar hooligan capable of writing great songs. They were tough but clever.

When Aero and I started listening to Stray in 1970, they had an infinite cachet too. The rock snobs may not have liked Stray but the new breed of young hooligans did. And Stray were barely older than us. It's a very important thing with heroes, that even if they be god-like they should not be so god-like that you couldn't one day be that good yourself. There must always be an aspect of, 'Hey they're just like us. I'm gonna do that one day.' Stray made their first album when they were all about sixteen. Some management company who'd have put them in matching dungarees and given them some piece of chart-fodder to sing didn't sidetrack them. They made a great big menacing fuck-off racket. They also had a light show, which was way ahead of anybody else's on the circuit at the time, and a famous exploding dustbin that had been known to blow holes in stages. I liked the way Steve Gadd handled the mike stand. He wasn't as flash as Rod Stewart but he made the mike look like he belonged behind it. It made you want to grab a kitchen broom and practise his moves. And of course, I did.

So it is very much with Rod Stewart and Steve Gadd in mind that I blag my first job as a singer with Colchester's finest, The Mightly Plod. And one day in early April 1973, after a scant two weeks' rehearsals, your singer finds himself in a vehicle on the A12, heading towards his first professional gig. The gig is at a girls' school near Epping Forest. I am just twenty years old, nervous, and still learning the lyrics. I don't want my fellow members to know just how fragile I am. After doing a sound check in the school hall we tart ourselves up: make-up, clothes and boots. Then we're on. The whole audience is teenage girls, lots of them, all screaming. We are going down a storm. In fact, when we take our break, the roadies and some of the teachers at the school have to form a barrier between the band and the girls so that we can get out to the classroom that serves as our dressing room.

I have never come across anything like this before, or at least not this side of daydreaming. We have to barricade ourselves in the room. Girls are outside, banging on the windows and calling to us. Is this what happens when you're in a pop group? I ask myself. Why the fuck did I sit around taking drugs for two years and getting myself in shit when I could have been doing this, all of it without any drink or drugs? When we go back onstage after the break, I take a handful of the band's badges to throw to the audience. A mistake. As soon as I produce them, the two front rows surge forward and mob me and the roadies have to step in and push the girls back. I cannot believe this. We drive away with the screams still ringing in our ears. Are all our gigs to be like this?

No. By complete contrast, the next gig we play is at a disco in Stevenage. The audience here are hard nuts, they're first-generation skinheads now in their mid-to-late twenties, who've grown their crops out. Their girlfriends are hard-faced, new-town disco girls. The music the DJ is playing is mainstream seventies soul. It's not looking good. When we go onstage, there are whistles and catcalls at our appearance. Our songs go down to hostile silence and hard stares. We are due to do three sets. When we've finished our second, there's a nasty hairs-standing-up-on-the-back-of-the-neck feeling. The club manager is very nice about it. He says that it's not our fault and that we're playing well, but he adds that they're a funny crowd tonight. He says that for our own safety, we should not play our third set.

There's no back-way out of this place. As the disco is in a large modern building, several floors up, we will have to walk through the crowd to make our exit. The roadies stay on to break the gear down and load up. We will leave, as early as possible and as quickly as possible so there's little time to get changed. The manager escorts us through the packed disco. The crowd parts slightly, leaving us a small corridor to file through with our guitars. We feel nervous like hostages, unsure of whether we are to be freed or executed. I am the last in the file. The people, who seem to tower over us, only glare at us as we make our exit. There's an eerie silence, because no music is playing at the time. One of the hard-faced women stretches her hand out as we walk slowly through the crowd and deliberately touches my heaped, lacquered hair, in a mixture of curiosity and contempt. It is less than not very nice at all. And then we're out, running through the car park in the deserted new-town centre, then homewards. And so the answer is no, all gigs are not like the one at the girls' school in Epping Forest.

Over the next few days we play a series of gigs, none of them as good as the first but none as bad as the second. We play at Derby, locally in Suffolk, and at a huge place in Margate. Within a short few weeks I feel like a veteran. It's surprising how quickly I've picked it up. Ironically enough, it brings me into contact with the law again. What is it about me that police and customs officers won't leave me alone? Do I have some sort of postcode stamp on my forehead, which only they can see and which reads, 'Give this bloke a really hard time, officer'? Well do I?

They never stopped for years. It was like being Keith Richards but without the fun or the money. Customs hassled me for fifteen years, strip searches, the lot. I was a good polite boy, but it never helped me. So one day I cured them of it.

I went through customs at several ports and airports, stage clothes on, swigging a bottle of vodka, smoking where it said 'No Smoking' and shouting, 'Come on you bastards!' I flicked V-signs at all the security cameras and began to undo my trousers while yelling, 'Bum search? Yes please!' They couldn't wait to get rid of me. They've stopped doing it now, so I've called the war off and I don't go abroad much anymore. They can't blame me for it as they made my life a misery. They did it to a lot of musicians.

It's strange that when you belong to one of the few British industries which have consistently helped to create wealth for this country over the past few decades, that you get shaken down just because you look a bit different. All the time, there's probably some android in a suit, walking coolly through with an attaché case full of Charlie. So, you want stupid, Mr Customs Officer? I've got stupid. One famous band I know has roadies who got so fucked off with the attentions of customs that they now routinely smear crunchy peanut butter in their bum cracks before the plane touches down in England, because they know they're going to get searched.

But getting back to the story. One night, we've played a gig in Kent and we stop at a service station in the small hours, for tea and toast. For some reason, I'm behind the rest of the lads in the queue, and they're already sitting down at a table as I come up to the checkout with my tray. There's a shadow over me. It turns out to be two policemen, they're glowering at me, 'Alright son, give us your keys.' I ask them what keys they mean. 'Don't fuck us about mate. Your car keys.' I explain to them that I don't have any keys, I don't have a car and I can't even drive. They don't believe me. They're getting very annoyed now. When they ask me how I got here, I tell them that I'm in a band and point to the roadies and band members sitting down several tables away. They escort me over to the table, 'Is he with you?' Everybody shakes their head and mumbles no. They grab hold of me and start to take me away.

At this point, the lads realise something is up and tell the officers that I am after all, the singer with their band. By now, I am very pissed off and shaken up. The reason for it all? Someone with longish hair has done a hit-and-run further along the road. I look like I 'might be the type', and they think I seem 'a bit pale and shaken'. Everybody, band, roadies and policemen are laughing about this. I am not laughing. It's too close to earlier experiences of mine, which my band mates know nothing about yet. I finally get to eat my toast and drink my lukewarm tea. I go home in a very bad mood.

Apart from this incident, I can't remember much about singing in that band that I didn't like. In the late summer of that first year, after I'd finally finished with the legal system, after Bachelor Johnny, our new guitarist, had replaced Paul, rock and roll replaced drugs as the biggest thing in my life. A couple of times, coming home from gigs that autumn, I'd say words to the effect of, 'Thank God I'm not pissing around with drugs anymore.'

And Stix would say, in his usual abrupt manner, 'Yeah, well we've cured you now, Zap.'

And Jack would say, 'Fuck that, Zap. You're in a rock and roll band now.'

They had cured me, and I bloody well was in a rock and roll band. I will never forget them for it.

And I could probably regale you with a hundred more gig stories; drink stories and sundry misdemeanours involving women, but they wouldn't be extraordinary. You'd have had to have been there really. Suffice to say that it was generally I who got myself into trouble, and even then, not so much trouble and not such good stories attached to it, that they couldn't be equalled or bettered by people in other bands, or even people who weren't in bands at all, if it comes to that. There are still a few tales worth telling, however…

You get used to playing certain roles in life. One of mine used to be getting myself into scrapes where someone else would have to bale me out. Sometimes the roles are reversed and the scrapee gets a chance to bale out someone else. Come with me to 1973. It's Colchester on a Saturday night. I've just had a forty-eight hour bug and am feeling a bit weak so I'm not a prime player tonight. We don't have a gig on, and Big Nik has decided that nothing else will do but we must all pile in the back of the Plod van and go to the beach at East Mersea where there's some kind of a party going on.

For some reason we have a large old sofa in the back of the van. It's decided that we'll use it to make our entrance.

I sit cross-legged on it; I'm dressed all in white. Five or six people carry the sofa and me down the slope onto the beach. This wacky entrance is Big Nik's idea and is intended to make me look like some sort of holy figure being carried by cult members. It only partially works, as when we get down to the huge driftwood fire, people's attention is elsewhere.

In front of the fire are two men, both naked. One is bent over with his hands on his thighs while the other appears to be sodomising him with slow and deliberate strokes. The one bending down is shouting, 'Up the bum, Gerald!'

The one doing the thrusting is shouting, 'Oooh! Ah! That's better, Gerald. Anymore, Gerald?'

The other Gerald is replying, 'Ooh! Ah! Right up the bum, Gerald!'

It goes on for about fifteen minutes, watched by a crowd of about seventy hysterical people who are applauding and cannot believe what they are seeing. Who are these guys? No idea. Nobody seemed to know. Never saw them before, or since.

Now I'm not drinking this night, so I can remember most of this. We very nearly prang the van on the way home, and the sofa goes rolling around in the back causing much fear. We're back in Colchester after midnight and I am on top of the multi-storey car park, now demolished, which used to sit on top of the bus garage. I am with Bachelor Johnny, Plod's guitarist. We are both lying down looking over the edge of it. Seemingly miles below, a squad car is patrolling around looking for us. They shine torches up. I'm hissing at Johnny, 'Keep your fucking head down.' Johnny, quiet man of Colchester's finest, has decided to climb round the metal grille, designed to stop idiots climbing the multi-storey car park. With the optimism of the fairly pissed, he's succeeded. I've gone in after him to get him down because one, I can climb and two, I'm sober.

The policemen have obviously been told that someone's been seen on the top of the car park but they can't be bothered to follow us up there. They get back into the panda car and drive off. Johnny and I walk down through the deserted levels of the huge concrete building. With a little bit of clinging and, 'Now put your foot down,' I manage to get him round the barrier, down the slope and back on the street. Things like this have probably been happening on Saturday nights for hundreds of years, in every town in Britain, but it's the only time that I can remember doing something like it, stone cold sober for the good of another human being. I've risked life and arrest many times, but being an egocentric bastard, only once can I remember doing it for someone else. Strangest night I've ever spent not drinking. And how did we eventually get Johnny back to Big Nik's place? Reader, I carried him.

Twenty-one

Aladdin Strain
Colchester, Essex, May-July 1973

Colchester's satin-flared finest are off the road. The departure of Paul, our best musician – a guitarist who could do Jimmy Page solos note-for-note – has knackered us. His leaving was precipitated by a number of things: personality clashes with Big Nik our roadie/manager; to a lesser extent, personality clashes with me. He's a down-to-earth working musician and didn't particularly like my foppish hundred-mile-an-hour wackiness. He's got a reasonably paid job waiting if he quits this glamorous penury we call the pop business. He has a girlfriend who wants a greater commitment. More importantly, we suspect that he has received a better offer from a more professionally behaved band.

I mean, we're none of us exactly stable personalities, but one day, we're sitting in Big Nik's flat in the house on Hangover Hill, on a bright sunny morning and Paul just breaks down and starts to cry. This shocks Stix and me. I'm actually scared because I don't want the band to break up. This band has changed my life. It's given me stability. I was heading for the gate marked Crashed and Burned before I joined this band. Oh, I'm still on probation. I still have the occasional relapse and swallow a load of pills, but the point is that being in a band has given me something to live for. I must be the only person in the world who ever joined a rock band to become drug-free. Now it looks as if it might be taken away from me.

The other members understand the pressure, of course. In 1973, parents, fiancées or employers do not see being in a glam-rock band as a good thing. But we are young and we don't care. However, the sheer depth of Paul's misery is a shocking thing to watch. Eventually, he just slinks off. A few days later we hear he's left the band, taken his share of the kitty and the gear and gone. So now we're *sans* guitarist, short of money, out of work and off the road. We were doing three or four gigs a week before this, rehearsing, sleeping late and generally behaving like low-rent pop stars, endless impressionable young women following us around and offering to be our girlfriends. The best two months of my life. And it's over.

Stix and I are working as early morning cleaners in Tesco's, seven till nine, six mornings per week. Is it hard for rock and rollers getting up that early? We honestly have no idea, since we usually stay up all night and then go into work. It's easier, and anyway, I can't remember anyone owning an alarm clock. This state of affairs won't last for too long, however.

One evening, we convene on Hangover Hill and we meet our new guitarist. He's called John. He's got this fallen haystack of black curly hair. He doesn't look like a glam-rocker, he looks more like a refugee from a West-Coast psychedelic band. Previous experience? He played in a heavy three-piece called Meat-Axe Jackson. He's not such a versatile guitarist as Paul and he's disconcertingly quiet and polite but there's something about him. He's a nice bloke. We decide that we like him after one audition. We have him gift-wrapped and take him away. Within a year he will become Bachelor Johnny, cigar-smoking Clint Eastwood fan, band philosopher and the phantom piss-pourer of Leicester Square. More importantly he will teach us all about drinking. Oddly enough, although we don't learn the fact until a good few months later, Stix and Jack have both met John before. Prior to my joining, a weird bearded guy had accosted the members of Plod at their third gig to ask if they knew of any good places to rehearse. The previous singer, Steve, and Stix, had more or less ignored Johnny because at that point they were only interested in female visitors to the dressing room.

With John in the band, come two great fringe benefits. John shares a house at the bottom of Hangover Hill, a two-minute lurch down the road from us. It's full of university students and all sorts of interesting visitors, some of who will become friends and later part-time roadies of ours. In one case, a rather exotic half-Corsican girl will become my girlfriend for a year, leading to an inevitable loins-on-fire-followed-by-heartbreak situation. That, prurient reader, is a story for another day.

The other fringe benefit is that John, being a recent economics graduate, is a life-long member of the faculty. This entitles him, as well as us, to rehearse for free in a disused science lab in a lovely old building in the university's grounds. We also get to use their bar, taunt the students, meet posh middle-class girls and generally get back some of the rates we pay, or rather, the rates we would have paid if we'd been rate-paying types of people. The boys in the band never really did understand how John had wangled the deal but this apparently is what you have to do.

You behave like a good boy, study for your exams and get to university. Then you tell the authorities that in order to further the pursuit of art, you've formed a University Experimental Music Society. After a bit of nodding, form

157

signing and all the rest, they give you this room to rehearse in, and the electricity. When they finally move you out of the room which they allocated to you, they even apologise and allocate you another room, then later a hut. Even though you may have left three years ago, even if the other members of your band are clods from the nearby town. And you can lock your gear in there. And their security guys regularly patrol the place to make sure that nothing is stolen. It's a brilliant deal. But I suspect that the real reason it all occurs is simply because they have forgotten about you. And that the allocation of free rooms to various university societies is merely a case of some bored clerk ticking a piece of paper once in a blue moon. The upshot of these circumstances is that the preening fops of The Mighty Plod now have a free and warm rehearsal place until the end of their career. It comes complete with built-in social life and access to two cheap bars. Top wangle, eh reader?

We weren't the only occupants of these comfortable rehearsal rooms, however. A group of students whom we came to know as the Stan Laurel Band also rehearsed there. Their drummer, a sceptical American called Dave, became friends with Stix. Their guitarists, Paul and Brian, were twin brothers from Barrow-in-Furness and their bass player, Chopper, wore a classic sulky pout and hardly every said anything. I mention this band because they were so very different to us in music and attitude. They had the edge on us musically, but they didn't write their own songs. They were appalled that I dressed up, put on make-up and wanted to become famous. For the Stan Laurel Band, music was the big deal. Months of circling each other like wary dogs finally led to a catchphrase that has never left me.

Sitting idly around over a few beers one evening, the northern lads and I got to discuss our respective motivations. One of them asked me, 'So why are you in a band then, Zap?' I explained about the fun, the drink and the possibility of meeting more women. I added that it was great being able to walk around knowing I wasn't just another android, that it was a chance to stick two fingers up at everyone who'd ever put me down. They asked me about my background and they expressed amazement that I'd been a working lad from a working background. Because of the way I spoke, they'd assumed that I was some kind of public schoolboy. It was my turn to be surprised. I explained that the only way for someone like me to get out of the gutter was through boxing, football or singing in a rock group and that I couldn't fight or play football. Then they asked me if I thought that being in a band made me better than anyone else.

'Of course it fucking does,' I said. 'That's why I wanna do it.'

Paul shook his head sadly and said, 'You're a nice guy Zap, but yer dead corroopt.'

I took this as a great compliment and whenever I said anything, for months afterwards, John and Stix used to chorus, 'You're a nice guy, Zap, but yer dead corroopt.'

Bachelor Johnny is of Irish parentage. Although he doesn't have an Irish accent, he has all of the other advantages and few of the small flaws of that wonderful nation. He is sage and convivial and tells good stories. He is slightly older than Stix and me and, since he is also educated, we soon begin to look to him for answers to the mysteries of life, matters concerning affairs of the heart and the future trajectory of our pop career.

Bachelor Johnny decides that we need to make a demo tape and take it to London. He's got a BSc so he should know. A student in John's house lends us a good reel-to-reel tape machine and his services and we duly spend two nights and a weekend recording four songs of mine. We

159

make cassette copies of the songs and we play it to Big Nik. Big Nik reassures us that the recordings are utter crap. He also adds that Mr and Mrs Evans, two floors up from him, didn't like it either. We thank him for his opinion and play it to some of the students in Bachelor Johnny's house. They're not crazy about it either.

John is not to be deterred though. He makes an appointment with an agent/record company bloke in Edgware, London. He makes a good reel-to-reel copy of the demo and refreshes himself with Guinness while doing so. The band is on their way. Can you hear that noise? The noise of rustling and primping? Why, it is the members of Plod tarting themselves up to go to the big city. Your preening singer here needs no bidding to get spammed-up. He hasn't worn any shoes all summer, in order to show off his red toenail varnish. His long straw-coloured hair is already thick with cheap lacquer. Perhaps the normal Dusty Springfield eye make-up is not quite extreme enough on this occasion though. So he applies even more. Offset by the torn black lacy blouse, the tailcoat, the black fingernail varnish and the twenty-eight-inch-waist purple loons he's squeezed himself into, it all looks *so* right.

Stix is more tastefully restrained in a black satin jacket and starry T-shirt, with only a touch of make-up. Jack Stardust, son of a Polish fish-breeder and our bassist? Well Jack has done what he can, bless him and now at least looks like a member of a rock band. The biggest surprise is Bachelor Johnny himself: white jacket, flowery shirt, floppy hat with hippy scarf round it, bell-bottom trousers, Chelsea boots and best of all, a really big thing round his neck which screams, 'HI THERE EVERYBODY. I AM A STRING OF BEADS. NOW FUCK OFF!' John looks great, or at least, he would do, were we a 1967 Moby Grape album cover rather than a 1973 glam-rock band. With this sartorial know-how and a knicker-melting demo tape, the like of which has not assailed the music industry's ears since 'Ziggy Stardust', how could we fail? Just watch us now.

Our four gallants are now sashaying down a north London street in the blazing summer heat. People stare occasionally, naturally. They're not used to seeing real stars in ordinary daylight settings. The valiant musicians locate the building, walk up the staircase and wait in the outer office. Soon enough they are invited into the presence of the Kingmaker. They array themselves in his office opposite his desk. He must be really impressed. He can't stop staring at the guitarist's hat and beads. And that weird singer! How much black eye make-up can one guy wear? The pop stars don't say much. Only a hint of their pride and general sass is given away by a flicker in the eyes, which intimates, 'Wait till you hear our tape. Because nothing in popular music is ever going to be the same again.'

Bachelor Johnny hands over the seven-inch reel of tape. The man puts it in his machine, laces it up and flicks the function lever over to PLAY. We wait. Tape hiss. We wait. More tape hiss, a very familiar sound in today's fast-moving go-ahead music industry. After five minutes of tape hiss, John ventures that perhaps he'd inadvertently rewound the demo out tail-side when he made it and that we merely need to flip the spool over onto its other side to hear The Demo Which Will Change The World. The Kingmaker is courtly enough to agree with this explanation and he turns the tape over.

A familiar sound comes from the speakers. Everything about it is perfect. As the afternoon sunlight beams down into the office, illuminating specks of dust like a miniature galaxy, the stabbing guitars and delicious three-part harmonies of the music seem to fill up the room. It is instantly recognizable and very commercial. The members of Colchester's finest stare at each other in surprise. They know it very well. It is the first track of *Sgt Pepper's Lonely Hearts Club Band*. And the musicians on the tape are playing it brilliantly. They should be. They are The Beatles.

Back in the car, as we head back up the A12 towards Colchester, Bachelor Johnny is still puzzled, but philosophical. We aren't sure whether the Kingmaker was impressed with us or not. It might have helped if we'd picked up the correct demo-tape from the sideboard, of course. It might have helped if we'd copied the right tape. We didn't know. One thing was for certain however: we were headed for the top.

Later that evening, while relaxing among the pile of album sleeves and old music papers which served as John's living room, John came sauntering in with the tea and said, 'Well... I suppose we'd better turn the telly on to see if we're famous yet.' One other curious thing came out of all this: Bachelor Johnny never wore those beads again.

That summer of 1973 would have been perfect but for one thing: I managed to get myself into deep shit once again. The nature of the problem preyed on me daily. The other members of the band didn't yet know a great deal about it, but while our general muddled optimism drove us ever onwards to refitting our ship, recording early demos and generally getting to know each other, there was one great black cloud following me around. My attempts at keeping it at bay met with varying success.

Our lives are never just one single melody running from A to B. Very often, like a Bach composition listened to for the first time, you hear the twist and turn of the top line. You notice the bass line underpinning and counterpointing it. The top line turns back on itself and reverses sometimes, and while your uneducated ear is still trying to unravel this, you suddenly notice a middle line like the third skein of a plait. It weaves in and out of the bass and top line, completely at home with either or both. And yet it does something all of its own. It has its own separate identity. A bonehead rock listener such as I was, upon noticing this intricacy for the first time is almost indignant, 'How the fuck did he do that?' Here follows my middle line...

Twenty-two

The Long Bad Friday
North London, May-August 1973

In any good story and with anyone who's ever lived dangerously or stupidly there's always got to be one last mission, hasn't there? For instance, a few years ago a good friend of mine had to leave the town we were both living in. It was One Last Mission time. Scarred all over his body from a varied career involving violence, Georgie had settled down, found a woman and was now a genial retired geezer in his forties, living off a bit of labouring and pints bought for him by softer chaps who wanted to hear his tales. No one doubted that he had done what he'd done, or that he could still do it if required.

We got on well, I suppose, because I was able to tell him stories back. I'd never made a pretence of ever having been any sort of a hard man. Georgie said that I made him laugh. I neither condemned nor condoned his world; I just listened. People who don't live conventionally don't necessarily all inhabit the same world, but the worlds often overlap. As I have said before the gangsters need their minstrels and jesters too. There's a common language that is understood and part of this language is a certain discretion.

Once, when I was having trouble with a record company who owed me money, Georgie and another bloke offered to go down to London and visit the company concerned. They spent a couple of pints trying to persuade me of the wisdom of this. I politely refused. They asked me why. I told them that I'd been brought up to fight my own battles and that, though I was most grateful for their offer, I felt that it would somehow be cheating if I solved my problems this way. I also knew, of course, that if I availed myself of their services, that at some point, the favour might be called in, and, as is so often the way of these things, the favour might be called in years later and at a most inconvenient time.

A few months after I'd turned down the favour, Georgie said to me over a drink, 'You know that time we offered to sort your problems out for you, and you turned us down?' I nodded. Georgie said, 'We gave you points for that. We'd have done it alright, but we respected you a lot more for not having taken us up on it.' And then Georgie told me that he had to go away. Didn't know whether he'd be back. He'd got to like the town, his woman and his friends, but he had one more thing to do. I don't exactly know what it was that Georgie had to do, but he left early. And when he left, I had a dreadful foreboding and a feeling that I might not see him again. But he came back. I never asked him how it went. He just said that that was the last one. He did indeed settle down, and stayed where he was till he died naturally.

Now, my own life, while being sedate compared to some, has also not been without its little dramas. I had hoped, by late May of 1973, having moved areas, broken my level of drug-taking down to the occasional aberration, M'lud, joined a working pop group, that my troubles were behind me. With my convictions for possession and vandalism both dished and done, fines paid and my probation now comfortably into its first year, I just wanted to immerse myself in pop music and song writing, so why had I been in this police cell in north London for the past few hours? What was I doing with a speed comedown and the remains of make-up all over my face? This was my one last mission.

The Mighty Plod has had to come off the road to learn a new set, refit the ship as it were. With a sunny bank holiday coming up, a little bit of money in my pocket, I have a few days spare. I decide to go and visit my old friends in Hertfordshire, scene of my earlier undoing, to show them the new cleaned-up and working rock singer. To make things more interesting and to save some money, I hitch from Colchester to St Albans. I spend the weekend seeing friends, not drinking and, oh alright, I drop a few blues.

On the Sunday I meet Jeremy. Jeremy is a posh little prat from quite a moneyed background, who has run off the rails somewhat. For reasons best known to himself, he wishes to acquire about 500 pills. He knows who has them, but since the gentleman concerned doesn't know him, he requires an introduction. Well how does this affect me, Jeremy? He tells me that the gentleman concerned, an old acquaintance of mine, would accept that he, Jeremy, was a kosher customer if I attested to his kosherness. I am a little bit uneasy about this.

Benny, the vendor of the amphetamine tablets is an old mate of mine, I wouldn't mind seeing him. But Jeremy, a rather ineffectual Bambi-eyed public schoolboy, a couple of years my junior, I don't know about him. Perhaps it's because he reminds me a little of a younger version of my old friend Aero, that I eventually soften. He probably just wants to look good in front of his posh mates. I agree to escort him on his run. Benny, whom I haven't seen for months and months has obviously moved on to bigger things and now lives about twenty miles away in north London.

I need a lift to London anyway. I've got to be back to rehearse on Tuesday. Jeremy will drive me up to London in his flash sports car. I will go and have a cup of tea and a yarn with Benny. Jeremy and Benny may complete whatever transaction they will and then Jeremy will drop me at the nearest tube station and I will go back to my nice new life as a pop singer. The next afternoon, I get in Jeremy's car, we go to an address in north London and we meet Benny. At Benny's house are two hippy chicks doing some cooking, a tough-looking London geezer rolling a joint and Benny's girlfriend, an old friend of mine, just getting up. It's a picture of domesticity, albeit domesticity of the type depicted in the Donald Cammell film, *Performance*. Benny, sporting a hennaed Rod Stewart haircut and no little eye make-up, greets me by giving me fifteen blues, which, out of recklessness, I swallow in one go. He informs me that the police are keen to interview him with regard to stolen motors and some firearms.

I ask him confidentially, if he feels at all worried about events. He winks at me, 'Well I hardly fink they're gonna be launchin' a nationwide man-hunt, Mart. Know what I mean?' The pills kick in and I begin to relax a bit. Benny's girlfriend invites me up to her room. I tell her all about the glam-rock band that I'm singing in now. She wants me to show her how much make-up I wear. We start plastering on eye make-up and lipstick. We're having a real laugh. Benny's gone out to find the pills for Jeremy. The two hippy chicks are still mucking about in the kitchen. The tough London geezer and Jeremy are sitting in an uneasy silence in the living room. I'm now really out of it. I'd also like to go, but I can't.

Suddenly there's a knock at the door. I can hear a woman asking for Phil or somebody. The hippy girl who's gone to the door says there's no one here of that name, but the woman is quite insistent and is trying to push her way in. The hippy girl is trying to push her out. Then there's a cry and a crash. The next thing we know, there are police everywhere. They've come in through the front, the back, even the window. There are yellow Labradors, men shouting, people being thrown against walls. I rise from my seat. Someone shouts, 'Sit down!' I sit down.

They search me. Luckily I'm wearing hipster trousers with no pockets, no underwear, moccasins with no socks on, a tiny skinny-rib jumper, and tons of make-up with my hair back-combed into a heap. I've got eight fags, no money and no lighter. My tiny bag of possessions is round the corner in Jeremy's flash car. A detective sergeant spends five minutes shouting questions at me, but it's no use, because I actually don't know anything. I'm speeding my nuts off and fairly confused.

Then I'm in a Black Maria, on its way to a police station. After shouting at me again, they throw me in a cell with Jeremy and another young guy. We can hear someone being banged around in the cell next door. I've got to get this make-up off. When I ring the bell, a florid Met sergeant turns up. 'What?' I ask him if I can have some water and tissues. They bring me the water and I use some rough loo paper to clean the worst of the make-up off. Jeremy tells me when I manage to remove most of it. My face is raw and the pills are wearing off. I'm beginning to feel severely depressed now. I wish I'd stayed at home and taken up my dad's offer to dig a trench and fill it with hardcore for a garden path. I mean I'm good at that, and they can't throw you in a cell for it.

Hours later, two detectives pull me out of the cell and march me down the corridor. I wonder if I'm going to get a kicking. 'Sign this.' I examine the piece of paper. It's light green with lots of space on it. I recognise it as a statement sheet. They want me to sign it. In the infamously corrupt 1970s, the Metropolitan Police want me to sign a statement sheet. I affect to examine it. The policeman bawls at me, 'What are you reading it for, you bloody wanker?' I tell the detective sergeant, as politely that I can, that I cannot sign something without having read it thoroughly first. 'Either you sign this now, or we lock you up again.' I tell him that they can't keep me indefinitely. 'We can keep you as long as we bloody like. Now sign it!' I decline. The detective shouts to the red-faced uniform sergeant, 'Take David fucking Bowie here and lock him up again.'

The sergeant pulls me down the corridor at double speed and pushes me back into the cell. My cellmates get similar treatment. Let me see, we were arrested at about four in the afternoon and it is now really late at night. We're there for more hours. I try to sleep. The door clangs open again. All three of us are marched down the corridor. The police present me with something to sign. This time it's smaller and buff-coloured. It's an acknowledgement of bail for twenty-five quid, in my own recognizance. They want to see me back here in twenty-eight days. They may or may not charge me. They cannot tell me what they will charge me with if they do. They have found small amounts of cannabis, amphetamines, barbiturates and heroin in the house. Although they have found nothing about my person, this does not necessarily mean that I won't later be charged with something found on the premises. We are turned out into the cold dawn somewhere after four.

What has happened? Well I'm not a hundred per cent certain, but this is what I think it was. There was a massive sweep of various drug factories in the West Country on this particular weekend. It took up much drug-squad manpower. The Mets, therefore, were assigned the task of clearing-out certain properties in London. It may have accounted for the fact that there were twenty-six of us in the rather run-down cells of this suburban police station on this quiet bank holiday Monday. And that, if the house, which I visited, really was an important target, they'd certainly mistimed their raid. Another odd thing was that for a while at least, the investigating officers seemed to think that I was somebody important and that I actually lived in the house. It may have explained why they wouldn't believe that I'd never been there before in my life. As for Benny, I don't know what happened to him. He wasn't there, and I never heard of him again.

Jeremy drove us back to Hertfordshire and I crashed out on someone's couch for a few hours. It was a very depressed young pop singer, on bail for twenty-eight days, who eventually snuck back to Essex with his tail between his legs that Tuesday. I just wondered what it was I'd managed to do to get myself in this terrible mess. I'd been to a house in an area of London that I'd never ever visited before. I'd sat in that house for about forty minutes. In that time, because I was trying to blag a lift home, because I had to take one last peek at my old life, my new life was about to collapse. I really felt like I'd blown it. I mean, they could charge me with anything they wanted. There'd be no waiving breach of probation this time. They'd throw the fucking book at me.

Every morning of those twenty-eight days, I woke up thinking that there'd be a knock at the door, a summons to attend the police station and a charge. Every night I went to bed and I thought about what was at stake: my band, my freedom, everything. I entertained suicide again. I wasn't going to do time in the nick. The twenty-eighth day came up. As I didn't have enough money to get down to London, I went into the local village station, told the village constable what the situation was and asked him to contact the north London coppers to tell them that I had duly presented myself.

He couldn't have been nicer. He got in contact with them, asked if I was being charged and told them that I had no money. As he was on the phone, I could see him nodding and saying, 'Yes. Right. Yes. OK. I see.' When he finished, he told me that if it was up to him, I wouldn't have to go, but they were insisting on seeing me and that I would have to get the train fare and report to the north London nick as soon as possible. I went home, borrowed the money from my mum and made the interminable journey back down there. Surely this must be it? They were definitely going to charge me with something.

A detective sergeant told me that the inspector in charge of my case had been injured. Investigations had been put on hold and I was being rebailed for another twenty-eight days. The bastards! They'd dragged me all the way down there from north Essex, just to spend two minutes rebailing me. Now I was going to spend another twenty-eight mornings worrying myself sick over what would happen. I carried on rehearsing with the lads. I also came clean with them and told them what had happened. It has to be said that they weren't particularly sympathetic or supportive. The sort of scrapes I got myself into weren't really in any of their frames of reference. Apart from all that, it would be a nuisance for the band if the singer got jailed.

After the longest twenty-eight days I have ever lived through, I didn't mess about. I just went straight into the north London nick late one Friday afternoon, squared my shoulders and braced myself for the worst. I saw Jeremy briefly. He looked scared. I was taken into a room by the bad-tempered detective sergeant who'd originally dealt with me. 'The inspector dealing with this case is still in hospital. We must inform you that we have found certain substances in the house and have had them analysed.

However, we now know that you weren't living there. It has been decided that this time, no charges are to be pressed.' The disbelief and relief must have beaconed out of me. He leaned over the desk and spoke straight into my face, close up. 'But we know what you were doing there, sonny. And we know what you'd had. And if we ever find anything to connect you with this sort of thing again, I will personally come along to wherever it is that you and your pop group are playing and drag you off the stage myself. And then we will get you into a cell and your fucking feet won't touch. D'you understand?'

'Yes, sergeant. Thank you, sergeant. Does this mean I can go now?'

He looked at me like I was rubbish. 'Yes.'

I walked down the steps of the nick out into the London street. Jeremy hadn't been charged with anything either. I looked at him. I was looking at a doe-eyed, scared kid of eighteen. They could have thrown the book at us. I didn't know him that well, but we'd both been through the same hellish fifty-six days together. We got about a hundred yards down the road and turned a corner. In the middle of rush hour in north London on a Friday afternoon, we were jumping up and down, hugging each other, shaking each other's hands and whooping and yelling. I don't know if anyone on the street was looking at us or not. I was high on the best drug of all, freedom.

That was the last time I ever saw Jeremy. On 1 August 1973, I walked down Colchester High Street on a sunny morning and promised myself that I was never going to do anything so stupid, ever again. The twentieth summer of my life began right there. I went back to rehearsing with Colchester's finest and thought myself the luckiest bloke in the world. Although over the years I've had the odd bit of this and that, that was really the end of my time as a teenage drug fiend. It's funny, because I occasionally see young lads now and I get into conversation with them. They give me all the macho spiel about how much stuff they're doing, and how they know gangsters, and how I wouldn't know anything about their tough world, but it's OK as they know how to look after themselves. I don't even bother to argue with them. I just say, 'Yeah. Right.'

Twenty-Three

Back to the Draining Board
Colchester, September 1973

I have heard it said, by people who help recovering drug addicts, that when a young person begins using lots of drugs, their natural social and emotional maturing processes are arrested until such time as they stop. Thereafter, the recovering drug user begins a slow, and sometimes painful, development into adulthood. In my own case, I wasn't addicted to any one drug. I was addicted to drugs in general and the idea of taking them.

My band mates, Bachelor Johnny, Stix and Jack, had practically no experience of drug-taking, beyond the odd pull on a joint at a party. They weren't, therefore, the best people to help me. In spite of this, in their own way, they did help me. I wasn't looking for help, although I probably needed it. When someone ceases drug-use as their main raison d'être, they need something that will help to fill the gap. In my case, it was rock and roll and to an extent, alcohol. The kind of piss-water that I drank was vastly less damaging than the stuff it had replaced.

However, in the early months of leaving the druggy lifestyle behind, I could never encounter any situation or sensation without also thinking, 'Yeah, this would be really great if I was tripping/speeding/stoned.' If I ever mentioned this, in my friends' company, much piss-taking and barracking would go on.

They'd say, 'Yeah, maan. Wow, maan!' Quite rightly, they thought it was tedious and boring. And so, after a while, I stopped it. It also occurred to me that they might have been slightly nervous and even faintly appalled by my previous lifestyle. In the end, I just got out of the habit of talking about it.

When Colchester's finest came off the road in the spring of 1973, what little money we'd had from gigs also ceased. Stix and I had worked as early morning cleaners in a supermarket, but it was never enough. In the two months where I'd been on bail, prior to the police deciding that I wasn't going to be charged with anything, I'd subsisted on a few quid from cleaning and the odd gardening job. There seemed no point in doing anything during that time. After all, I could be in really deep trouble. I might even end up in jail. It was a miserable and sobering time for me. After I was let off the hook in early August, apart from rehearsing, I just wandered around Colchester, or cycled around the Essex lanes on a borrowed boneshaker, high on the euphoria of my new freedom.

I had no girlfriend, having finished with the last one after I'd got in trouble. It seemed simpler. I had no money. I stayed in my parents' village and did the odd gardening job or I crashed over at Nik's flat on Hangover Hill. During this time, apart from smoking, I was drug-free and hardly even drank. I'd take a bus over to Maldon, walk out to Goldhanger and walk along the saltings. I'd walk over the old Roman causeway to Osea Island in the River Blackwater and sit in a field by myself looking at the late summer heat haze over the marshes. I will never forget that time. I was trying to grow up. It was my own private summer.

Round about the middle of August, I had one of my famous work-ethic attacks. There was an ad in the paper for a kitchen porter in a Colchester bistro. I walked into the place late one afternoon, and I started the job the next morning. My duties consisted of cleaning the restaurant and the toilets, a bit of humping and lumping and washing up dishes. I was to work four days a week and there'd be extra work if I wanted it. It wasn't great money, it never is in catering, but it would be perfect, as a way of getting a basic wage for a job that wouldn't impinge on my band activities.

After being in a rock band, everything as far as I was concerned was just another rotten job. At least it was an honest rotten job. There were no prospects, but no pressures. I did not take a briefcase full of dirty dishes home with me to do every night. Before I went into the place, things were dirty. After I left, they were clean. I got paid. End of story. For the best part of the next thirteen years, apart from singing, playing and writing, washing up and cleaning is all I did. My workmates were often young, middle-class people on their way somewhere else, students, people doing MAs in drama or English. Often they were posh, horsey or arty girls, filling in time before they married army officers or bought nice little restaurants of their own. Occasionally, they were people like myself: musicians, actors or artists who were trying to support themselves.

It was my first experience of seeing the straight, provincial English middle-classes at close quarters. I now learned that bread wasn't white. It was this heavy, indigestible grainy stuff, which couldn't easily be sliced to fit into a toaster. I came across my first black pepper mill, which no matter how hard I shook it, would not give up any pepper. I learned that garlic wasn't a powder to be used with the greatest caution, but a lumpy thing consisting of bulbs and cloves, which was to be used with wild abandon. I learned that salt was a crystal stuff, laid out on the tables in little ramekins, and crumbled over one's food. I learned that we read *The Daily Telegraph* or *The Times* and not *The Mirror*, and that we didn't say, yep, yeah or even yes, but hummed distractedly and said, 'Oh errm, yaah.' I learned that if we liked a morsel of this or that, we said, 'Mmm, delish!' We also made a lot of noises that sound like the noise a kitten makes when you jab it with a compass point, a sort of 'Eoww!' noise. Or we said, 'Aioo! Hoow sooper!' We didn't put our ethnic blankets on a bed; we hung them on the wall. That's if the wall wasn't already covered in Hessian. We didn't like comfortable seats either. This is why we made the customers all sit on rock-hard, high-backed church pews. I'll tell you, for your son of a squaddy here, partly brought up by grandparents who had dinner at lunchtime, it was all a bit of an education.

Working in this place wasn't anything like working in the kitchens of the big hotel where I'd previously worked. Here, the gruff mateyness and foul language of City & Guilds-trained chefs who'd bowled saucepans at my legs and shouted, 'Straight back please, Sunshine!' was completely absent. You hardly ever saw the owners of those sorts of places. In this new place, you might be working a few feet away from the owner. It could all get a bit *Fawlty Towers* sometimes. The owner was actually a nice bloke, an ex-officer from the Paras. He had a way of barking orders at you, and was brusque at times but also unexpectedly kind at other times. The trouble was he was partly deaf, so I was told, from too much time spent on the rifle ranges. He'd often want something done instantly, when he'd just told you that he wanted something else done instantly. It used to drive me bloody nuts sometimes, because you didn't get a chance to explain anything to him.

It has to be said, that your hero here was possibly a little bit over-sensitive, due to his past habits and his slow recovery from the cessation of them. One day, I'd just finished my normal restaurant cleaning jobs, and I noticed that one of the tables was wobbly and leaning at a strange angle. It was a pine, crossbar construction, which was fixed to a low wall partition. It was a table for two, often favoured by lovers, or by businessmen doing lunchtime deals. The problem with this table was that it needed the bolts in its support struts tightened up at regular intervals. When I examined the table, I was alarmed to find that the bolt underneath wasn't just loose; it had nearly come out. I located the special spanner for the job and was grappling around under the table when the owner interrupted me.

'Martin. I thought I asked you to do the windows?'

I managed to stutter out, 'Yes. I was coming to them but this table will...'

'Look, just get them done will you?'

'But this table, it's...'

'You've always got an answer for everything, haven't you? Just get on with it.'

I made one more attempt before lunch to try to convey the importance of what I'd been trying to do, but he would have none of it. At this point, the vengeful petulant side of me took over and I just thought, 'Well fuck you, Charlie!' I said nothing, and I waited. Sure enough, halfway through an extremely busy lunchtime, two large businessmen were digging into their well-done steak in garlic butter and untouched salads when the whole table just collapsed. The carafe of wine, the grub, the glasses and the bread pannier went all over their suits, their laps and the floor.

A waitress came roaring into the kitchen, 'Table nine's collapsed!' Big chaos all round. Your washer-up here went out into the side-alley with a roll-up, killing himself with laughter.

One morning, I was hoovering the place when I found two five-pound notes under a table. It's not a lot of money now but in those days it was about two thirds of my weekly pay. I took the money into the kitchen and told them where I'd found it. A day or two later, the owner gave me one of the fivers back and told me that the customer who'd lost the money was so impressed with my honesty that he was giving me half of it. Oh yeah? Well I'm not sure. In a small bar or restaurant business, when money starts going missing, things can get very awkward among the staff, if somebody's got light fingers. Everyone is under suspicion until that person is discovered with fingers in the till. More commonly, things get too hot and the thefts dry up. In the intervening period, small thefts in a small place can make for a horrible working atmosphere. So was I being tested? I think I may have been, but it worked out to my advantage. A couple of weeks later, the owner and his wife went on holiday for two weeks, left me with the keys of the restaurant and some petty cash and asked me if I'd like to clean the place, top to bottom. A big cleaning project was what I was good at, and I was working by myself. When they came back, they paid me well over the odds, and I felt for the first time in years that I was a trusted and efficient human being, rather than a useless space cadet who was only good for singing in rock bands.

I also remember thinking how brilliant it was getting paid. I could buy books and clothes, and pay my mum back all of the money she'd lent me when I was broke. It probably sounds vaguely pathetic to someone who's never been in any kind of trouble but at the time, I felt like I was on the road home. One evening in October of that year, I was walking down Colchester High Street on a Friday with money in my pocket. It was just getting dark and there was that hazy gold and rose western sky which you get when it's going to be a cold night, and a great black pall of smoke above the buildings. Crowds of people were staring up, and I heard the nee-naa, nee-naa of fire appliances. Woolworth's was burning down. Groups of school children and shop people were all standing, chatting amiably. Funny old world isn't it? People go around with scowls on their faces all day, but you give them one burning department store to gather round and everybody's happy.

Down at our guitarist's house, St Guinness', at the bottom of Hangover Hill, the students had all come back from the summer holiday. It was my first experience of university students. I used to think, 'Gosh, I bet they're really clever.' Some of them had three or four shelves of books and none of them by Ian Fleming or Denis Wheatley. They were all feminists and Marxists, things I hadn't really encountered much up until then. They spent a lot of time involved in arguments. It got quite passionate at times, but then nothing happened, especially not any kind of housework. Among the people whom I'd known up until this time, an argument was generally a short thing, which later resulted in a fight. It certainly wasn't something that you enjoyed, looked forward to or found stimulating.

In earlier days, if someone said to me, 'Oh Tel had a bit of an argument with Ron,' I would usually expect the next bit to run, 'so they took it outside and now Ron's agreed not to keep chatting Carol up anymore. Until they unwire his jaws.' With these students it would be, 'Ah…but I don't think that Valerie Solanas was an extremist, as such. When she shot and wounded Andy Warhol, maybe she hadn't found the answer. But,' (pause for meaningful pay-off line) 'she may have been seeking a new way of asking the question.' (Followed by a triumphant gleam.) They'd be hurling authors' names around and citing this writer and that writer, whereas I'd be thinking, 'Hmm, I'm sure this all is very clever but have you got anything by Slade?'

As far as I was concerned an intellect was an unwieldy millstone that seemed to cause a great deal of dissatisfaction to its owner and took up loads of time at the expense of the cleaning. One or two of the students, especially the women, treated me with the kind of fascination that you might reserve for a member of a lost jungle tribe who had learned the rudiments of English. Stix was more recognizably intelligent and the male students were quick to notice this and converse with him. I, on the other hand, whose ambition stretched no farther than singing in a band, shagging a dream rock chick, drinking lots of lager and maybe buying some pad to do it all in, was viewed with a mixture of curiosity and wariness

Another thing that was a bit controversial was my choice of job. Concerned onlookers would ask, 'But how long do you think you can wash up dishes for?' Forever, if necessary. 'But you've got a good brain.' Very charitable of you to say so, but even if it's true, why waste my good brain on some employer or boring university course? Where's my drink? Got anything by The Pink Fairies? Why don't you clean up around here?

I also learned the difference between an anarchist and a Marxist. A Marxist will steal your chairs and lease them back to you under an approved manifesto. An anarchist will steal your chairs because he's cold and he needs firewood, but if you're cold too, at least the anarchist will invite you in to sit around your burning chairs and get warm. The Marxist will still be having a meeting about it, while you freeze to death outside.

Having said all of this, I began to like some of the students a great deal. They could be witty and interesting, and they seemed to be just as fucked-up about everything as I was, in some cases, even more so. At least I'd been a working lad. Students were pro the workers. Though it struck me that when these people talked about the workers

181

and What The Workers Wanted, which they did frequently, they hadn't actually come across many workers. On the odd occasions when students of my acquaintance got holiday jobs, they'd come home knackered, with tales of woe about how the workers needed re-educating before they were ready for revolution. In other words, the students often discovered the same things as I had about the workers: the workers want to get paid, get laid more often, do less work, own more things, take loads of holidays and receive less hassle. What's wrong with that?

Some students went out on picket lines, out of solidarity with the workers. The girls would get their bottoms pinched. The boys would have the piss taken out of them. The police would knock them around. Their dads would bail them out. What do we want? Not sure. When do we want it? Er... And then when it was all over, most of them got jobs as civil servants, teachers, social workers, and polytechnic lecturers. And I'm glad they did, because they were nice people. You need people like that, but their destiny was stamped through them like the word Blackpool is stamped through seaside rock, and like the word PRAT was stamped through me.

And so in the mornings, I went into the bistro and washed the plates of the bourgeoisie. In the evenings I rehearsed with the band whom I believed would be my passport out of having to do what I was told. At weekends I went up and down the A12 with Colchester's finest and played low-rent pop star to any pissed-up bunch of boneheads who wanted to watch, because I didn't know what else to do. I could only go forward, because there was no way I was going to risk going back. And what else? It was fun. That's all.

Twenty-four

The Case of the Strange Bottles
The A12, Mid-October 1973

Colchester's finest, The Mighty Plod, had been in training for the whole summer. When Paul left and Bachelor Johnny joined, we'd had to take stock of ourselves. Sure we were a glam-rock band. That is, we wore the gear and the make-up, had the attitude and very much fell into a Sweet/Slade bracket. And we'd done lots of gigs, far more and further afield than almost any other band in Colchester. But from the time I joined in early March of 1973, until the time Paul the guitarist left in late May, we were essentially a covers band.

This was fine by Stix, who since the tender age of sixteen had been corresponding with agents in a very grown-up, letters 'n' contracts sort of fashion. The agents were, of course, blissfully unaware of his age and giving us anything up to five gigs a week. It was fine by Big Nik, who had the not unreasonable belief that the best thing for a working band was lots of work. But there was a niggling feeling in some quarters that if we really wanted to move up we'd have to have our own songs. Jack, God bless him for it, thought that we should be more of our own men. I had been writing songs since I was fourteen and was keen for us to have a set all of our own. The over-riding opinion

183

however, was that if we wanted to work we wouldn't get away with writing our own stuff.

When Bachelor Johnny joined, a quiet strand of defiance came with him. John also wrote songs, or as he was fond of saying, he wrote 'numbers' – riffy rock compositions. Whereas, he said, I wrote songs. Stix was half-swayed when he heard the separate efforts of Bachelor Johnny and I. Always interested in the technical side of drumming, our strange inventions were more of a challenge to him than the chart fodder we'd been learning. At the same time, he was not disposed to risking the loss of gigs he'd fought for because of our artistic self-indulgence. Big Nik was far more blunt on the matter, 'You're not gonna do that rubbish that Zap's writing!' Things got a little heated at the house on Hangover Hill. Had I joined a pop group so I could succumb to the orthodoxy of commerce? It shouldn't be a case of, 'Can we get away with it?' We were in a rock band for fuck's sake! We should be able to do what we wanted.

Bachelor Johnny, far less volatile than The Singer With Two Chips On Each Shoulder, just quietly said yes to everything then did what he bloody well wanted, while I went roaring into passionate battle on behalf of Art. Stix and I had fierce arguments about what we should do. In spite of it all, we began writing and rehearsing our own stuff, planning to sneak it into the sets from time to time. I even wrote a four-part mini pop opera called *My Friend Jean*. Naturally, it was dreadful. Down the dark corridor of creation are two doors. One is labelled Great Ideas and the other is called Pretentious Wank. Because the corridor is so very dark, it is very easy to go through the wrong door, and I frequently did. However, I believed then, as I believe now, that if you never enter the corridor at all, then nothing will ever happen.

We cannot all be Lennon and McCartney. We cannot all be Jimi Hendrix. The trouble with the music industry is that its youngest prodigies are those most often held up as examples of the industry norm. The truth, however, is that most of us struggle for a long time before we begin to understand the rudiments of the songwriter's craft. Bachelor Johnny and I were no exceptions. And while we struggled, we did so in the face of a legion of critics: our fellow band members, our roadies, the students who lived in John's house, anyone who read the music papers, our girlfriends, and the man in the pub. Everyone, in fact.

They all knew where we were going wrong and what we should be doing about it. I can't imagine a chair-maker, an electrician or a baker who was learning the ropes, ever having to put up with what young songwriters do. They'd give up. And we'd all be sitting in dark rooms, on plastic milk crates, feeling hungry. Come to think of it, that's what it was like most weeks on Hangover Hill anyway. But then, assuming that John and I had fought our corners, written the songs, persuaded everyone to learn them and slipped them into the set, what might happen? What usually happened? This did.

We have driven to a place somewhere near Norwich. It is a pub. The landlord has already told us that he, 'hoop you dun't play nuth'n too heavy.' The last band that 'played heavy' round here didn't go down too well. 'Heavy' includes Deep Purple covers like 'Smook on the Worta' (as pronounced by our landlord). A bit of 'Status Quoo' will probably 'goo down alright', however. Providing it's at the end of the night, of course. Our hearts are already heavy. Oh and naturally, there's no food, only crisps. Because this is East Anglia and we're not here to fucking enjoy ourselves.

Eight o'clock and the audience begin to drift in. They certainly don't look like they've come to see Colchester's finest. In fact they look very straight indeed. I often used to wonder where very ugly, badly dressed, stupid people used to go to meet each other. I used to wonder how they found each other, disseminated their fashion tips, got off with each other and later bred the generations of ugly, badly dressed, stupid people of the future. I used to wonder how, when a dreadful record was released, that all of these people would telepathically seem to know about it. And then go out and buy it so that it got to the top of the pop charts. I wondered if there was some secret brotherhood, a radio station I hadn't yet managed to tune into. But I think I do know where they meet now. They get summoned to all these pubs on Friday and Saturday nights by some strange means and then the landlords of the pubs are given an agent's number. The agent then telephones or writes to The Mighty Plod and we go and do a gig for them. Which is why, as Stix used to say, four musicians would drive miles and miles to go to a place they didn't want to be, to play tunes they didn't want to play, to a bunch of people who didn't want to listen to them.

In tonight's case, we go up on stage at the appointed time, to play the first of two forty-five minute sets. We've barely struck up the first chords when, as if by magic, the whole audience disappear into the other bar and stay there until we've come off. When we come offstage for our twenty-minute break, the jukebox is switched back on. As if by magic again, the whole audience, beer-glasses, handbags and all, come back into the function room and start dancing to it. When we go back onstage, they bugger off again.

I am amazed by their behaviour. It was as if they'd decided they didn't like us before we'd even packed the van up and left Colchester. We may as well be doing our own material, I reason. What does it matter if they're not even watching or listening? The brewery says the landlord's got to provide entertainment. The landlord has to phone an agent. The agent has to provide a band. And we have to play. But that doesn't mean the audience has to listen, does it? And OK, we may not have been the best band in the world but we weren't bad. And we did perform danceable current pop hits. In all probability this sort of thing was going on in pubs all over England and happening to loads of bands like us. Nonetheless it was hard not to take it personally sometimes.

And what was the Musicians' Union doing during this time? Give up? Well I'll tell you. They were issuing stickers that said 'Keep Music Live'. But what if people didn't want music to be kept live? Why, we might end up in a situation where DJs, the people who only put the records on the turntables, became more important than musicians, the people who played the music; a situation where, if it was the will of the people, pubs would become more like discos and have bouncers on the door in most towns. In the end, DJs might become really big stars, people start idolising them and saying things like, 'Wow! That guy really knows how to put a record on the turntable doesn't he?' No Martin. Now you're just being paranoid. It's stupid of course. How could it possibly happen?

The Musicians' Union has a firm stance on this sort of thing. It is all set down in its rulebook, which is printed in Old Norse. At some later date during the mid-eighties, the armed might of the combined branches of the Union's eastern wing sent a recommendation to the national body of the Musicians' Union that a new logo be designed for the Union tie. With a no-nonsense, cutting-edge approach like that, it was no wonder that Bachelor Johnny had such little trouble persuading us to join the MU. Yeah, you had to sit through meetings occasionally. Yeah, you had to cough up your dues. Sure. But think of the benefits. You got 150 quid's worth of insurance cover for your instruments. Though I think that the thing that really sold the idea of joining the Union to me was the cut and thrust of it all, watching cabaret organists bickering over the minutes of the last meeting with seaside bandleaders, before they all rushed off to the bar during the break, like school kids running out of the gates. And if a music biz with shit-for-brains and a cash register for a heart was robbing a generation of young rock and rollers blind, well what the hell? We were in showbiz. We could take it.

And in these intoxicating days of being part of Colchester's finest, I don't mind. I don't mind the audiences who hate you before you've even got to the place. I don't mind the arguments over the material. At least I didn't conform and join the army. Because in the army you end up going to places miles away, where nobody likes you much. In the army, there are long periods of boredom, only mitigated by brief periods of fear and relief. You get hungry, sleepless, and cold. And the only thing you can depend upon is the small group of comrades you came out with. And it's nothing like being in a rock band, because in the army, you get fed and paid every once in a while.

But there is balm in Gilead, fair reader. In the dark of the Plod van, Bachelor Johnny is fumbling in his gig bag. He produces a mysterious bottle. Now he produces a bottle opener. He drinks the contents of the bottle, produces another bottle and repeats this procedure three or four times. He seems content and philosophical, jocular even. The drummer and the singer are studying him with great interest. What is this elixir that he carries with him to a gig? He explains to us guileless boys that the liquid relaxes, rejuvenates and helps to ease the hurts inflicted by the world. Stix and I haven't had much experience of drinking; Stix, because he is only seventeen and has little knowledge of the world, and I because I've taken so many drugs between the ages of seventeen and twenty that I scarcely had time to fit alcohol into the schedule, loftily pronouncing it as a 'low-drive drug for low-drive people'. My point of view is about to change quite radically.

Shortly before the next engagement, Stix and I pay a visit to an off-licence over the road from St Guinness', where Bachelor Johnny so conveniently lives. From this point onwards we never look back. After gigs on wet autumn nights, as the Plod van wends its way home from the farthest outposts of East Anglia's entertainment frontier, Stix, Bachelor Johnny and I are tooled up. The back of the van becomes a shimmering place, a kind of gentlemen's club if you wish, where the conversation sparkles, wit and banter abound and we coast gently down towards the twinkling landing lights of all our best tomorrows. We surprise ourselves with our own erudition and charm. How could we have been so wrong about ourselves? Are we not the best rock group on the planet? Of course we are. Of course we are. Our sticky little hands are on Madame Fortune's thigh, and there is a twinkle in her eye. And oh, the dame is up for it tonight. Big or small, she'll take us all. Prats.

Twenty-five

Chocks Away
East Anglia, November 1973

And so, with a handful of inaugural gigs to break the ice after a long summer refit, Colchester's finest are well and truly back into the old routine. And eastern England shall know us by the rumble of our Transit van, by our stupidly tight loon pants and by the oaths and foul ditties that emanate from us. There are certain small rural towns in East Anglia whose traditions run richly through them like the blue veins in a well-matured truckle of Stilton cheese. One of these traditions is that the boys from all the smaller villages in a given town's environs will make their way into that town on a Friday and Saturday night and attempt to physically assault each other. This particular ritual, marinated in time itself, is all the better if it is fuelled by ill-restrained alcohol consumption. It is also essential that a central venue be provided for the night's gladiatorial exertions and that a group of musicians be engaged, in order to provide an accompaniment to it all.

And the towns themselves? Ah, I remember their names as if it were yesterday: Hadleigh of the Sloping Stage; East Dereham of the Sunshine Rooms; Acle of the Holiday Broads. It was the mid-seventies. Our audience were stocky village lads, on great four-inch platform shoes, their King-

Edward arses squeezed into trousers tight at the top and yet baggy all the way down, their shirt collars sticking out of their jacket lapels like glider wings, and homicide in their inkwell eyes. They walked as if each had forgotten to take the coat hanger out of his jacket, the pins out of his shirt, and the cardboard labels out of his trousers. But they were our audience, and we their musicians. So we had to rub along as best we could.

Bachelor Johnny, our guitarist, is well and truly broken in by now. We are returning to Debenham for the first time since our triumphant début there some months before he joined. Debenham likes us. Debenham has rebooked us. It has a spanking new village hall and we are to perform here. And so on a freezing cold and misty autumn evening, the Plod van rolls up, disgorges its pouting cargo and their musical instruments and prepares for the festivities. The arrangement is that, as well as playing, if we provide a disco to fill the gaps, we will get extra money. Bachelor Johnny has had a brainwave: if he stays in for a night or two, he can make up a tape of guaranteed toe-tappers, blast it out through our PA in between our playing times and save the cost of getting a tedious DJ on board. The members of the band think that this is a capital idea and so we entrust him with the job.

The playing itself goes as well as can be expected. It is actually a good gig. The front few rows of the audience are made up of pretty-ish country girls staring up at the musicians. The singer is prancing and flouncing around. The drummer and bassist are working precisely. And the guitarist, in a green midi-length dress, women's boots and his scrubby beard looks well...er, striking. Our dispute with the management of the venue really begins with the matter of our improvised disco sounds.

Far from hearing the current hits such as Suzie Quatro, The Detroit Spinners, The O-Jays and the fabulous Osmonds, the audience are getting a blast of something entirely unexpected: a drawn-out affair by Quicksilver Messenger Service for instance; a doleful number by Mogul Thrash. In fact, what ensues from the speakers on this night would be fine for say, a San Francisco all-night freak-out in mid-1967. But it becomes apparent that it's patently unsuitable for Debenham village hall in October of 1973. Worse is to come, however. Bachelor Johnny, while relaxing with a Guinness or two, has also allowed bits of speech from the ITV *News at Ten* to creep onto the tape in the gaps between songs.

Hence, the gap between a Moby Grape wig-out and a Curtis Mayfield track, might be punctuated by two minutes of Reginald Bosanquet giving us the low-down on the bread strike or the three-day week. Bachelor Johnny is perfectly OK with this and sits in the dressing room patiently placating a not unnaturally aggrieved venue manager. Stix and Jack are keeping out of the way. I am laughing hysterically at the whole affair and the punters are looking puzzled and having difficulty dancing to the *News at Ten*. The venue manager is, yes, a bit cross. He agrees to knock it out of our wages. Big Nik does not agree. There's a bit of an argument. I throw an ashtray. We exit in some disgrace. We don't return. The art and money equation is never an easy one, reader. Such experiences coarsen the delicate sensibilities of musicians and we sometimes forget ourselves and behave badly.

One of the chief souces of revenue for working pop groups in East Anglia is of course the humble RAF base. Colchester's finest played many of these in our time. Many bachelors are to be found at such places. Unmarried enlisted men want to meet girls. Unfortunately, air bases are noisy and require lots of room for tank-busting fighter-bombers to take off and land in. Consequently, they are often situated miles from civilization and their gallant men must drive into nearby towns to meet females. The RAF has a solution to this problem. They provide buses to and from the local towns, so that interested spinsters can be transported to the bases and meet the lovelorn airmen.

The kind of women who may be found embarking on these mercy wagons during the early seventies, unhappily, are not necessarily the Venuses we anticipate. Many seem to be on the incautious side of forty, with a husband on, say, a night shift. We often noticed that white PVC boots, orange woollen trouser suits, or untenably short skirts were common attire among them. There was a tendency to wear much face powder. Perms were tight and often curly. Lipstick tended to be worn very bright and just under the nose. It was sometimes advisable, for our own safety, to view them only in the reflections of our guitar scratch-plates. To be fair, the RAF lads seemed pleased enough with the women's arrival and since we ourselves weren't in the women's sights why would we care too much?

Only once did I allow one of these goddesses to get near to me. I couldn't stop her. As I left the stage after completing the first set, she came thundering across the dance floor, looked me in the eye, and thrust her hand straight down the front of my hipsters. Cupping her hand round my knackers and pausing for a good assessment of my penis girth, she said, 'Just wanted to see what you'd got down there, boy.' And then she cackled and looked at her friends, whom were all shrieking with laughter – quite a shocking experience for a boy of my tender years. I would learn to live with it. There was no counselling back in those frontier days and the mental scars took a long time to heal.

At a base in Lincolnshire, we were given a dressing room but no sink to piss in. Pissing in the sink was a tradition with us. We did it whether they gave us a bog or not. This wasn't just discourtesy. Once you'd got full make-up and effeminate clothes on, you didn't want to have to share a urinal with a group of snorting psychopaths, who may have been too dim to realise that you were the cabaret, and, therefore, allowed to look like that. This particular dressing room didn't even have a sink.

Luckily we found an old tombola drum. It was of the revolving type with a crank handle for mixing up the raffle tickets, or the printed-paper numbers. It stood in a sturdy stand, which was lucky really, because an awful lot of piss went into it that night. We pissed in it, our roadies pissed in it. I believe even a couple of the RAF types, who came backstage, pissed in it. There was a good three gallons or so in it by the end of a long evening.

The gig went well enough. The airmen staggered out. The women tucked their knickers into their handbags and got back on the bus. And then came the sound of marching feet. I asked a half-cut airman what was happening. He informed me that the military police were doing a snap-inspection, to make sure that everything was in apple-pie order, after the dance. He said that they usually checked the dressing room. Our ears pricked up at this. Bachelor Johnny and I realised that there was still a tombola drum half full of piss in there. We ran in. 'Just making sure we haven't left any er...leads, yeah leads, that's right. In there.' Reader, you have no idea how heavy a tombola drum half full of piss is, once you've lifted it out of its stand.

John and I managed to get the casement window open and in the darkness of the dressing room, we lifted the wobbling drum over to the window and tipped the contents out into the night. We were a couple of floors up so we'd expected an almighty splash. What we didn't expect was the shout of 'Oi!' from below, or the man and woman's voice, or the fading curses as we rushed out and walked innocently back into the hall. Where had we tipped all the piss? No bloody idea. I've spent years wondering what really happened. But life is full of mysteries isn't it? Though I do find that alcohol is often involved, in cases where these mysteries occur.

By the autumn of 1973, Bachelor Johnny had demonstrated to Stix and I that the strange elixir that he drank on the way back from gigs was indeed very beneficial. We had learned from him however, that each man must find his own elixir. John's personal quest and his Irish heritage dictated that his preferred choice was Guinness. Stix and I found that lager was good for us – very sensible too, beer with trainer-wheels, if you like. Soon though, we found that large amounts of lager had its drawbacks on long journeys.

Big Nik had many virtues as a roadie but patience was not one of them. If we were doing a gig in the outlands of Norfolk or Rutland, for instance, Nik would want to drive home as quickly as possible. How well I remember his clarion call, 'Out the road, wanker!' In fact if he were in that kind of mood we'd be pushed to stop for food, let alone frequent pisses. Stix and I were in a quandary. We needed to drink, yes. But lager consumption meant we needed frequent pit-stops, and yet Big Nik was reluctant to stop more than once every hundred miles. Oh, we toyed with the idea of an arrangement involving funnels and siphon pipes, which could be trailed out of the Transit van's sliding doors. We considered all sorts of civilized alternatives.

The uncivilized alternative was to open an empty beer can with a tin opener, piss in it, pass it along the back row in the darkness and hand it to Sav, the roadie nearest the offside door. Sav would then jettison either can or contents out into the Anglian countryside. A can of warm piss being handed to you in the darkness is not for aesthetic souls. Improvisational as we all were, when we were younger and more rustic, the situation was not ideal. Quite apart from that, it was self-limiting. Drink enough on any one occasion and one's accuracy diminished, with sometimes, unpleasing results. Nik, however, was resolute. He would not stop.

I applied all of my artistic inventiveness to solving our problem. And Stix applied his considerable intellect to it. We had an idea. What we needed was condensed beer! Something that would get us three times as drunk, in half the time, for a reasonable price and yet still retain the essential beer buzz, without having to stop for so many piss-breaks. Round about this time a lager company began making something called Special Brew. We did some trials with it. It revolutionized life in the back of the van. It was not a well-known drink then and didn't have the ill repute bordering on stigma, which is associated with it in our current moral climate. I like to think, that in our own way, we helped pioneer the use of Special Brew.

Stix and I generally referred to the drink as 'Neck Oil'. Even now, I have a sneaking affection for it and will drink one or two in polite company, regardless of the suspicious looks that my drinking of it causes among more genteel friends. With the neck oil trials completed, we now had our solution to the drinking-versus-pit-stop conundrum and it was full steam ahead for the rest of our time together. Neck oil, it must be pointed out, is a wonderful servant but a sadistic and tyrannical dominatrix. Here is a cautionary story.

One night after a gig, we were too drunk to impinge on Nik's hospitality. Nik could be quite strict. And besides, he lived with June, who was a lovely woman and highly tolerant, but wouldn't brook downright barbarism. Since it was one of the many university holidays, and some of the students were away, we decided, at Bachelor Johnny's invitation to keep the back-of-the-van party going back at his house. It was the first night that I'd only drunk Special Brew to the exclusion of all else. I drank it at the gig, I drank it coming home from the gig and I drank it back at the house. Bachelor Johnny put me to bed in the large room, which he and his brother Harry shared during normal term-time.

I awoke in the small hours absolutely bursting for a piss. I couldn't find the light. I tried to find the door. Eventually I found it. The door handle, however, seemed to be made of wires. In the pitch-blackness, I kept trying to open it. After some time had passed, I realised that the door handle was, in fact, an electric guitar. It had been a false lead. I tried walking around in the darkness. There was a thump. One of the huge speaker cabinets in the room fell onto a bed. I realised that the other bed was near a window. After some walking, I managed to find the bed. From then on, it was short work to find the sash window, hurl it open and engage in one of the longest pisses I'd ever experienced. Whole ideas for album concepts occurred while I was doing it. I finished and shut the window. I walked around in the darkness for a bit longer to try and find my way back to my bed. It seemed to be taking some time. Then I slept.

I wasn't overly concerned that I'd pissed out of the window. After all, there was only a dark and narrow side-alley below, which no one in the house used much. And there were no next-door neighbours, except for a repair garage that was now closed. And anyway, better to piss out of the window than piss in the room. In the morning, I awoke with not so much a hangover, as the feeling that I really needed to be found a place in some kind of a hospice as soon as possible. I remembered the problems I'd had with finding the door during the night. I noticed an electric guitar on its side. I remembered the speaker falling off the dresser. And yes, there was the speaker, precariously hanging over the bed on which it had fallen.

Finally, I remembered the piss. Did I really do that? I asked myself. I crawled over to the window, hauled it open and hung out of it to see if there were any signs of micturition in the alley down below. There was nothing. Two windows along however, down in the overgrown weeds of the narrow alley, were signs that someone had taken a monumental leak during recent hours. And yet a couple, both students, had occupied the room in question. This meant that I must have somehow pissed out of their window.

To have pissed out of their window, I would have had to find my way out of my room, along the corridor and opened the door to their room. I would have had to walk to the other end of their room, over their bodies, because their mattress was by the window, and then opened the window. And then standing on the mattress where the couple was sleeping, I would have had to piss out of the window, close the window, walk back over their bodies, back down the corridor and then find my room, find my bed and go back to sleep. I mean…how? And nobody said anything to me the next day. I mean I didn't ask or anything. But there were no funny looks or strange atmospheres in the house when we all eventually got up.

But I looked out of the window again. There was no mistaking it. I'd pissed out of a window, two windows along from the actual window of the room I was in. And I swear that I never left the room. You explain it to me. Coincidence? Some kind of telekinetic urination? Or one of the many mysteries of Special Brew? When I told the boys about it, they just sort of shrugged. Except for Jack, who said, 'That sounds like a pretty out-of-your-head type beer you've bin drinkin' there, boy.' And you know what? He wasn't far wrong.

Twenty-six

The Night Before Christmas (One)
Ipswich, Late December 1973

We were sitting around Big Nik's flat, in the house on Hangover Hill, on a Friday night. Appropriately enough, the place is now some sort of a Colchester community mental health unit. It was heading into mean midwinter, the long dark days down to Christmas. We, the members of The Mighty Plod, Colchester's leading bunch of young glam-rock wastrels were twiddling our thumbs and ballbagging about our lack of progress, when the news came through that we had a gig: two nights at the Gear Shift in Ipswich.

This news cheered us immensely. We hadn't got a lot on the books. It was ninety quid for the two nights. We normally went out for thirty. What was the catch? We were about to find out. We had just one rehearsal to prepare ourselves for the Friday/Saturday-night stint.

It was the beginning of a long relationship with the Gear Shift which would become to Plod what the Kaiserkeller was to The Beatles. The upstairs club was in Ipswich's old market centre. I have always really liked Ipswich, for it has a rough and good-humoured friendliness, a mood that I've always found lacking in Colchester. The Gear Shift was Ipswich's main and probably only late-night drinking dive.

Colchester, at the time, didn't have such a place. The club stayed open until about two, far too late for us young boys. Being the only late watering hole, it had an interesting clientele: villainous-looking men and their molls, dockside gays with muscles, hard faces and steel combs with sharpened points, the odd pill-pusher, a handful of working girls, foreign sailors, English matelots and lots of beefy-arsed American airmen from the nearby bases. Apart from this, the place was a magnet for every drunk and gold-digging ditch-pig that could still walk on two legs when the town pubs disgorged their last customers.

It may not have been an ideal audience for your gorgeous glamsters here but it was a top recipe for a punch-up. The Gear Shift, which was above a pub, held about a hundred people. Very often, however, far more were allowed in. They had six bouncers. I mean that's a lot of bouncers for such a small joint and, on a good night, it was just about the right number. When the Gear Shift went up, it went up like a saloon brawl in a Western.

Our dressing room, or what passed for one, was a lumber-room with a few chairs in it and lots of bottles and cans. The door hung and curtsied on one hinge. The stage was a postage stamp that we extended with beer crates. Crammed into its tiny space with Stix's crash cymbals lacerating my back, Bachelor Johnny's amp howling in my ear and Jack's bass-stack throbbing on my right, I began the first set of what was to be our baptism of fire. The punters liked it rough, which was just as well, because that's how we played it.

We did two sets and seemed to go down well. They actually liked us. Jake, a huge Jamaican bouncer, told us to play a third set. We grumbled but we did it. After one in the morning he came into our dressing room and told us to get out there and play a fourth set. We were knackered. We hadn't been told we were playing a fourth set. I produced my union card in a vain attempt to be vaguely official and demanded to see the club manager, whom I hadn't yet met.

Jake protested, 'Ah maan, he don't wanna be disturbed. He's godda headache.'

'We've played the best part of three hours. I demand to see him.'

'He ain't gonna like dis, maan. You sure about dis?'

'Yeah.' I looked round at the others for support.

Jake went loping out and I smiled in satisfaction. Nothing happened for a while. Then the door crashed open. A huge man in a smart suit, flanked by two bouncers, stood in the doorway making the room look suddenly darker and a lot smaller. He flicked his lank hair back, stared at me and reaching into his immaculately tailored fob-pocket produced what I estimated to be about half an ounce of cannabis resin.

'Right,' he barked. 'Which one of you little toe-rags has been smoking this shit in my club?' We all looked at him in astonishment.

'How much longer do you want us to play, Mister?' I asked him.

'That's better,' he said. 'Now get out there and make a fucking noise!' He swept out with his two henchmen and we went out onstage and gave it some stick.

We finished our set; the bouncers threw the punters out, except for a few girls. We began covering the gear over. One of the bouncers came over and gestured towards the bar, 'The manager would like you to have a drink with him.' It was an order. The manager was lounging on the bar. Like many rufty-tufty geezers he had a beautiful, if over-ornamented wife. She kept looking at my body like she was considering the idea of having it wrapped and taken home. This made me nervous.

'Sandra. Get this boy a drink. He's thirsty.' To me, 'Whatchoo 'avin'?'

'Pinta Tuborg please.'

'You're 'avin' a short.'

'Alright then. Southern Comfort.'

And so on and so on... Like all villains to all fey entertainers, the manager was displaying gruff kindness, the easy magnanimity of the very powerful. I wasn't even in this guy's football match. I was...'nuffin''. Nuffin' is by no means an insult. Men like this live in a kingdom. The kingdom has its own kings, queens, dukes, athelings and thanes, but when they have a feast, they need their jesters and their minstrels. If they don't have their cabaret, they can't boast a feast, so they're kind to us. It's a very ancient symbiotic relationship and you can see examples of it all the way from Roman emperors right down to the Krays.

The manager was, in his own words, 'Well pleased', and was looking forward to us returning on the morrow. There might even be more work in the offing. We understood we were to be punctual. We understood we were playing four sets. We understood everything. We left.

Twenty-seven

The Night Before Christmas (Two)
Ipswich, Late December 1973

I had a bad cold. It had gone onto my chest. So now I had a mild fever, which gave everything an air of unreality. It was Saturday night at the fabulous Gear Shift, thrumming hub of Ipswich's entertainment wheel. We'd survived the Friday night. We were on our second set and roaring out a cover of 'Cum On Feel The Noize'. The place was chocka, its dance floor absolutely heaving. I could feel the heat coming off the dancers. Even though I was singing, I didn't seem to be in my own body due to my fever. It was like I was outside myself watching myself perform.

But something odd was happening on the dance floor. People seemed to be floating backwards, except for an American airman and a Dutch sailor still in uniform. They were doing what looked like a high speed Twist routine. Three other Dutch sailors appeared, then more American airmen. One of the sailors fell. Two English sailors appeared. An American fell. There was blood. It was a vicious punch-up. But in my head it seemed to be happening in silent slow motion. The whole dance floor went up.

The PA speakers, two cabinets and two columns began to rock as the bodies hit them. Our roadies, Nik and Sav, took one side each in a well-practised routine and leaned their full weight on the stacks from behind to keep the things from falling backwards. I would have been terrified if I hadn't been feeling so strange. The dance floor was just a blur now, of boots, heads, fists and bottles. From out of this mess came Jake's head and one of his hands, right near to where I was singing. He shouted above the noise, 'Keep fockin' playin', maan. Keep fockin' playin'!' We kept fockin' playin'.

Suddenly, all six bouncers retreated from the fray. Had the punters got the better of them? No way. The fragile flowers of The Mighty Plod were about to witness a technique. The bouncers regrouped and forced a wedge into the middle of the fight. They simultaneously seemed to floor six of the main fighters, who went down like spud sacks. Next they formed a sort of human corridor to the top of the club stairs. Along this corridor, they threw their opponents in rapid succession, subduing them with heads or fists on the way through before pushing them down the staircase. They ejected about twenty people in the space of a couple of minutes. Three bouncers stayed upstairs as a rearguard, while the other three followed the ejectees downstairs and threw them out on the street, locking the double glass doors behind them. I had never seen such slick work in my life. It deserves to be written down.

Later on that night, in a gap between songs, there was a huge bang and the sound of screaming. Four gentlemen had returned in a large car, and emptied a shotgun into the front doors downstairs blowing glass all over the foyer. Fortunately, no one was in the way and so the incident ended happily, all things considered. These were our instructions then: If at any point during our recitation, the ladies and gentlemen on the dance floor should find cause to disagree with each other in a physical fashion, we were to continue our work vigorously and in a conscientious manner. We were to, 'Keep fockin' playin', maan.'

I was twenty years old, Stix was seventeen, Jack and Bachelor Johnny were grand old men of twenty-two. We found the experience scary. The women were very naughty, and the men were very rough. We were skinny kids in make-up, torn blouses and tight trousers. One pair of my canary yellow hipster loons were so tight that the only way I could get them on, was to lie on the dressing room floor, while the roadies took one leg each and eased them up my thighs. Add to this, the size seven high-heeled women's boots I used to squeeze into and it made for a very peculiar sort of walk, if nothing else. I like to think, however, that I cut rather a dash. Some of the huge American airmen took a far less charitable view of me. This could be quite unnerving, say, in the toilet, standing at the urinal between two of them during my breaks.

If there wasn't an available sink in our dressing room, Stix and I usually went to the pisser in pairs, which made things look even more dodgy, clad as he was on occasions, in hot-pants and gold lurex tights. We never got in any trouble though. I don't think the Yanks actually believed what they were seeing. Nevertheless, I did sometimes feel like I imagine a zebra feels, while drinking at a watering hole in between two lions.

Once, when we were having a break, the dressing room door crashed open, and framed in the doorway was the biggest American I'd ever seen. 'A'm a fight'n' muthafucker from Noo Yawk!' he bawled. 'You guys the fuck'n' baand? Where's aal the balls?' Oh prithee kind sir, but we have no idea what you're crapping on about. 'Wimmin, boy! Wimmin! Chicks! Ya know? Ah thought you guys'd be knee deep in pussy. When Ah wanna woman, Ah jest hop orn. A-huk-huk-huk!' Well quite sir. I expect you do sir. But at this point we are taking a well-earned rest so could you possibly leave us in peace to discuss the pressing matter of whether we begin the next set with Quo's 'Paper Plane' or possibly our very own 'Phil the Cleaner'? This was the general nature of encounters with our public at this point in our career, mildly interesting but ultimately unedifying.

The music which the DJ played while we were having our breaks was heavy funk, which over time I began to develop a taste for. He also played a lot of Barry White. At that time Barry White was just beginning to break over here, and I can never hear a Barry White record without being transported back to the Gear Shift. I'd never been much of a clubbing guy up until then but my experiences during those early years have ensured that I never subsequently became one. Anthropologically speaking though, the Gear Shift was a fascinating place. Here I could observe man and woman at play in an endless and delicate courtship pavane older than time itself. Last Turkey In The Shop was a particular favourite of mine. I now recount it to you for your own delectation.

After the band had finished our last 'Shakin' All Over' or 'Johnny B Goode', we would exit the stage, thanking our patrons, and then retire with a beer to watch the drunk and those without partners come to what conclusions they could. Thus, a broken-nosed beef baron would shyly approach what I can only describe as a rhino in a dress and ask her if she wished to dance. If the offer were accepted, the male would then lurch over to the hapless DJ and slur, ' "Paper Roses" by Marie Osmond, mate.' The DJ might reply that that particular disc wasn't on his play list at that point. The beef baron would then say, louder, 'No mate. You're playing "Paper Roses", alright?' The record would go on.

Returning to his chosen one, the male would then get her in a clinch which involved grinding his thigh into her crotch and dribbling down her neck while the pair of them went round in slow circles on one spot. The whole spectacle was redolent of watching a sack of spuds in a suit that had been tightly tied to a badly loaded bag of grapefruit revolving on an invisible turntable. An enduring image there, and deeply challenging. I hesitate to speculate, when desire came to its fruition, later on that bosky evening, precisely what raptures Cupid had lined up for these lovers. But I shan't dwell on it here. You may have just eaten. Thus did the apple-cheeked young hopefuls of The Mighty Plod have their delicate senses awakened by rude old Grandmother Reality, with her cackles in our ears and her horny hands all over our little pink plums.

Shortly after Christmas, Big Nik and Stix came up with, 'Good news lads. The Gear Shift loved us. We're their kind of band. We've got a residency!' It was true. We would play there Thursday, Friday and Saturday nights every other week. Four sets a night, three nights on the trot, once a fortnight, until further notice. With all the punch-ups, drunken servicemen, swamp-donkeys, honey-monsters, tadger-grabbers, pill-pushers, morons and space cadets we could put up with. What more could any four boys want?

Twenty-eight

Brickies in Bacofoil
Colchester, Mid-February 1974

Stix, Jack and Harry broke the divan bed. They'd been giving a drunken, clothes-on display of humping each other when one of the bed's legs snapped and it collapsed on one side. The woman whose bed it was was palpably upset about it but made those sorts of it-doesn't-matter-really noises that genteel hostesses sometimes do. It had after all been her mistake to invite us to the party. She was a waitress who worked at the restaurant where I washed up dishes. Her name was Bibi and she was much older than me, say about twenty-seven. She was buxom, had a posh voice and wore lots of dark eye-make up. Bibi had something to do with the theatre and I believe she ended up being a wardrobe mistress in the West End. At this point, however, she was still learning her trade at the university theatre and waitressing part-time.

I had a bit of a thing about Bibi, so when she said to me, 'Our production finishes on Saturday and we're having a bit of a closing-night bash. Perhaps you'd like to come along, and why not bring some of your friends from your pop group,' I was excited.

I shouted, 'Hubba wow-wow, baby! Any chance of me assailing the velvet canal between your thighs with my

209

lurve gondola?' This is actually not what I said at all, but I probably thought it.

Bibi said that there would be lots of interesting young actresses there as well as the usual student theatre types. I tried to explain to her that pop musicians were a roistering bunch of young rips who were fond of horseplay and generally up to a bit of a lark. I swear that I genuinely did try to give her a get-out clause. But Bibi wasn't having any of it. 'Oh nonsense. We're theatre people. There's not a lot that can shock us, you know.' Well it's your funeral, lady.

After our gig, six of us had turned up at Bibi's big house with cider and a few cans of light ale and had been ushered into a polite gathering with restrained lighting, quiet conversation and the discreet tinkle of wine glasses. Now there was a broken divan bed and the sound of someone shouting, 'because I just don't trust fucking communists, that's why!' Bachelor Johnny had got hold of an amp and guitar and was sitting on a stool in their living room singing an extremely long and drunken version of some song which went, 'I'm goin' down to Noo Orleans.' He sang it over and over again at top volume. Harry, Bachelor Johnny's twin brother, was trying to make amends for the bed damage and was being very genial but of no use at all and I was wondering why the actors were chatting each other up instead of the actresses. We didn't know any gay people in those days. In fact the whole thing was a complete mystery to me. This is why when Bibi's husband started pouring lots of wine down my neck and telling me that I had, 'a very interesting face', I didn't mind in the slightest. I just thought, 'God. They're dead friendly these theatre types. I always used to think they were a bit snotty.' I asked him, 'any more wine about, Squire?' The friendly theatre bloke took me by the hand, led me into the kitchen and showed me two huge boxes and several bottles on the table. It was more wine than I'd ever seen before in a place that didn't actually sell it.

'Red or white?' he asked. I took a big bottle of red, unscrewed the top of it and took a good pull on it. He looked slightly taken aback. 'Don't you want a glass?'

'Nah. That's all right, chief. I've got a bottle now.' He laughed awkwardly at me. We went and sat down again in the very arty living room. I was quite happy to converse with him. It was when I found his hand on my dick that I began to suspect that all was not as it might be. 'Where's Bibi?' I asked.

'Oh, she's probably gone to bed with her boyfriend. She does her thing and I kinda do mine.'

Even through my extreme drunkenness, I felt the spade of disappointment clang loudly on the back of my skull. I also felt the hatpin of alarm as it jabbed me in the back of the neck. I think this was the moment when I realised that I was one hundred per cent heterosexual. For all that foppishness, make-up and general mimsiness that went with glam-rock, there was very little genuine lavender in the movement. We were in fact a bunch of brickies in Bacofoil, plumbers in lipstick. I, with my black nail varnish and women's deodorants was the nearest thing that The Mighty Plod had to a first lady in this band. How effeminate was I? Why, the roadies used to arm-wrestle each other to share a tent with me on tour. It was because I didn't smell like a polecat I suppose. Not that the other guys did either. It was just...well the van could get a bit whiffy on long trips and I always liked to arrive smelling like a tart's boudoir. Women seemed to like it anyway and at least I didn't smell of Eau de Dettol or Essence de Soldering Iron, like Jack.

I've had this argument time and time again with gay and bisexual mates. I do not believe that everybody is bisexual.

I don't mind what people do with what appendages to what apertures and never have. There are certain good friends of mine who happen to be queer (I understand this word has now been reclaimed), and whenever I meet them, they light up my little life, because they are clever and funny and in every way good. However, this does not mean I want to get into bed with them anymore than they want to get in bed with me.

Anyway, getting back to the story: so here I am, wrecked with no chance of a sausage and doughnut situation with Bibi. Her husband's trying to muck about with me because I'm pretty, drunk and stupid – or at least I'm pretty stupid and drunk. I'd like to be able to say that I exited the place with dignity and aplomb, but to tell you the truth I can't remember how or when I left. All I know is that I woke up on the floor of Big Nik's flat the next morning, with half a bottle of wine and an award-winning hangover. As soon as I was able, I also managed to ascertain that I was still a virgin in all my concave departments and that there were no undue signs of wear-and-tear in the tummy-banana region. In fact there were no telltale splashes or stains whatsoever, apart from a fair amount of wine down my shirt.

Stix seemed to have fared slightly better and was invited to the home of a young actress where everything proceeded more or less as we would expect until six in the morning, when Stix realised that he had woken up looking at the wrong wallpaper. The incident ended a tad acrimoniously but our drummer, the pin-up of The Mighty Plod, put it all down to experience. The central lesson we all learned from this is that theatre people as a rule, don't generally get on that well with hairy wazzocks in rock bands. But why ever would they?

Twenty-nine

Local Lad Makes Mess
East London and Colchester, March 1974

'...but with some interesting, self-penned songs and the amazing choreography of their lead singer, the winners are... Plod!'

And with these words, Colchester's finest have just become national semi-finalists in the *Melody Maker* Rock and Folk Contest 1974. During the quarter-finals we have thrashed other bands such as Jerry the Ferret, Mile End, and Grood to go through to the next stage. Most importantly we have beaten Fritz, our hometown rivals. Fritz have a brilliant sixteen-year-old guitarist called Steve. Steve dismisses all other guitarists except Hendrix. He can play like Hendrix. But he cannot write songs. In fact he has written his first song for this competition. It's called 'Rock 'n' Roll Woman'. And then his wah-wah pedal goes wrong in the middle of it. Panic. And relax.

The judges prefer our songs, which tonight, ladies and gentlemen, are 'Neo City' and 'Malice In Wonderland'. And yes, I know that the last title has been thought of by other artists since then but we had it first, so nyah-nyah-nyah. Naturally the fey young fellows of Plod, or at least three of us, have gone right over the top with the silly clothes and the make-up. Next to us, the other bands look like a bunch of carpet-fitters. And so for once, we are little lower than the angels. Much celebration and whanger waving in the Plod van this night, as we rumble our way back up the A12 to Colchester – home of nothing in particular.

Within a week, and much to the chagrin of our critics at home, a photo of me, the size of a packet of B&H King Size cigarettes appears on page thirty-seven of *Melody Maker* magazine. The other lads are only slightly miffed that they've been clipped from the shot, since a large headline above the pic proclaims, 'PLOD TO VICTORY'. But me? Oh my dears. On the outside is a modest smile. But on the inside, ticker tape is raining down. Men in skyscrapers high above my parade are popping champagne corks and breaking out the cigars. I am standing in a huge open-top Daimler with Brigitte Bardot by my side while a crowd of sceptical former girlfriends, teachers, employers, and relatives look on with deep resentment. It's my first bit of rock press. After this long struggle, who could possibly hold it against me?

Colchester could, that's who. A day after the picture comes out, I'm sitting downstairs in a café in town when a voice across the table goes, 'What shitty local band managed to get their fucking picture in *Melody Maker* then?' It was typical really. And it carried on wherever we went. People don't like it when you do something. Like two trains sitting in a station, when one train slowly begins to pull out of the station, for a few seconds, nobody on either train is exactly sure which one is moving. When it becomes apparent that it's not theirs, there's a slight disappointment involved. This gives rise to the great English put-down. How dare you do something! You've just emphasised my own stasis. And to do that is the very height of bad manners. And so they slag you. And the more you do, the more they slag you. In some places, you

might get a little support, or a murmured acknowledgement. But in small-town England, if you try and climb out
of the pit, don't expect anyone to help you get out. More
likely they will grab your legs and try to pull you back
down again for daring to have the arrogance to even think
you could try. They're quite happy for you to be bad or to
fail. For that only serves to confirm what they believe; that
nothing good ever came out of here, and nothing can ever
come to any good. So there's no point in even trying.

No matter though, the weather's set fair for Colchester's
greatest jessies right now. We have secured that all-
important support slot with a major-label band at the local
tech college. This is a big deal for us. The band is Warhorse,
an aptly named lumbering big band connected with one of
Rick Wakeman's more grandiose projects. Younger readers
may not remember the time when dinosaurs walked the
earth, but let me tell you, neo-classical rock concepts were
doing great business back then. The label sponsoring
tonight's particular mastodon is Atlantic, on which, more
later.

Plod intend to go right over the top with regard to this
one. It's our chance to show the big boys and the locals
how real rock stars play the game. Bachelor Johnny has
excelled himself tonight. He's wearing all white, plus huge
wraparound shades and stack-heeled boots. He looks like
Roxy Music's Phil Manzanera. Full marks to the geezer. I
am wearing my torn black lacy blouse, those trousers, high
heels, Dusty Springfield make-up (girls, that woman had a
lot to answer for) and black nail varnish. I'm also kitted out
with a stuffed dog on a chain and lots of blood capsules.

Well the gig goes great, if you discount a little bit of
Bachelor Johhny losing it at the beginning while he gets
used to playing his guitar through a much louder rig. But
good old Stix and Jack are ably manning the engine room,

I'm throwing myself about and screaming and it's marvellous until...black out, and silence. Somebody – could have been me, could have been Sav – has tripped over a plug and brought the whole show to a halt. The main band's roadies are less than pleased about this. After five minutes or so, they manage to get it all up and running again. We finish our set and exit the stage.

My girlfriend is a little upset. While clapping at the end of one of our early numbers, someone leans over to her and asks, 'Why are you clapping them?' She replies that it was because we were good. The voice says, 'No they're not. They're crap. Everyone knows they're crap.' What it is to have home-town support, hey? I'm also told that two girls have had to be taken out of the auditorium because of my shenanigans with the blood capsules. Nevertheless a small crowd of deviants does seem to have taken a shine to us. This annoys the sullen ranks of the prematurely bearded that comprise Colchester's rock cognoscenti.

But I am just about to insult my first celebrity of the spring, which is almost a tradition over here on Planet Newell. Naturally, I'm not watching the main band. Why should I when there is Special Brew to be downed? I have kept my promise to Big Nik and the others in the band not to be drunk onstage. But now... I am going to have a drink. Sitting there in full kit, make-up running, I see a familiar-looking man come into the dressing room. He used to be a big pop star in the sixties, with a string of hits. But right now he is head of A&R, (that's the bloke who signs up bands) at Atlantic Records. This is an important fellow.

I ask him what he is doing in our dressing room. He walks right up to me and almost like a scene from a bad TV rock series says, 'Hi. I'm Dave Dee. Now where have I seen you before?'

I reply, 'Aw, I dunno man. What dustbins d'you hang around?' He laughs awkwardly. He doesn't have the bearing of a man who is used to musicians being rude to him. Alarm bells are beginning to ring for Bachelor Johnny and Stix now. They realise that I am 'on one' and that this bloke might very well want to help us. Too late, I've started up again. All my resentment over powerful major labels begins to spill out. I finger his herring-bone, football player-style jacket. 'My mum used to be a big fan of yours, y'know.' I move in closer, breathing Special Brew in his face and whisper, 'Is it true that you have to sleep with A&R men to get a record contract these days? Go on. What about it?'

I was unable to say anymore after this, because a roadie's hand was clamped over my mouth and two people dragged me out of the dressing room and down the stairs. As soon as the hand was off my mouth, I screamed abuse at the top of my lungs up the stairwell. Boy was there a row over that. I got all the usual, 'Do you realise that this guy could have signed us up?' And then a bit of, 'Why do you behave like this?' But there was no point talking to me when I was in that kind of mood. As far as I was concerned, it was us versus the world, and no way were we selling out to the first smarmy fellow that deigned to walk into our dressing room. And Dave Dee, if you're reading this now, I'm sorry. That's if you even remember it. But it did happen. It was my fault. I've grown up now, well a bit. And I did actually like some of your records. Oh, except for 'Wreck of the Antoinette'.

Well, some bands say, no sell-out. I actually lived it. None of this helped poor, bewildered peace-loving Bachelor Johnny or precociously business-minded Stix who were now brushing Mr Dee down and trying to obtain a pledge that he would listen to our demo tape. Mr Dee having been suitably brushed down, an address was obtained. A few days later, a demo tape was despatched to the address. About a week after that, the demo tape was despatched smartly back with a standard rejection letter: Dear so and so, we regret that the type of music which you do is not what we are looking for at the moment. Why don't you just give up, you hopeless schmucks? Or perhaps you might care to try some other branch of the entertainment industry, such as TV repairs, blah-de-blah.

The receipt of our demo only served to fuel my argument that all record-company people were parasites and bastards, who needed to be killed, but Bachelor Johnny was quietly disappointed in me. He didn't say so but it was in his eyes as I launched into yet another them and us rant. Stix's opinion was a standard issue, 'Zap, you're a pretty good songwriter but you know nothing about business so why don't you keep your mouth shut.' I was in the wrong, and I knew it, so I tried to button it a bit more after that. Didn't work though.

Thirty

When You Are Forty
Norfolk, Late March 1974

After our triumph at the *Melody Maker* Rock Contest, it was pretty much business as usual for The Mighty Plod. We did what rock bands do. We gigged. We rehearsed. We drank. We worried about money. A continued harangue from a disgruntled Big Nik led to yet more bickering. The ever-practical Nik's latest song was that we had to get a four-hour rock set (he meant cover versions) together, and then we could go out and play in Greece and Turkey. As far as Nik was concerned, we'd never get any work doing 'that rubbish that Johnny and Zap are writing.'

Jack the bassist's song was, 'we need a proper touring van with reclining aircraft-style seats.' Bachelor Johnny's song was, 'the pub's got an extension tonight.' Stix and I didn't care what the song was, as we weren't really listening. If you divided up on a pie chart what we were interested in, about fifty per cent of the pie might be allocated to what we could eat, drink, smoke or listen to. Another forty per cent might concern itself with young women – the getting of them and the keeping or dumping of them. This left a slender ten per cent, which was allocated to Any Other Business. Any Other Business included the state of the world, politics, health and welfare, other people's feelings, our families and listening to what Big Nik thought. Any Other Business had to do a big job for a little piece of pie.

Despite our cavalier attitude, we did sometimes get depressed about things. If we were sufficiently battered at the wrong time by anyone outside the band, it would get us down. One evening, while heading out to a humdrum rehearsal, Stix remarked that his parents had given him a severe roasting when he'd risked visiting them. He said that they'd concluded their lecture with, 'Ah, but what are you going to do when you're forty?'

I replied, 'My parents quite often say that, too.'

Jack said, 'So do mine.' Bachelor Johnny nodded sagely and said, 'Yeah, mine say that too.'

We wondered what this magical number forty had to do with anything. After some discussion, the subject having lost any interest, we filed it under Any Other Business. On the other hand, it did provide us with a valuable catchphrase. Afterwards, whenever anyone was discussing anything serious or the subject was getting boring, we'd look meaningfully at the speaker and say, 'Ah, but what are you going to do when you're forty?'

Eric Coates' *Dam Busters'* theme became something of a favourite during long trips in the van, after Jack had compared the van interior to the cockpit of a Lancaster bomber. Roadies and band members would begin humming it while the others would imitate the sound of whistling bombs and crackling radio announcements. Sav, as bomb-aimer, would occasionally open a sliding door and direct a bottle of piss at a road sign as we bawled the tune out in the darkness. Once, Nik noticed a van in a lay-by, which was obviously being used for courtship. He slowed the van down to a crawl, allowing the band members to roar out, 'Wooaarrrr! Shagging!' before coasting slowly away singing *The Dam Busters* at the tops of our voices. Little things eh? And we wondered why we didn't get invited to grown-up parties.

One time, when I was expecting a girlfriend to visit, I borrowed a room at St Guinness' from Bachelor Johnny. I had to hit the sack early that night, because she was arriving early the next day from abroad and she didn't like me drinking huge amounts. I didn't want her to see me hungover, hair in a bird's nest and gagging for a hair-of-the-dog, so I selflessly left the pub early after a few beers and went to bed. Sometime during the small hours, a group of band members and friends snuck quietly into the room where I was sleeping and began softly humming *The Dam Busters*, like a choir around my bed. They built the tune up in volume until they were roaring at the top of their voices. Waking up to find my bed surrounded by shadowy, singing figures with bottles in their hands, freaked me out, because I'd been suffering from a series of acid flashbacks. I wasn't really sure whether it had happened or not, until they told me the next day.

And so, with *The Dam Busters'* theme fairly fixed in your minds, unscrew that bottle top, spark up that fag and amble with me back to the spring of 1974. The question is, what happened to my earlier heroes, the members of the rock band, Stray? This is a salutary lesson for would-be rock stars. I always swore that if I ever wrote a book about the pop biz, I'd call it *Being Brilliant Is Simply Not Enough*. Not enough? Irrelevant, more like. I used to think that pop stars practised in bedrooms till their fingers bled, that they formed bands, did gigs, got good, got signed, got better and got famous. The truth of the matter is that many of our idols were at stage school. They were child stars pushed by pushy parents, or their parents knew somebody influential, or they went to public school and had that instilled sense

221

of what to do, what to say, where to hang out. It's no good just being good at music. You have to want money and you have to want fame and you have to want those two things in huge amounts. And you have to want them really, really badly. You can tell all the lies you want to a credibility-hungry rock press later on.

Failing qualifying for any of the above, you must hook up with a manager who does. Ideally, he'll be a public schoolboy with a tortured underside – let's say strict Catholic or Jewish. He'll have a good dab of male ego – he might have a weakness for racing cars or gee gees – but this drive will be offset by a strong feminine principle. He should know about paintings, classical music and theatre. What held back The Mighty Plod and, in this case, the members of Stray, was not having this kind of manager.

Plod got a gig at the Royal Links Pavilion in Cromer, on the north Norfolk coast. When Stix told me that we were to be supporting Stray I was so excited that I nearly handed my fags round. It was only three years earlier that I'd been one of an army of teenagers who used to think Stray were the saviours of the world. I'd seen them play at the Temple in Wardour Street as a pilled-up eighteen-year-old. I used to listen to their second album, *Suicide*, about six times a day. Now I was actually going to be playing on the same stage as them. It's had to convey how I felt about it.

I had seriously expected Stray to be superstars by this time. Four Shepherds Bush teenagers barely older than we were, Stray had risen out of the London 'toilet circuit' in early 1970. They had been the youngest band ever to play London's Roundhouse and had been signed to Transatlantic when the members were about seventeen. They were tipped as the next Led Zeppelin and had a die-hard following of young oiks like me who were getting increasingly fed up with the progressive noodlings of other bands. When you're a seventeen-year old with spots,

Chernobyl in your trousers and a frantic wanking schedule you do not need The Incredible String Band. You want Uriah Heep, The Pink Fairies, Hawkwind and Stray.

So how is it that a band like Stray, who'd worked so hard, had such good material and such a following, didn't make it to the next level? I knew nothing about the music industry then; I didn't know how an industry can reject enduring talent which has worked for its living, and yet catapult to fame two biscuit packers with shit-for-brains and a silly dance-ditty guffed out by the songwriting team at This'll Do Publishing Ltd. You tell me how that works, because I haven't figured it.

As soon as I came off the stage in Cromer, I went bouncing down into Stray's dressing room to meet the chaps. Del Bromham, their guitarist and songwriter, had gone out for some grub but I met the other three members. They didn't seem as enthusiastic about their own band as I was. They looked knackered and pissed-off, like battle-weary troops. They were also pretty stoned. They certainly weren't in the mood to meet a waggy-tailed puppy of a fan. I asked Steve, the singer and my earlier role model, where the famous light show and exploding dustbins were. He told me that Stray didn't use them anymore. It was time for the band to get psyched up and ready to go on, so I wished them a good gig and discreetly drifted out. I was feeling a bit let down. I'd finally met my heroes and they seemed to be having a hard day of it.

And then they went on. Their set was taut and hard in comparison with my own band. They'd lost none of their power. In short, they delivered. I realised that they'd saved all their energy for the stage. It had been unreasonable and naive of me to expect to find them leaping around the dressing room as well, not when they whacked it out at this rate. After the gig, I hung around the stage, feeling disconsolate and waiting for the roadies to finish loading our gear into the van, when I felt someone tap me on the shoulder. It was Del Bromham. He smiled cheerily at me and said, 'that was a pokey sound you got out of those bass-bins of yours. Did you build them yourselves?' He meant our sound had been powerful. I explained to him that Jack and Bachelor Johnny had built the big speakers because we couldn't afford to buy new ones. Del told me that we had the makings of a good band and that we should keep going, because we were going to make it one of these days. He said that he'd been watching us and that we'd performed well. I couldn't believe it. And even if it wasn't true I'll never forget his kindness for saying it.

Stray were basically knackered by management who'd failed to seize the opportunities. Towards the end of their career, through a chance meeting, Charlie Kray briefly managed them, however, by this time their hour had passed. With Charlie holding the reins they found some sectors of the music business unwilling to work with them, although it must be added that gig payments were never late.

I don't believe that any energy is ever truly wasted. Even if it mutates, it always gets passed down the line somewhere. That Stray never got their due is the music-industry's loss as much as ours, but as I went out in the world, I met all sorts of rock musicians of my vintage who had been inspired or energised by Stray in some way, including members, and this is telling, of The Damned and XTC. There are many other stories of great musicians who failed to fulfil their potential. I do not, by the way, include myself in this pantheon; any misfortune that may have befallen me was my own stupid fault. I had the errant belief that all you had to do was write some tunes, strut your stuff and muck around a lot and that somehow, something brilliant would happen.

Music-biz success is comprised of five basic ingredients: right sound; right time; right place; right look and right age. The first four of these, you can have some influence upon, but talent often takes a long time to develop and the whole of that time, the clock is ticking away. Like a game of bar billiards, the bar comes down and the balls don't come back. Then it won't matter how brilliant your material, or how charismatic your stage show, you will not be signed. Everyone who reads this will know a friend or some guy in a pub who has an amazing talent, but never made it.

There's no point in being bitter about it. Sure, there's an element of luck, but there's also an element of hard work. A great man once said after being told he was lucky, 'Yep. Seems like the harder I work, the luckier I get.' And disgruntled artists have been bitching that they 'woz robbed' since Juvenal's time. Sometimes, you just don't make it. And even if you do, the view from the summit isn't always what you thought it would be when you finally do reach it. I've met a handful of my former heroes and become good friends with several of them. And they all bear some sort of scar, bewilderment or permanent fragility as a result of their success. So don't believe your own press – good or bad – and take it a little easier on your body and whatever you decide to put inside it.

And I had a helluvva time, didn't I? And I'm still working, and still awake, and no one has been made homeless from any of my activities – apart from myself. No children went to bed hungry as a result of anything I did. A couple of women got slightly irritated maybe. And one or two people got worried about me for a while, but like thousands of my fellow baby boomers, I eventually grew up. In a way. And I take my place at last in a society that has been mostly pretty tolerant of me, all things considered. As for the drugs: my God, what a prat. I could probably have got the whole business over and done with in a month, if I'd had one of those glossy wall-planners that major record companies use.

Mums and Dads: be nice to the little geniuses you've spawned. Little geniuses: be nice to your mums and dads. They go through a very difficult stage when you're a teenager. Young would-be pop star: keep poncing around in front of that mirror, for it is your heritage. Record industry: wake up and listen. Or fuck off. It's only music. Lastly, elders: stop asking youngsters what they're going to do when they're forty. They already know. They're going to become you.

Thirty-one

This Little Ziggy Went to Market
Colchester, Spring 1974

So I was shagging this girl in a broom cupboard after a gig... It was probably close to midnight and I'd had some lager and a drop of wine. It was her idea. I wasn't looking for it or anything, quite the opposite. I'd just played one of the worst gigs of my life. Not hip enough to be the New York Dolls and not commercial enough to be The Sweet, we lumbered up and down the A12 in Big Nik's grumbling old Ford Transit van learning how to be rock stars.

Most of the time we'd kept ourselves on the road by playing dodgy cover versions of Slade, Steppenwolf, Rory Gallagher, Status Quo and T Rex in what Stix called 'the great working-class playgrounds of East Anglia'. This time however, we'd got a proper gig at Essex University, where we could play our own songs. This engagement was in a building called the Hexagon, which is now a restaurant. It was quite a privilege to have wangled such a gig. We mostly played pubs and clubs, since college and university gigs were monopolised by big London record companies who needed to push those acts they'd invested money in. Somehow we'd got this gig. Our getting it was a big deal and all of us were keyed up about it.

Plod were not a popular band with Colchester's cognoscenti. Colchester liked its bands to be bluesy and hard rocking like Free or progressive like Pink Floyd or Genesis. Colchester's rock cognoscenti were a bunch of hard-arsed bikers, ex-soldiers and drinkin' dopin' hippie dockers. The students of Essex University on the other hand liked The Doobie Brothers, Little Feat and The Eagles. Except for the girls, who liked Bowie and Roxy Music, but then birds usually do have better taste and more vision. What nobody liked was…us. We plastered make-up all over ourselves, wore satin trousers and girlie blouses. We had stacks or high-heeled boots and posed a lot. We preferred drink to dope and our music was a messy thrash of botched chords and ill-conceived songs with pretentious lyrics about being beaten by cruel girls and losing our minds. Sound good? Believe me, it wasn't.

On top of all this we were foul-mouthed, cocky and absolutely convinced that we were star material. There was, I suppose, a little bit of jealousy directed towards us. Still in our teens and early twenties, we were younger than most of the existing local bands. And we had a stage act. I used to climb things and do a kind of epileptic shimmy that I'd pinched from Arthur Brown and Roger Chapman. Sometimes I chewed blood capsules or dragged unlikely props onstage with me, such as a stuffed dog on a length of chain. Stix wore green leather hot pants, gold lurex tights and blue lipstick. Bachelor Johnny periodically wore a midi-length Biba dress on stage.

At last we had this big home-town gig and we'd won our heat of the *Melody Maker* Rock Contest hadn't we? As far as Colchester was concerned, we were still that bunch of mouthy young upstarts who'd rejected the idea of doing an endless blues jam in the key of A. They weren't to know how hard we'd worked. That we'd notched up ninety-odd gigs. That by the time the summer was over, we'd have more or less ditched the glam-rock stuff and stumbled at last on the art of song writing.

We told everyone that we were going to show Colchester. Meanwhile Colchester was waiting for us. Some people had even told us that they were going along just to slag us off. Our changing room was on an upper level, looking down on the dance-floor auditorium. The roadies had set the gear up, including a primitive monitoring system that would, for the first time, allow me to hear myself onstage. The place was packed. But as we went through to the stage area I had a bad feeling. Someone called my name, but above that sound I could already hear people shouting, 'Fuck off. You're crap.' A crushed can went over my head, as did a lot of things in those days. I couldn't believe that people would be so hostile to a band they hadn't even heard yet.

A girl, who was probably one of our only fans, had made me some trousers out of tonic-liner material. She'd cautioned me against wearing them because of the fabric's flimsiness. But no, I had to have my glammy trousers. So the girl ran them up on the machine in a hurry and I put them on. The band sparked up and roared into a furious thrash called 'Neo City'. To my horror, I found I couldn't hear myself at all. The sound was all over the place, a vast tuneless roar. Telepathic panic set in, as if the four of us were on a sledge whizzing down a steep hill, with our hair blowing back, simultaneously screaming, 'Aaarrgh!'

As soon as the number crunched to its logical halt, a roadie ran up and told us that the new monitor system had blown up. Five or six hundred people were jeering and shouting at us. Bachelor Johnny smashed into another song as I did my best to figure out where we were and what I was singing. Any lead singer/frontman from a seventies glam-rock band will tell you: when the sound's not going right, leap up and down a lot. Be visual. Taking a high speed run from one side of the stage to another, I leapt as high as I could in a scissor-kick. As I landed, I felt my bottom half go cold. My stage trousers had split right down the front of both legs.

The gig ground on wretchedly for another forty tortuous minutes until we finally exited to an anti-applause of whistles, boos, cans and paper aeroplanes. I felt completely humiliated and depressed. Jack was having a shouting match with the roadie about the blown fuse. Bachelor Johnny was trying, as he always did, to mediate. Stix had fucked off for a drink. I went upstairs and looked miserably down from the upper level to the dance floor below. The previously hostile crowd were now happily doing a wall-to-wall boogie to the swinging sounds of Tina Turner's 'Nutbush City Limits'. It was what they did every Saturday night at Essex Uni, from the record's release in 1973 until 'Saturday Night Fever' came out in 1978.

I remember standing upstairs looking at them for ages, thinking, 'There's got to be something better than this. What do I have to do?' And then I thought about the waitresses in the restaurant where I washed up, and how, on Tuesday morning they would ask me how it went. And then I thought about not going into any of Colchester's pubs for at least a year. And then I thought about maybe giving it all up and only going for long walks across the fields where I didn't have to see anyone any more.

And then this blonde girl I knew appeared at my side and asked me if I was alright. She gave me an open bottle of wine, which I downed half of in one gulp. She put her arm around me, led me to the other side of the deserted upstairs landing and she opened a door which turned out to be a cleaning cupboard full of Jeyes fluid and brooms. She pulled me in after her and pulled the door to. Then she lifted and parted her checked cheesecloth skirt, under which she wore nothing. She lifted one of her legs up onto a cleaning bucket. And then, standing up in a broom cupboard at Essex University, above what is now the Hexagon Restaurant, she shagged me. She didn't have to do that. But it was very nice of her.

Thirty-two

In Plod We Trust
Central London, May 1974

The big day has arrived. The national semi-finals of the *Melody Maker* Rock and Folk Contest are upon us and Colchester's finest are girding their young loins, honing their chops, sharpening their licks and generally bracing themselves for the win which will catapult them to pop fame. On this day, it is Bachelor Johnny, guitarist, wise man and seer, who will be the hero of the hour. Stix will be the dutiful drummer. Jack will be uncharacteristically badly behaved, and Zap, your winsome young singer here, will have his work cut out wrenching disaster from the jaws of defeat. But fret not – he'll do it.

I have fallen over. I'm not dead drunk, but I'm drunk enough to have tripped up halfway down the aisles of seats of the London auditorium. Four people at a table, who were previously studying a band on the stage and making notes on their papers, have stopped doing so. I am sprawled headlong in front of their table and have possibly jogged their writing as I grabbed one of the table legs on the way down. I find myself looking up at an attractive-looking woman in her early thirties. In a soft northern accent, she asks me if I'm alright. 'Could you tell me where the toilet is please?' I ask. The other people at her table are pretending that they haven't seen me.

The woman points in the direction of the toilets. As I rise to my feet, I realise what I have done. I have fallen over drunk in front of the judges' table. I'm not bothered about it. I know it will get me points in the van on the way home but there is a feeling growing inside me that I'm not courting, so much as bound in holy wedlock to disaster. The woman judge, who has so kindly asked about my well-being, smiles at me understandingly. I notice she looks slightly tired. I'd never seen the singer Elkie Brooks close up before. I wonder if she remembers the make-up-caked drunk she directed to the toilet that May afternoon in the mid-seventies?

Events leading up to this day have not augured well for us. Bachelor Johnny had injured a part of his anatomy some months earlier. He needed a simple operation to sort it out. I say the operation is simple, but it's painful if done when an adult. Bachelor Johnny had selflessly cancelled this operation once already, because of gigging commitments. He was about to have it finally, and it had been touch and go as to whether we'd be able to do this competition, because he was in a lot of pain.

After lots of concerned chat between Stix and John and me, it had been decided we had to do this gig. We were in good time. We met up at St Guinness', Johnny's house at the bottom of Hangover Hill, picked up the gear and proceeded to a side street just over the road, to load the Plod van.

Everything all right so far? Good. We're on time, everyone is present and the van is loaded. But God never opens a door without he slams someone's dick in the sash window round about the same time.

Jack and Nik never did get on that well. I mean, Stix and I bickered from time to time like a couple of growing wolf cubs, but mostly we were allies against the forces of common sense which were ranged against us. Big Nik with his scathing tongue and quick wit and Jack with his stubborn quirkiness – he's always held up the band for certain rituals like washing his hair or having his tea before a gig – made a fiery match sometimes. Before we'd even moved forward on our way to the competition, Nik, who was driving, opened the side panel of the window. Jack protested that he'd just washed his hair and that he'd get a cold. Nik told Jack he was sick of breathing in all the smoke and wanted the window open. Jack leaned forward and closed it. Nik opened it. Jack closed it. The van moved off. Nik opened the window. Jack closed it. Nik jammed the brakes on. Bachelor Johnny, sitting in the front seat, struggling to put his seat belt on, shot forward, smacking his head hard into the windscreen. Nik and Jack, oblivious to all this, carried on arguing. Stix and I, realising that Bachelor Johnny had taken a bash, got the side door open and hauled Johnny out. He was dazed and shaky. We leaned him against the side of the van to steady him. The argument was still raging inside the van as Stix went round to try and referee.

At that point, Nik started the van up again and it jerked forward. Bachelor Johnny, with nothing to support him now, began to fall out into the road. I caught him just in time and held him up. He was in pain, on painkillers, had been bashed on the head and now had tumbled into the road. Johnny was shaking and mumbling to me, 'Let's just blow it out, man.' It wasn't like John. He was normally such a trouper. I could see he was in a bad way. I began to panic a bit. Nik and Jack were still arguing. And now Stix and I were in the unlikely roles of peacemakers. Everyone was swearing and trying to sort it out.

In the end we made John a cup of tea back at the house, wrapped him in a blanket, in case shock set in, and loaded him back in the van about fifteen minutes later. He'd recovered enough once we got to the contest. But I hadn't. I don't think the band really had as a whole. And one last little upset: what often happened when we did gigs, was that the rest of the band would go on, plug in, spark up and then I'd come running out to hit the first verse with a bang for maximum impact. On this occasion there was some complete prat of a stage manager backstage, playing Border collie to the bands. While I was waiting for my colleagues to spark up, this prat was saying, 'Why aren't you on yet?' I tried to explain to him that it was part of the show but he wasn't listening. He mistook my reluctance to go on as stage fright and began literally pushing me out of the wings. I toyed with the idea of whacking him, but I knew there'd be big trouble if I did and anyway we'd had enough trouble for one day. I ran on. We weren't bad, I suppose. But with Bachelor Johnny nowhere near full-throttle and me over-compensating with the stage act, it wasn't our finest ten minutes really. It probably didn't help that I made all my usual rude remarks from the stage to audience, judges, and anyone out there. Anyway, we fucked it up big style and we knew it.

With a good two hours before the results of the contest were announced, how do you think the members of Colchester's finest filled in the diamond-studded minutes? Why, we drank. Even Jack. Especially the normally sensible Jack. Stix and I stayed longer at the bar than most. I even befriended a singer from a Hastings band who was kind enough to give me a toke on some particularly average bush he was smoking. When we rejoined John and Jack in the auditorium, Jack was bawling out insults at the other bands. Stix, Jack and I sat in a pile of cans and crisp packets and felt considerably more cheery than when we'd arrived.

We were conspicuous by our bad behaviour, especially Jack. Every so often we'd notice one or other of the judges craning their necks and peering over in our direction to see where the noise was coming from. And later, as if there had been any doubt in the matter, I managed to fall flat on my face in front of Elkie Brooks. Ah, golden memories. We had to assist Jack back to the transport. Nik was less than pleased. Bachelor Johnny slept while Stix and I carried on drinking. Another 'victory' for Colchester's finest as we trundled back up the A12 still taking the piss out of the Yes-soundalike trio who'd won the contest. We'd been especially taken with the chubby singer and his pink-satin dungarees.

When *Melody Maker* came out the following week, we got a couple of scathing lines about being, 'a fag-rock band whose singer had kissed the lead guitarist mid-number.' The band that won the competition got a recording contract and an appearance on *The Old Grey Whistle Test* and were never heard of again. Mind you, neither were we.

Under normal circumstances, we might have got a post-mortem and a dressing-down from Nik for our unprofessional behaviour. Since the day's bad start had been partly due to him however, it never happened. As far as we were concerned, we'd blown it. But we'd live to fight another day. There would be other gigs, other bars. Bachelor Johhny would get his anatomy sorted out and Martin Newell would wake up on the floor next morning, swallow two painkillers and walk up Hangover Hill to face another day's kitchen-portering.

Thirty-three

A Taste of the North
Leeds, June 1974

There is a Mick Ronson solo album track called 'Music is Lethal'. The lyrics describe a 'Prince of the alleys', stumbling, in his search for wine, and are credited to an Italian songwriter called Battisti. The translation is by David Bowie. The song is possibly pretentious. It's certainly over-dramatic and over-produced. And I still love it to death. Slag it off on Planet Newell and be assured that someone will come over and flame you in your bed.

Naturally, I identified with it. What glam-rock singer from Colchester wouldn't? I was weird, arty, brilliant and doomed. So very, very doomed. My audiences at Ipswich's Gearshift would not have been aware of the extent of my doom, but I like to think that there were pretty strong hints of what was to come in the sheer pain that I injected into Plod's cover version of Rory Gallagher's 'Messing With the Kid'.

None of this arty strangeness explained why I was standing on a moor near Halifax with a knotted hankie on my head, my trouser legs rolled up to my knees and shouting at passing cars, 'We're going to Leeeds! Leeeds!' Stix and one of our roadies were doing exactly the same thing and it all seemed to make sense at the time. A coach

237

load of people en route to Harry Ramsden's fish and chip emporium, regarded us with only mild interest. We were on our first northern tour. That's one cancelled club gig in Halifax and a couple of dodgy pub gigs in Leeds to you, matey boy.

Stix conducted one of the more valuable contributions to nutritional research during this period. And it cost the government nothing. Realising that expending money on food meant that he had less to spend on beer, Stix reasoned that since peanuts were full of protein and beer had a certain food value, he could probably live off peanuts and beer for the full three days of the tour. This would free up money for extra beer rations, at the same time as providing enough energy to do the job of drumming. Stix was eighteen years old and known to be highly intelligent. We had to lend his theory some credence and for the first two days the experiment did seem to be working.

On day three of the experiment, however, Stix discovered he was suffering from an ailment that we later came to know as 'yellow peanut-water disease'. And so the research was reluctantly discontinued. Bachelor Johnny was, as ever, sage after the event. He told of a similar thing, which had happened to his twin brother Harry, who in not dissimilar circumstances had, 'written off a perfectly good pair of underpants and had been forced to throw them in a bin at a bus garage in Istanbul.'

It was certainly colder in the north; particularly up on top of the moors. I can't even remember why we drove up on them that weekend, but we had a Ford Transit van, and by golly we were going to use it. The Mighty Plod spent a vast chunk of their lives in that van. Big Nik and Sav had done it up and separated the gear from the musicians by putting in a plywood tongue-and-groove-look partition. They installed a row of old Rover seats in the back. My seat was behind the driver. It was here that I held court, told jokes, ate cold spaghetti out of cans, read, slept, drank, entertained women friends and touched up my make-up. I could almost say I grew up in that van but for the fact that being in Colchester's premier glam-rock group had nothing whatsoever to do with growing up.

Jack could be entertaining on tour. The son of a Polish fish-breeder, Jack had been given the stage name of Jack Stardust by my predecessor, Steve. It was a nickname that Jack hated, however, and so we didn't use it much. Jack was a fellow of rough-hewn manners. He had once walked into a bedroom whilst I was naked, with a young Australian woman astride me, and shouted, 'Come on, Zap. Get that over with, we're going out to the pub.'

The young woman had carried on oblivious, while I exclaimed indignantly, 'Bloody hell, Jack. Have you no decorum?'

Jack just stood there looking at us and after a pause enquired, 'So are you ready then, or what?'

A less glamour-orientated person would be hard to imagine. Jack wouldn't wear any make-up and he had to be nagged into dressing up for the stage. But he was a cheerful sod most of the time, a good, solid heavy-rock bassist and bloody handy with anything electrical. He was rumoured to put Dettol in his bath and to sleep with his socks under his pillow when he was travelling. He wasn't particularly broad-minded and could be easily rattled by our antics. Stix and I did all the usual boys-in-the-back-of-the-van stuff, waving our whangers around and so forth. Jack would turn round in the front seat and find himself facing someone's dong. This was one way of 'Jack-baiting', and it continued sporadically on long journeys until a weary roadie produced a cold spoon from the glove compartment and took a dispassionate swipe at the offending organ.

Another game I played, if Jack was sitting in the back of the van, was to remove all of my clothes while he was asleep and sit there reading a music paper, so that when he woke up he found himself sitting next to a naked body. 'Oh, for Christ sakes! Put your clothes on, man.' I'd tell him that we'd decided we'd be a better band if we started a new movement and all got naked sometimes. I'd tell him this quite sincerely and ask him what he thought of the plan. Nakedness in general was a great weapon in my fight against boredom. On one occasion, at a Trust House Forte service station, I noticed two coach loads of German tourists queuing patiently for their snacks. The queue spanned the length of the building's long windows as they shuffled tiredly towards the cash desk with their trays of food. I wonder if any of them still remember the man naked except for make-up and boots who ran across the floodlit courtyard in front of them as they gazed out into the darkness?

Tony Blair, by this time was probably at Oxford. Other young men of our age group were pushing back barriers, and forging important careers. Our contemporaries growing up in the seventies were dynamic and go ahead, laying the foundations for building families, empires, governments. They were making the world a better place. We, on the other hand, were waving our whangers in the back of a Transit van up and down England's great highways.

Our Saturday gig for the northern tour was a pub called the Fford Green. When I say pub, it was more like a workingmen's club, with rows of Formica-topped tables in the room where we were to play. It was a real taste of the north for us Essex boys. The dressing room was full of black-and-white eight-by-ten promotion pictures of previous acts that graced the stage. One picture I remember was of two middle-aged Jimmy Savile look-alikes. They were grinning at the camera, as they held their guitars, tuning heads to the ground, crossed over like swords. They rejoiced under the name of Huf 'n' Puf. I never forgot them. I can't understand why they weren't massive. I scanned *Melody Maker* and the pop charts each week for signs of some meteoric ascent. But nothing. The music industry is indeed fickle.

Showtime came and we crashed into our usual commercial pop set. This usually began with Quo's 'Paper Plane' or T Rex's '20th Century Boy'. During our drinks break the place filled up with old Teds. These were not young reproduction rockabilly types; they were genuine old Teds in drapes and bootlace ties, big lardy geezers in their early forties who used Duckhams on their quiffs and smelt of chip oil and Tetley's bitter. And they looked very hard indeed. We finished the first number in our second set, a cover of the Doobie Brothers' song 'Long Train Running'. One of them reached up and grabbed me by my black lace blouse, 'Can yoo plair Rocknrorl?' It wasn't a question it was an order.

I replied, 'Well we can...but...'

He looked menacingly at me and said, 'Well yer better play it son or yer fookin' dead.'

We roared into 'Good Golly Miss Molly', followed it with 'Shakin' All Over' and hurriedly went straight into 'Wipeout'. It was during an extended version of 'Johnny B Goode' that I noticed the stage had grown dark and the drum-kit was wobbling around. A dozen or so beefy Teds were up on stage doing some weird fifties-style dancing. I could hardly move for the bastards and I could feel the floorboards straining and shifting with the weight of it all. We were going down brilliantly. We ran out of rock-and-roll standards after about forty minutes. Bachelor Johnny said to me, 'repeat the set. They're too pissed to notice. Just keep the fucker going.' We finished the set and the Teds drank up and went home.

The landlord was a very strange bloke. I'd heard stories from other bands that on some occasions he cleared the punters out at closing time by donning a policeman's helmet and a truncheon. He came over to where we were breaking the gear down and loading it into the Transit. We thought he'd be pleased with us. Not a bit of it. He shouted that if we didn't hurry up and get the gear out, he'd throw it out himself. And I will never forget his parting words, 'We've 'ad some top-class acts in this pub. But you lot...were first rairt roobish! Now tek yer fookin' money and fook off!'

In the van later, Stix said, 'I think one of the things about the north is that the people are so friendly.' Bachelor Johnny made jokes about Huf 'n' Puf and I smoked cigarettes and sulked. I later found out via a friend of the agent who'd booked us that the landlord had told him what a great band we were and how well we'd gone down. When I asked why he'd been so horrible to us, I was told, 'Oh, he's always like that. It's just his way.' Aye. The north.

In spite of this, we came to love the trips up north. The audiences and the people were generally warmer and more responsive than their counterparts in reserved East Anglia. The first northerners we met had a cheerful get-it-down-yer-neck attitude to drinking that was much more in keeping with our own ideas. We were sometimes treated with astonishing kindness if we needed a place to stay and I at least was very taken with the scenery outside Leeds and Halifax. If we played well and played hard we were always given a good reception. On the whole, we thought, the north was a good thing.

As we drove home to Colchester in the early hours of the Monday morning after the Fford Green gig, I began another valuable experiment with cider, lager and

Carlsberg Special Brew. Stix was taking it easier because of the yellow peanut-water disease. We'd just got over the border into Essex and as the sun came up over the Colne Valley, I shouted to Big Nik, 'Stop the van!'

It was a beautiful summer morning. A low mist rolled across the fields, the foliage was deep green after recent rain, and, in the distance, a rooster crowed from a tumbledown medieval barn. On mornings like this you believe that time-slips can occur and if you listen hard, you are convinced that you can hear the echo of some Saxon woodcutter's axe deep within the ancient bluebell-scented forest.

Unfortunately, all of this passed me by. This was because I was down on my knees by the side of the road, scorching the grass with a man-sized hughie. The acrid brown vomit poured out of me like a bath emptying, as Jack leaned out of the van yelling encouragement. Stix, ever the gentleman, held my hair back for me as I went in for second, third and fourth hurls.

We hit Colchester early on the Monday morning. We could see people going to work. We could see schoolchildren waiting for buses to take them to their processing plants. We could see all of Colchester looking miserable and pissed-off about things. And I was still drunk. I'd done some gigs, and I was going nowhere but up, and it was brilliant, and I thought, 'Wow, this is the job for me.'

Thirty-four

Clacton Is God
Colchester and London, Late Autumn 1974

Come with me, children, for another walk down Hangover Hill. Not to the house at the top of the hill where Big Nik and Stix live, but to our other gang hut, St Guinness', at the bottom of the hill. Colchester's flimsiest had appropriated this dark former orphanage with gothic windows. It was home to Bachelor Johnny and several students of sociology and incomprehensible gobbledegook.

In the autumn of 1973 there was a party there. Upon seeing Bachelor Johnny at the makeshift bar in the kitchen, I issued the standard Plod greeting. This involved grabbing a fellow's hips from behind and making thrusting pelvic movements at his arse. Optional etiquette included grabbing his crotch while shouting, 'How's yer bag, y'old bastard?'

He turned round in extreme surprise, pushed himself away and asked, 'Who the fuck are you?' I looked him in the eye and noticed a complete lack of recognition, even though I'd been sharing a rehearsal room and several bars with him for some months. A helpful bystander explained to me that this was not John.

'Well it fucking looks like him,' I shouted. I had, in fact, just introduced myself to Harry, Bachelor Johnny's identical, and I mean identical, twin brother, whose existence I had hitherto been unaware of.

Harry, although he looked exactly like John, was very different in character. Harry was streetwise, whereas John was a philosopher and a dreamer. Harry, like most of us, recognised that two of the main reasons why young men join pop groups are because they think they're going to make money and meet girls. But in his previous pop group Harry lost money and he didn't meet any girls. So what did he do? He started working as a roadie for an established Colchester pop-harmony-covers band. They were called The Shay. Catchline: ten strings, five skins, four guys. And they worked. So Harry got paid.

What did Harry do next? He sold some of his music equipment, bought himself a sports car and some snazzy shirts and started drinking at an all-female teacher training college over Clacton way. Harry had both money and girlfriends and for him at least, Clacton was God. Stix and I used to discuss this a great deal and looked up to Harry as a kind of alternative success story. Harry also came up with our favourite catchphrase of the time, 'You're full up.' This referred to both bullshit and drunkenness.

Harry was as handy a bassist as his twin was a guitarist, so he was invited to join our rehearsal roommates, The Stan Laurel Band. This move was not popular with a small group of girl students who'd fancied their previous bassist, the gorgeous pouting Chopper. After a small demonstration by these girls, chanting, 'We want Chopper!' at Harry's debut gig, Harry took to wearing checked woollen carpet slippers for every performance. This dismayed his band mates but amused the members of The Mighty Plod.

Considering that Plod were the nearest thing that Colchester had to pop stars, we didn't do exactly brilliantly for female companions. It may have been something to do with the fact that we were boorish, sexist, rude, drunken and broke most of the time, or it could have just been that we seemed unattainable. Stix's girlfriend was a sixth-former. She was pretty, quiet and intelligent and after Plod's first northern trip made him a bag of Scotch eggs to make sure he didn't starve like the rest of us often did. Certain women regarded Stix and I as being a very bad thing. Yet out of the whole band Stix was the only one who managed to maintain a steady relationship with a female.

My own girlfriends were forever leaving me. I could never understand it. Looking back on it all, my chief function as far as women were concerned seems to have been to illustrate to them that they actually needed a relationship with someone who was more stable or normal. It took me years to understand that young women didn't necessarily want a madman in make-up, keeping them up until five in the morning doing Jimmy Saville impressions while standing up in bed drinking Special Brew. Close friends would later try to console me by explaining that she left me because, 'you were just too much to take, maan. She couldn't 'andle it any more.'

Bachelor Johnny didn't have a girlfriend for ages. Neither did Jack. I always liked real women, as opposed to flimsy student girls. I preferred big, dangerous, dirty women with erection-demolishing cackles and a few laughter lines and crow's-feet. Women who'd drag you by your dick into the bedroom and flick you your dinner money in the morning after they'd drained your dairy. Unfortunately, women like that tend to like villains, rather than fey, skinny twenty-one-year olds who sing in dodgy rock bands. For the most part therefore, I went out with anyone who was dumb enough to put up with me. Admittedly, there were a few girls who used to follow us around, but you tended not to get too tangled up with them because it nearly always led to misunderstandings and trouble. As Billy Bragg once said, 'There are only two things that get you into trouble in this world; your signature and your dick.' You learned to keep a semi-professional distance, if you could.

Harry, on the other hand, seemed very worldly. One night he brought this dangerously sophisticated woman with a black cocktail dress and gold jewellery round. She had high heels and lots of leg, and womanly make-up instead of student glam. We'll call her Roxanne. I was completely impressed, and not a little envious. The thing about Roxanne though was that she seemed to be a bit of a rock 'n' roller too. She came to see us play and Harry said she had some connections in London. She told us that she could get us some gigs. This is what happened.

Roxanne came to a gig in a club called Bottoms, off Leicester Square. She brought some bloke from the music biz whom we will call Dennis. Dennis was apparently in a position to do something for us. I can't remember what, but it was all jolly exciting at the time. The club was a few floors up. The lift was all purple velvet and mirrors. This was not a toilet. People with 'OK yah' voices were saying things like, 'Yah, I can geddit for yoo, but it's gaying to cost yoo abite twenny graand.' The waitresses were handsome West-Indian girls, tall with graceful Nefertiti necks. Like the lift, the club was decorated throughout with velvet and mirrors. We played our set, went down well, got paid, packed up and left. One number had gone down very well. It was a breakneck-speed version of The Beatles' 'I Saw Her Standing There'. I remember it, because they asked for an encore.

It wasn't until years later that I realised where we'd performed. Off Leicester Square? Several floors up in a lift? We had played what used to be a very famous old club. The place was the exclusive club where The Beatles, The Stones, The Who and the whole sixties rock aristocracy used to slide off to for a quiet drink when the hysteria got too much. The lift, which we'd remarked on and taken the piss out of, was probably the same one which Lennon and Harrison had thought was on fire, after a dodgy dentist had slipped them their first dose of LSD one night in 1965. Without knowing it at the time, Colchester's finest had just played the Ad Lib Club. Well, I say we didn't know it. Stix did. He'd got us the gig. He was good like that. This gig proved one of the amazing things about London. It doesn't matter what you do or where you do it, someone has probably done it there in the same place, long before you. The small two square miles or so of central London is full of clubs that have all been other clubs or whorehouses long before you were even thought of.

One of the gigs that Roxanne got us that autumn, through the good offices of Dennis, was rather more eventful, at least for me. It was a huge entertainment complex, somewhere off the Strand. It was called Global Village. It will be better known to some of my gay colleagues as a club called Heaven. We were to play two houses. We played our first set, they cleared the punters out and then a new lot came in. I can't remember much about the set but I do remember the audience were quite well shod and that I'd obliged them with the usual tight trousers/loads of make-up and no shirt sort of thing. Lots of leaping about and hey, what's this? Why it's a young woman pulling me down a corridor.

Now, the dressing rooms were downstairs below stage level, and the backstage doors led out to the Charing Cross arches where at that time, all the alcoholics used to swig their Milk of Amnesia from bottles and tins. I knew this because we'd parked our Transit van there earlier. I seem to recall that it was the girl's idea to go and inspect the van, but I didn't object to the plan. I told the helpful, dinner-suited security man that I was going out to the van to get some spare stage clothes. I also told him I would knock twice when I wanted to come back in. He nodded understandingly, locked the door firmly behind me and I went out into the darkness with the girl.

As for the visit to the van, what can I tell you? The young woman seemed very keen. She seemed to have one achievement in mind. As is so often the case, the incident was hurried, tawdry and culminated in some moist ghastliness. She made her excuses and just went. I had understood that she liked rock groups a great deal and that her specialist subject was singers. Having helped her with her research I now had to get back into the club. Unfortunately, all the knocking in the world didn't have the desired effect of regaining entry to Global Village.

This was now a doubly sticky situation. I was barefoot. I was wearing only the hipster canary-yellow flares. My hair was heaped and lacquered. I was wearing huge amounts of make-up and I was bare-chested. I was also under Charing Cross arches on a freezing night with only the distant sound of traffic and the nearer sound of arguing alcoholic down-and-outs for consolation. A running man is harder to stop than a walking man, so with this thought in mind, I began to run through the arches, dodging the staggering drunks and hurdling the prone ones. I cut my foot on something but kept running.

Eventually I emerged onto a busy West-End side street, full of people coming out of theatres, who tried to look the other way. I ran up onto the Strand. I was now too worried about missing the second set to worry about my appearance or the cold. At last I found the club's front door. I banged on the glass for them to let me in. A belligerent security man shook his head at me and told me to piss off. I banged again and tried to tell him that I was the singer in the band that night. He made threatening gestures with his fist. After a while he finally opened the door. I somehow sensed that he didn't believe anything I was saying. Luckily for me, two women who'd been at the front of the stage during the first set were leaving the club and said something like, 'Good set tonight.'

At this I beseeched them to tell this idiot who I was. He bought it. I was back in. As I was coming down the corridor to the dressing room, I could see a very glamorous older woman with what looked like her two minders entering our dressing room. And then I heard her posh voice boom, 'Where's the youth with the tight trousers?' She repeated the question. Who was she? Reader, I have no idea, because by that time I'd had quite enough for one night so I hid in another empty dressing room until she'd gone.

When I eventually rejoined the boys in the band, there was much laughter about this woman, the predatory nature of her, and what might have befallen me if I'd stayed around. Only Jack seemed to remember that I'd disappeared to the van quite some time earlier. 'Oi Zap,' he asked, 'did you plumb it?' No Jack. We played chess.

Thirty-five

Winter of the Disco Tent
Colchester and London, Winter 1974-Spring 1975

There is only so much roadwork and rehearsal that a bunch of young dudes can do before they'll either break up or get good. Plod broke up eventually, but first we got good. All that rehearsing in the shed at the back of Essex Uni, all that primitive recording on my old Sony sound-on-sound machine, eighteen months of playing dancehalls, seaside clubs, college supports, nightclubs and any toilet that would have us, had muscled us up. I believe the expression is 'dues-paying'. But since the expression is mostly used by the jazzers and sundry other musos who'd scorned us at the outset, I mention it only out of utter contempt. The facts of the matter were that we were now not the shambolic bunch of young chancers who'd initially blundered out onto the stage together at the beginning.

By November of 1974, glam-rock as we'd known it was all but dead. I saw this as no excuse for me to stop wearing mascara and tight trousers, of course, but the band as a whole, had developed into something slightly more sinewy and more manly. Our listening tastes had become more eclectic. I'd become quite interested in early Steely Dan. I was obsessed with Steve Miller's album, *Number 5*. I also listened to a lot of French music: Leo Ferré, Jacques Higelin

251

and Jacques Brel. Bachelor Johnny had got me interested in West-Coast bands such as Quicksilver and Moby Grape. We all listened to Rory Gallagher. Stix liked Dave Brubeck, Love, and The Beach Boys. With a mixture like that, something weird was going to happen our music.

Bachelor Johnny and I had started to write songs together. He started hitting on some very strange chord patterns and I'd begun slipping into writing lyrics for them and pointing up the melodies. It all seemed to develop quite naturally. The songs were original and quirky if not actually immediate. We were beginning to become our own band. As news of our behaviour and increasingly strange material filtered back to the agents who gave us live work, we'd been getting less of it. Our duty was to be a human juke-box and play the hits of the day. The hits of the day, however, were not as good as they had been a year earlier, when glam-rock was still in full throttle. Slade and Sweet numbers had now been supplanted in our covers set by Ken Booth's cover of the Bread song, 'Everything I Own'. I could deal with that. I could even deal with covering Eric Clapton's version of 'I Shot the Sheriff'. But I had to draw a line somewhere.

During one of our increasingly sporadic and guilt-ridden 'better learn some chart covers, I suppose' rehearsals, I was appalled to find myself struggling with Carl Douglas' 'Kung Fu Fighting'. Something snapped in me right there and then. I think we performed it at one gig and then never did it again. Big Nik was becoming impatient with us. Stix and I bickered. Jack snorted, shook his mane and ballbagged about us supposedly being a rock-and-roll band. Bachelor Johnny said 'yeah, yeah' and carried on being Bachelor Johnny. But John and I had written 'Solaré', a bitterly sarcastic piss-take of a Martini commercial. We'd also written 'You Are What You Eat', the riff of which John had pinched from a Curtis Mayfield song. I'd written 'My Finest

Hour', a cowbell-driven rocker in a Beatle-ish minor seventh key. We had the makings of a good original set.

With a low mist on the fields, the sweet smell of smoke and over-ripe damsons on the air and a chubby autumn moon rising in the melted Mivvi sky come with me, once again, up the A12 to Norwich. Clear those crisp packets out of the back seats, and ignore those bottles and cans clinking around down the side somewhere and take your place on the knackered springs of Yesterday. Close your ears to sarcastic comments and filthy songs and lets see how our creativity is to be rewarded in this dead-man's gulch of a musical period between glam and punk. Welcome to the winter of the disco tent.

It is Sunday. We have got a gig at no less an emporium than Norwich Theatre Royal. This is a large, well-appointed venue in East Anglia's main city. Venue capacity is about twelve hundred we are told. Punters will be seated. There is a balcony and proper dressing rooms. We are supporting Cozy Powell's Hammer. Cozy Powell is one of rock's finest drummers. Who has he played with? Well, everyone, most notably Jeff Beck and Rod Stewart. The strange thing is that he's had a couple of chart hits this year, so he and his band have been playing top venues. Our agent, one of the last to give us work under the impression that we are a chart-covers band, has booked us in as support. Our agent will be coming to check out his boys tonight. Will we be doing our pop-covers set? Will we fuck.

Over now to Stix for his definition of an agent: some bastard with a leather coat, a large wallet and a broom cupboard with two telephones in it. Thank you. Over to our singer for a quick poetic background to the times: it's the autumn, heading for winter. I'm still washing up in the restaurant, but I don't care, because I'm in lurve with the Corsican girl. I walk around kicking leaves and dreaming strange dreams. I read Anaïs Nin books. I've been for my final visit to the clap clinic and I haven't got anything. This is an incredible relief because after the tawdry incident in the van under Charing Cross arches a month ago, it was looking a bit touch and go there for a minute. We touched. We went.

The clap clinic wasn't too traumatic. I think the waiting room was the worst. The door of the women's waiting room swung open as I walked past and I recognised at least two women whom I knew, sitting within. In the men's waiting room was the standard atmosphere of forced, nervy jocularity, and the usual suspects: three students, two local roughnecks, four soldiers, and a very respectable headmasterly looking sort of geezer. He was even more nervous than me. How do I know? He was buried in a copy of *Readers Digest*, which was upside down, and shaking slightly.

Our area was reputed to have had the highest VD figures in the country at the time. Colchester was a fatal combination of garrison, port and university. This was the official reason. The legend in my circles went as follows: the women at an all-female teacher-training college in a nearby coastal town would shag the rough boys from the fairground rides at the beginning of the summer season. The boys from the university and the colleges shagged the female teachers later. They passed it on to the female students at the uni. The boys from the town shagged the uni students. The girls from the town shagged the boys from the town. The boys from the town shagged everything. The soldiers shagged whatever they could, as well as bringing back stuff they'd caught while on tours of duty. And so half the town was on orange juice for six weeks at a time.

They had me up on the old table there with the paper liner. Then they took the piss, then the mid-stream piss, then a bit more piss and then some blood. Then they asked lots of questions. They got a small metal loop on a stick and shoved it into my Eskimo eye. The accompanying sensation of burning and tickling led me to spontaneously scrunch my toes up so violently, that I ripped the inner lining out of a perfectly good pair of Chelsea boots. I had a very kindly female doctor, however, and a couple of very friendly male nurses. They found nothing more than a tiny thing, which may have been a skin tag, may have been a venereal wart and may not even have been venereal at all. And I did absolutely the right thing coming. And they'd let me know about the smear test. And yes, I was to drop in any time I was worried. And there'd be a bit of a wait on the syphilis test.

I'm feeling good. I haven't got galloping yallerjack. Just as well, as my girlfriend is coming over from France at Christmas. I've been discharged from probation, which is the only discharge I want right now. Apart from all this, I haven't taken more than a couple of Dexedrine for over a year. My brain is beginning to unfreeze. Dreams are coming back. My mum asks me if I want a cup of tea one morning and when I say that I do, there are tears in her eyes. This is because it is the first occasion, in over three years that she hasn't had to ask me four times. I don't even smoke any dope. I mean, I'm drinking a bit, but I never could drink that much. Come to think of it, I wasn't even much good at taking drugs. I just did it a lot, that's all. Now I wander through the drizzly Colchester streets and the lanes of Essex villages and, for the first time ever, I begin to enjoy my life as an adult human being. I've been away for a long time, a very long time.

Let's go back to the gig. Colchester's finest step out onto the huge stage at Norwich Theatre Royal to find ourselves looking out at a packed house that are cheering and clapping before we've even started. Many of them are fourteen-year-old girls, and their parents. What the hell. Even while I'm leaping around from one end of the stage to the other, I'm thinking, 'If we had these kind of conditions all the time, it would be easy.' How could you be bad for a crowd like this? We're playing well. In a break between numbers Bachelor Johnny or Stix have to stop to adjust a bit of equipment and, for the first time, I find myself actually talking to the audience, as if they were a crowd of friends in a pub.

I start mucking around. I do a Deputy Dawg impression. They love it. This is like pantomime. Hey, we're in showbiz. They like the songs that John and I have written. They don't want to let us go, but I can see someone in the wings, making wind-it-up-now gestures to us. Buoyed with confidence I tell the audience, 'Sorry everybody. Looks like we've got to let the support band on now.' As I pass him in the darkened wings on my way back to the dressing room, Frankie, Cozy's singer, gives me a bit of a black look. He needn't have bothered. For once, I am not being rude or cocky. I am just so happy.

After Cozy's band had done their stuff, we even got our share of autograph hunters backstage. Getting into the van in the compound behind the venue, a small crowd of kids grabbed hold of me. The roadies had to drag me into the van, with kids still hanging from my arm. When I finally got my arm back, and Big Nik sped off out of the gates, my hand felt funny. The kids had stolen all the rings off my fingers. The sheer thrill of it all, after all the shit we'd been through, offset the loss of the rings. Maybe it sounds corny or naive, but a gig like this can keep you going through weeks of having to play the usual toilets.

This brings me neatly back to our agent. Was he there? Yep. Did he like us? Nope. It didn't matter that we'd gone down brilliantly. We'd been playing our own songs. For the purposes of work, it would have been better for us if we'd played a nice safe anaemic set of chart pop covers and maintained the Status Quo by playing 'Paper Plane' again. Maybe even done 'Kung Fu Fighting'. Either way, we'd blown it with him. We weren't going to be getting any more work from him from now on. We were guilty of thinking for ourselves. How could he ever trust us to go out and keep those androids dancing at weekends, now that we'd done this?

A little while after this gig, in December of 1974, we played at our local tech college again. After a patchy performance some months earlier, the social secretary had given us the benefit of the doubt and booked us for another support gig. This time we played as well as we had at Norwich. At some point over the summer we had gone to the crossroads and sold our souls to the devil. We weren't just a one-trick pony. Even some of our critics had to concede that we were beginning to get it right. This time I would go back to my place at the sinks of the restaurant where I washed up and when the waitresses asked me how it went, I wouldn't have to mumble, 'Oh…all right, y'know?' Because they'd already heard, because their friends had seen us. And we'd played a blinder.

So do you want the happy ending? That was the last time that Colchester's finest ever played in Colchester. We played a handful of gigs elsewhere. Then one day, my mum had a mysterious phone call. This foreign guy had rung up. He had heard a demo and wanted to meet us. He was from The Gambia. He had some very peculiar ideas, one of which was to put me in a Freddie Mercury-style white catsuit. I vetoed this. He also knew a promoter who wanted to book us for a tour abroad. The letter, which he couldn't read, was in French. Since I was the only one in the band who had any French at all, I looked at the letter. It appeared to be a contract for a two-week residency, quite well paid, in a top club in Beirut, which was a war zone at the time. More importantly, he wanted to book us into a studio, a good one. It was TMC in Tooting. The Glitter Band had just been recording there.

We spent two weeks rehearsing, and rehearsing, and rehearsing, until we were tight as a gnat's chuff. I cannot remember a time during my whole two years in the band when we worked together so cheerfully and so well. When the frosty January morning of the appointed session dawned, we rose early, without hangovers and took our places in the Plod van. We were ready to go up to 'Lunnun'.

We had a greasy breakfast in a café, went into the studio and in somewhere under twelve hours, recorded and completed half a dozen blistering tracks. We played the best we'd ever played. Even the engineer thought we were good. He hadn't come across such a hardworking, tight band for years. Go on. I bet he says that to all the bands. 'No, mate.' He assured us that he meant it. Who were we? And why weren't we famous yet? The Gambian guy showed up and heard the stuff, and signed us up, more or less on the spot.

Well let me tell you, there was no little jubilation in the Plod van as we headed back up the A12 in the early January darkness on this night. Harry raised the roof with his huzzas when we all got back. We drank and planned. After the pub, I sat in Bachelor Johnny's living room with my head spinning and my ears still whining from the hours in the studio, and I suppose we all crashed out and went to bed dreaming.

Then for a while, nothing happened. In common with many bands, we thought that once you'd inked the parchment your troubles were all over. Mostly however, it means they are just beginning. But in this case, nothing happened. Oh, Jack got his screwdriver out and fiddled with electronic gear while we waited. Stix got involved in a little side project with an old mate of his from school days, who was playing in a pick-up band for a soul-singer. Bachelor Johnny and Harry got on with their jobs and talked about moving to London. I nipped off to Montpellier, France, to see the beautiful Corsican girl. 'Jus' get your train fare 'ere, mah darleeng. Ah weel pay evairy theeng else.' I didn't need to be asked twice. I drank whisky all the way down to Marseilles, was picked up by two French girls in a dodgy motor and was sick on a beautiful mountainside overlooking the Côte d'Azur. I was pushed into a cold shower somewhere in Hyères and shagged senseless on an orthopaedic bed. Her sister was a physiotherapist. I can't remember much more. I also drank a lot of local rotgut and pastis, learned a bit of French and generally tried to behave internationally.

The ferry spat me out at Dover about three weeks later. In my absence, the others had fulfilled a couple of local gig obligations, most notably at Harwich's Vacuumatic Sports and Social Club. Big Nik suggested, as he had on so many previous occasions, that we stop pretending to be a band and just form a gentlemen's drinking club instead. We met round Bachelor Johnny's place, at St Guinness's, and we rehearsed a bit more. We waited, and we heard that a record might be coming out, a single. We argued and speculated about which one of the songs it might be, and we occasionally made a phone call. And we waited, and we waited. And, as so often occurs when you do nothing, nothing happens. Spring came mincing into the fields, and a light green haze came over the land. And I expect that the forsythias blossomed harsh yellow in the back gardens seen from trains.

And we just drifted apart. We never even broke up. We just drifted apart. And that was the end of Colchester's finest, The Mighty Plod, who had been through so much together. It was a great shame, because I loved that band, and I loved all the guys in it and around it, because they helped to save my life. They were great company, and I still think that if we'd stuck it out, we might really have done something. In an industry where lack of success is not necessarily the same thing as failure, we'd done alright really. The four members of Colchester's finest had stood laughing in God's lay-by and pissed up at the stars, because it was better than working, any old day of the week. And it still is.